D0871883

Sudden Shakespeare

Sudden Shakespeare

The Shaping of Shakespeare's Creative Thought

Philip Davis

ATHLONE
London

First published 1996 by
THE ATHLONE PRESS
1 Park Drive, London NW11 7SG

© Philip Davis, 1996

British Library Cataloguing in Publication Data
A catalogue record for this book is available
from the British Library

ISBN 0 485 11496 8   hb

Typeset by
Bibloset

Printed and bound in Great Britain by Bookcraft (Bath) Ltd.

For my mother and father
Sheila and Sid Davis

In Shakspeare there is a continual composition and decomposition of [the characters'] elements, a fermentation of every particle in the whole mass, by its alternate affinity or antipathy to other principles which are brought into contact with it. Till the experiment is tried, we do not know the result, the turn which the character will take in new circumstances. . . . Shakspeare's imagination is of the same plastic kind as his conception of character or passion. . . . He seems always hurrying from his subject, even while describing it; but the stroke, like the lightning's, is sure as it is sudden.

(William Hazlitt, 'On Shakspeare and Milton', *Lectures on the English Poets*)

Contents

Note on Texts and Editions

Unless otherwise indicated, references are to the New Arden editions ('Arden 2'). With *Antony and Cleopatra*, *Othello* and *Richard II*, however, references are to the New Cambridge editions which offer distinct advantages in these particular cases. I have supplemented Kenneth Muir's New Arden *King Lear* by reference to Jay L. Halio's *The Tragedy of King Lear* (Cambridge) and René Weis's Longman edition with its parallel text of Quarto and Folio. Likewise, with regard to *Hamlet*, I have consulted Philip Edwards's New Cambridge edition whilst quoting from Harold Jenkins's New Arden. I have also found much profit in Stephen Orgel's Oxford edition of *The Tempest* and R.A. Foakes's *A Midsummer Night's Dream* in the New Cambridge Shakespeare. I have used John Kerrigan's fine edition of *The Sonnets* (Penguin). Students should consult Folio facsimiles (which I have used in particular in Chapter One) and the Oxford *Complete Works* edited by Stanley Wells, Gary Taylor, John Jowett and William Montgomery.

Introduction

In his essay on *Hamlet* Hazlitt says:

> Other dramatic writers give us very fine versions and paraphrases of nature: but Shakespeare, together with his own comments, gives us the original text.

This present work is an attempt to stay close to that 'original text' which Hazlitt says that Shakespeare offers. I wanted to try to avoid paraphrasing Shakespeare and thus making him tame and familiar – be it by moralizing Shakespeare, or humanising Shakespeare, or politicizing Shakespeare. I believe Shakespeare starts from language caught in and coming out of a particular tight predicament, not a relaxed opinion or fixed plan, and I wanted to find a means of imitating Shakespeare's way and following it. Above all, my aim was not to slow Shakespeare down with a commentator's clumsily retrospective words but to try to keep up with him and register the very moment of his making thought come into being. Shakespeare is, to use the word with which Malcolm describes Macbeth, 'sudden'. There is a bursting feeling about the plays; almost too much seems to be happening simultaneously. For Shakespeare works like the speed of lightning in *King Lear*: 'thought-executing' – no sooner carrying out a thought than destroying it.

Perhaps so-called 'close reading' is somewhat out of fashion, but I wanted to stay as close as possible to the very moment of utterance, to the very formation of those shapes and spaces and patterns that Shakespeare's imagination seemed intuitively to find and investigate. My first chapter is the fruit of that attempt to keep as close to Shakespeare as does Shakespeare's language to Shakespeare's imagination. I argue that Shakespeare thinks quickly and powerfully and intuitively because he thinks in terms of spaces and places and shapes, long before he thinks of humans or morals or principles. He is first of all a technical writer, getting himself into tight configurations of space and time which bring forth words – and only then meanings, arising out of them. The very space and

pressure of the events produces verbal thoughts – and only then
characters to fit and bear them. 'His mind and hand went together',
say Heminge and Condell of the speed of the master. In that way,
as Hazlitt suggests, Shakespeare gets into the very origin of things
again, as if for the first time. In his dramas of creation, evolution and
destruction, Shakespeare created a parallel world through which he
could lock into the creative life-force itself.

But if Shakespeare starts from what is technical, it is not because
the technical is his only or his main concern. On the contrary,
Shakespeare uses certain shapes and figures in order to generate a
language the speedy unfamiliarity of which may lead him beyond
those leisurely platitudes of human opinion and temperament that
otherwise all too consciously predetermine exploratory routes.

'Nature uttered itself in him, and came to self-awareness in him',
said Middleton Murry in his book on Shakespeare, 'in the sense of
Goethe's saying, that "Man is the first speech that Nature holds
with God".' The work of Shakespeare is a version of the original
text of life; his is like that first speech coming into being. These
are old-fashioned Romantic formulations to which in this present
book I try to give a Renaissance context in terms of rhetoric,
poetics, physics and cosmology – showing how again and again
Shakespeare makes and remakes whole worlds in his plays. Nature
abhors a vacuum, so does Shakespeare. His mind, its words, rush
into the spaces that emerge and develop in the unfolding of the
plays, as if called into being even as characters in his plays are called
into being and then shaped by the situations around them.

In Chapter One I show the Shakespearian dynamic working
across many plays; but where Chapter One deals mainly with
plenitude in space, Chapter Two is concerned with a correspondent
pressure in time. In Chapter Two I test my method and show its
specific applications by bringing it to bear on a single most complex
play, *Hamlet*, alongside *Measure for Measure*, *All's Well That Ends Well*
and *Coriolanus*. In *Hamlet* the Shakespearian generative dynamic –
that in a thousand different situations a man could be a thousand
different men yet each of them also bearing some relation to the
others – becomes a problem to the protagonist himself. I use that
other great Renaissance improviser, Montaigne, for purposes of
both comparison and contrast – comparing Montaigne's essays with
Shakespeare's plays as a way of working out the different forms

of being disclosed by each, with particular relation to matters of survival and character, comedy and tragedy, and commitment and belief. Indeterminacy in Shakespeare does not merely mean that at different times or from different positions you can think almost anything about something; it isn't simply about relativism, plurality, or scepticism. Shakespearian indeterminacy means that in any one matter there are always too many things that should be thought of simultaneously and cannot possibly be.

Chapter Three extends the application of the theory worked out in Chapter One to the histories and to the late plays – as public and personal histories respectively. I look at Shakespeare's impatience with simple linear sequences in the *Henry IV* plays and his fascination with complex shapes in *Richard II* and *The Winter's Tale*. I conclude, with particular reference to *The Tempest*, that Shakespeare does not have a single new philosophy of his own that can encompass at the 'macro' level the thousands of overlapping possibilities of human meaning offered at the 'micro' level of the plays' fast language. Instead he offers an almost infinite series of perspectives and combinations within what is none the less, ultimately, a finite condition governed by the fundamental repetition of old laws. His language produces thoughts that seem for a moment to go beyond the reaches of the human system and yet finally have to remain contained within it.

In Chapter Four I return to my method in Chapter One, continuing the attempt to try to reproduce something of what is implicit in the very meaning of Shakespeare's speed – with particular reference to theatre-time and the reality of performance. It is intrinsic to Shakespeare's vision that so much in the plays which seems as though it should be of *permanent* value is cast into a form whose performative life exists in the very force of *transience*. In Shakespeare some sudden thoughts become stabilized into action or into character but thousands of others – 'thoughts in their dumb cradles' – must 'perish by the way', not selected to make a major difference to the life depicted on the particular occasion. The best way to follow Shakespeare in this process is not by paraphrasing him or conceptualizing him, but by reperforming Shakespeare - be it through an actor on the stage or a reader from the page. By sudden mental performances we rediscover through Shakespeare a dramatic form of creative thinking, more deeply involved in the very processes of life than is our conventional view of what constitutes thought. Shakespeare does not offer messages but life-forces. He is, in Peter Brook's words, a creator not a communicator.

Liverpool has strong Shakespearian traditions in both academe and theatre. Accordingly, I am grateful to Professors Muir, Edwards and Bate of the University of Liverpool, and to Lee Beagley and Paula Simms of Kaboodle Productions. To Tim Langley and Brian Nellist, good men, I owe most of all. Thanks are also due to two great theatre-goers: Jane Davis and Angie Macmillan.

Chapter 1

'I Could Be Bounded in a Nutshell': Dramatic Space and Personal Place in Shakespeare

How did Shakespeare think?

The mysterious inscrutability of Shakespeare was a favourite theme of the Romantics. Keats fancied that if only we knew how Shakespeare sat in order to write *King Lear*, he might have a clue as to how the man operated. More recently, Ted Hughes like others before him has tried to explain the whole of Shakespeare by means of a central Shakespearian myth, seeking amidst the very diversity of his work one single key to understanding Shakespeare aright.

Would you pluck out the heart of my mystery? That is to say: is it the recourse of cranks, down the ages, to seek to find what Hughes called Shakespeare's original template, his underlying creative algebra?

I want to explore the possibility that there *is* an underlying matrix which forms the finite basis of Shakespeare's infinite variety. Russell Fraser's suggestion is my starting-point: 'A good way to read him is as the problem solver, intrigued by technical questions.'[1] For Shakespeare, I shall argue, is fundamentally interested in 'pattern' – not only in the familiar sense of decorative design and formal composition but in the first meaning given in the *Oxford English Dictionary*: an archetype, an example or model deserving imitation, and thence anything designed to serve as a matrix or mould. The Elizabethan divine Richard Hooker took God's law as the archetype for all other laws and ways of being on earth: 'That law which hath been the pattern to make, and card to guide the world by'.[2] In his own way, Shakespeare looks for derivative laws of creation in the patterning of his own work. 'Pattern in himself to know' (*Measure for Measure*, III ii 256).

Thus, to approach Shakespeare afresh, I believe we require both a less blandly human and a less rebarbatively political language than has sometimes been used in literary criticism during this century.

What is needed instead is an initially technical language which would be capable of responding suddenly – at a level prior to the settlement of definite human opinion – to the speed, transforming shape and even violence of Shakespeare's way of thinking as it comes *into* meaning. And we can learn that language from Shakespeare's own sense of pattern. In what follows I offer an attempt at identifying such a prior technical language, close to the way Shakespeare's imagination works. I call it the dynamics of space in Shakespeare's mind. It finally has cosmological implications, but it develops first of all out of Shakespeare's concern with rhyme-patterns.

1 ON RHYME

I am concerned with how much Shakespeare starts quite neutrally from the nature and deployment of poetic *space*: initially, the sense of space that results from the use of varying forms of *repetition* within the limitations of room enforced by *rhyme*. To begin with, take four famous lines from Sonnet 64:

> When I have seen the hungry ocean gain
> Advantage on the kingdom of the shore,
> And the firm soil win of the wat'ry main
> Increasing store with loss and loss with store . . .

By interchange, the land and the sea win and lose, lose and win in the very ebb and flow of their paradoxically wedded antagonism. This is not repetition as a form of redundancy; on the contrary the repetition and inversion seem to redouble the space available. Thus, what is technically so dense about the last line, in particular, is what William Empson speaking so long ago of the sonnets called 'an interpenetrating and, as it were, fluid unity'.[3] For though the last line eventually settles down into two mirroring half lines as in the punctuation of the 1609 Quarto:

> Increasing store with loss, and loss with store

none the less the reader is initially tempted to read through the mid-line caesura as in Kerrigan's edition:

> Increasing store with loss and loss –

until, once the land has thus gone too far, the sea, by a kind of counter-movement, takes over again and comes back into play:

> and loss with store

– thus restoring balance just as the rhyme is achieved:

> is it not most delightfull to see much excellentlie ordred in a small roome, or little gallantly disposed and made to fill up a space of like capacitie . . . ?[4]

'Increasing store with loss and loss with store' is a line that both expands and contracts 'with loss and loss with store': a fluid unity indeed such 'as makes the motion *certaine*, though the varietie be *infinite*'.[5] For the varyingly repeated rhythm of gain and loss between land and sea goes on infinitely but the same, like variations within a theme.

In what Samuel Daniel calls 'an Orbe of order and forme',[6] in a little world of its own, rhyme works both to restrain and to yield, as if the relation between rhyme and sense were itself something very like that between land and sea. So in the liquid movement of Sonnet 95 –

> That tongue that tells the story of thy days,
> (Making lascivious comments on thy sport)
> Cannot dispraise, but in a kind of praise,
> Naming thy name, blesses an ill report

this punctuation taken from the Quarto allows not only:

> Cannot dispraise but in a kind of praise;
> Naming thy name, blesses an ill report

but also:

> Cannot dispraise; but in a kind of praise,
> Naming thy name, blesses an ill report

– so that 'but in a kind of praise' for a second moves freely between both lines, looking before and after, closing and reopening the sense.

Created in limited space against the surrounding background of what is otherwise (says Daniel) an 'unformed Chaos', the little orb or world of the sonnet is like a history of the cosmos in small, for it offers an ordered plenitude of infinite riches in a little room. Shakespeare's lines so often have a momentarily double thickness: parts at once gaining and losing from each other, stealing and giving, suddenly finding room of their own not only despite but because of constraint. For the lines quoted from Sonnets 64 and 95 are only particularly brilliant examples of the basic movement characteristic of the turns made within a sonnet – to take even the conventional couplet-close to Sonnet 15:

And all in war with Time for love of you,
As he takes from you I engraft you new.

Again, of course, there is a comma rhythmically understood in the midst of that last line: 'Even as Time takes life and beauty from you, so I engraft you anew in this poem.' But that is not quite how it at first reads. In the dynamics of reading – or as Shakespeare puts it 'in war with Time' – 'you' and 'I' are, for a pre-grammatical moment in the blur of pronouns, as close spatially as words can be:

As he takes from you I engraft you new

– such that the registering of a second clause as suddenly and abruptly taking over from the first, precisely to compensate for it, seems an active achievement which does *justice* in the nick of time to the two now slightly differing occurrences of 'you' in the same line. A sharp change of *levels* occurs silently in the very midst of the apparently smooth, straightforward *line*. For a tiny second – 'from you I' – there was a momentary tension, almost immediately resolved, between (on the one hand) the space along the rhyme-line offered to the words as single unitary atoms and (on the other) the grammatical and then human meaning of the words when taken together. One sees in that moment, as formal space meets what fills it as meaning and the two marvellously become one, the poetry getting made again.

Something analogous may be seen to happen in the larger worlds of the early comic plays. *The Comedy of Errors*, for instance, starts with two sets of twins, symmetrically divided between Ephesus and Syracuse, who act like an enlarged equivalent of rhyme in partnership. The play is an expanded poem, starting from two simple and separated combinations meeting and remeeting in one place – on one side Antipholus of Syracuse and his servant Dromio of Syracuse, on the other Antipholus of Ephesus and his servant Dromio of Ephesus – and producing from that basic *simple* patterned matrix a rising series of increasingly *complex* transformative variations. What I shall be describing here is thus not a plot summary but a mechanism for the use of space.

For example, starting simply, consider what we may call level one in the series: in act I scene ii Antipholus of Syracuse is called home by Dromio of Ephesus: Antipholus of Syracuse has just sent his Dromio, Dromio of Syracuse, to wait for him at an inn and keep his money safe there, when Dromio of Ephesus enters to relay the message from Antipholus of Ephesus's wife. Thus enters Dromio of Ephesus, to complain of his master's tardiness, for the first error:

> *Syr. Ant.* What now? How chance thou art return'd so soon?
> *Eph. Drom.* Return'd so soon? rather approach'd too late.
>
> I ii 42–3

'Return'd' and 'approach'd', like 'soon' and 'late', exactly mark the different direction the two characters are mentally coming from. This Dromio denies he has received any money; this Antipholus denies he has a wife. Antipholus hits him, Dromio runs off. This is indeed simple.

But now comes the move to level two. By act II scene ii Antipholus of Syracuse has met up with his own Dromio of Syracuse again: this Dromio denies the previous conversation, Antipholus hits him (for what is to Antipholus a second time), then suddenly there enters Adriana, wife of Antipholus of Ephesus. She says: Why did you not come home? I sent Dromio for you and you beat him –

> *Syr. Ant.* Did you converse, sir, with this gentlewoman?
>   What is the course and drift of your compact?
> *Syr. Drom.* I, sir? I never saw her till this time.
> *Syr. Ant.* Villain, thou liest, for even her very words
>   Didst thou deliver to me on the mart.

Syr. Drom. I never spake with her in all my life.

                                                    II ii 160–5

This Antipholus and this Dromio were originally on the same side
and should still be so if this were still level one: for neither has
indeed ever seen Adriana in his life before. But now as Adriana
accuses this Antipholus of lying, when he denies all knowledge
of her, this Antipholus in turn accuses Dromio of lying when he
says the same thing. The symmetrical complications, the swopping
of partners, the reflection upon reflection in the play's mirrors, are
beginning to become almost self-generating.

By act IV scene iv the multiplication of levels is almost beyond
number. Antipholus of Ephesus has gone home only to find himself
shut out because the other Antipholus is reluctantly inside in his
place; moreover the gold which Antipholus of Ephesus gave
Dromio to pay for a chain was gold he mistakenly gave to
Dromio of Syracuse. Thus he both mistakes and is mistaken.
In act IV scene iv we now see act II scene ii through the
looking-glass:

> *Eph. Ant.* Say, wherefore didst thou lock me forth to-day,
>   And why dost thou deny the bag of gold?
> *Adriana*   I did not, gentle husband, lock thee forth.
> *Eph. Dro.* And gentle master, I receiv'd no gold;
>   But I confess, sir, that we were lock'd out.
> *Adriana*   Dissembling villain, thou speak'st false in both.
> *Eph. Ant.* Dissembling harlot, thou art false in all.

                                                    IV iv 93–9

The first line of the first speech of Antipholus of Ephesus is
directed at his wife, the second at his servant; the wife replies
in a single line of denial which is matched by the single line of
the servant's own denial; but then the servant adds one more line
which splits him off from the wife and links him back with the
husband his master; the wife then turns against the servant as the
husband had done just before, but the husband next turns against
her. The hapless but agile speech by Dromio of Ephesus is caught
in the very midst of the chaos, twisting and turning both ways. 'A
sentence is but a chevril glove to a good wit – how quickly the
wrong side may be turned outward' (*Twelfth Night*, III i 11–13).

It is striking here that what has become improvised chaos has itself as much order as order itself has. And it is equally striking that the genuinely touching bafflement, pain and quarrelling of the parts ('gentle husband . . . gentle master', 'Dissembling villain . . . Dissembling harlot') should still so make up one comic whole. 'I never heard/So *musical* a *discord*' (*A Midsummer Night's Dream*, IV i 116–17).

'Much excellentlie ordred in a *small* roome' may be expanded into a *large* one. But once Shakespeare gets into that larger room of the plays he then uses the very increase of space only to begin to contract again. By this means he creates an internal density to his works by the almost endlessly varied reworking, within themselves, of their first basic terms: Antipholus of Syracuse, Dromio of Ephesus, Antipholus of Ephesus, Dromio of Syracuse. Or consider another initially simple example. In the equally transformative *A Midsummer Night's Dream*, with Helena, Demetrius, Hermia, Lysander, Shakespeare's technical rule seems to be: where there are four, until the final resolution it shall always be three against one, rather than two plus two. In the play's first half it goes like this, in terms of 'odds' rather than 'evens':

> *Helena* O, teach me how you look, and with what art
>   You sway the motion of Demetrius' heart.
> *Hermia* I frown upon him; yet he loves me still.
> *Helena* O that your frowns would teach my smiles such skill!
> *Hermia* I give him curses; yet he gives me love.
> *Helena* O that my prayers could such affection move!
> *Hermia* The more I hate, the more he follows me.
> *Helena* The more I love, the more he hateth me.
>
> I i 192–9

At level one in Hermia's speeches we see the sonnet-like opposi-tions of what Puttenham aptly terms the cross-couple: 'because it takes me two contrary words as it were a paire of couples, and so makes them agree like good fellowes'.[7] But this is compounded at level two, where Helena's distress is multiplied by seeing itself in the mirror of Hermia's effortless and unwilling victory. And the two levels contrapuntally, indeed ironically, rhyme in together, as only true love should, through that technique of reversal which is one of Shakespeare's virtuoso hallmarks. By the second act of the play, moreover, through Puck's magic and another reverse variation, Helena and Hermia have changed places – and Helena cannot believe it. So Helena to Lysander:

> Wherefore was I to this keen mockery born?
> When at your hands did I deserve this scorn?
> Is't not enough, is't not enough, young man,
> That I did never, no, nor never can
> Deserve a sweet look from Demetrius' eye
> But you must flout my insufficiency?

II ii 122–7

Helena to Lysander *and* Demetrius:

> You both are rivals, and love Hermia;
> And now both rivals to mock Helena.
> A trim exploit, a manly enterprise,
> To conjure tears up in a poor maid's eyes
> With your derision!

III ii 155–9

Helena to Lysander and Demetrius *and* Hermia:

> *Lys.* *[to Hermia]* Why seek'st thou me? Could not this make
> thee know
>   The hate I bare thee made me leave thee so?
> *Hermia* You speak not as you think; it cannot be!
> *Helena* Lo, she is one of the confederacy!
>   Now I perceive they have conjoin'd all three
>   To fashion this false sport in spite of me.
>   Injurious Hermia! Most ungrateful maid!
>   Have you conspir'd, have you with these contriv'd,
>   To bait me with this foul derision?
>   Is all the counsel that we two have shar'd,
>   The sisters' vows, the hours that we have spent
>   When we have chid the hasty-footed time
>   For parting us – O, is all forgot?
>   All school-days' friendship, childhood innocence?

III ii 189–202

It is part of Shakespeare's technique to treat these people initially as though they were just numbers in his mechanical pattern of space. In that sense a scholar such as Marion Trousdale is right to treat a Shakespeare play technically 'as a rhetorical exercise' involving 'formulaic presentation, by which I mean the kinds of continuance that varying makes possible'.[8] And it is this initial immersion in sheer technique that sometimes makes Shakespeare seem blankly indifferent or inscrutable. But if that patterning is his starting-point, it is no more than that. Shakespeare first treats what is human not as if it were human but always as though it were something else – something formally repeatable and yet variable, something numerical or musical. For the more that in the first place one part of Shakespeare detachingly puts dramatis personae into formal numbers, the more in the second another part of him is then reactively provoked by a further mechanism to restore them as human content. Half sadly from within the play, half comically from just outside it, poor Helena thus resists in the second place what the rhymes seem to be giving her in the first, as if she were the helpless dupe of a happiness seen only through the looking-glass. She does not fit her image there. As Orlando says in *As You Like It*, 'O, how bitter a thing it is to look into happiness through another man's eyes' (V ii 41–3). Helena has to deny from her heart that she occupies the physical space or place the rhymes offer her – one: 'is't not enough . . . but you . . . ?'; two: 'And now *both* rivals to mock Helena'; and three: 'Lo, *she* is *one* of the confederacy!/Now I perceive they have conjoin'd all *three*.' Is't not enough, young man? It is not enough for Shakespeare. For then Shakespeare in his plenty adds another poignantly overlapping twist and turn. For even as we hear Helena's bitter reproach to Hermia, we simultaneously imagine Hermia's own equally helpless feelings: a Hermia as rejected now as was Helena before, but rejected also by Helena even as Helena unjustly thinks herself betrayed by Hermia – and what is more, by a Hermia occupying Helena's place even while poor Helena herself cannot vacate it.

Shakespeare's is always such a *full* world. By a relatively simple technique of varied repetition and repeated combination, a genuine comic complexity is exponentially generated out of a simple ground-plot of symmetrical kinship. Figures of rhetoric become springs of plot. The principle of creative combination, evolving so much difference out of such basic likeness, holds good at all levels starting from the very simplest elements:

quin etiam passim nostris in versibus ipsis
multa elementa vides multis communia verbis,
cum tamen iter se versus ac verba necesse est
confiteare alia ex aliis constare elementis;
non quo multa parum communis littera currat
aut nulla inter se duo sint ex omnibus isdem,
sed quia non volgo paria omnibus omnia constant.
sic aliis in rebus item communia multa
mutarum rerum cum sint primordia, verum
dissimili tamen inter se consistere
possunt . . .

A pregnant proof of this my *Verse* affords:
For there are Letters *common* to all Words,
Yet some of different *shapes* and *figures* joyn
To make each *different* Word, each *different* Line;
Not but that many are in shape the same
But all agree not in one common frame.
And so of other things, tho Things are made
Of many *common Seeds* in order laid,
Yet may the Compounds widely disagree.[9]

As with letters in words and words in verses, so with atoms
in elements and elements in compounds in the corresponding
vocabulary and grammar of the world's own composition. In
Shakespeare, as here with Lucretius, there is just that analogical link
between linguistic and natural effects. Such then is Shakespeare's
verbal chemistry creating such infinite variety out of a finite matrix.

For what Shakespeare does at one level with the definite frame
of rhyme, he does likewise at a larger level macrocosmically with
the framing space of plotting. Indeed, one can see, in small, those
two levels beginning to separate out from Shakespeare's saturated
solution, if we look at, say, a moment taken from *Love's Labour's
Lost*. Berowne is wooing his witty match, Rosaline - 'My gentle
sweet,' he says, 'Your wits make wise things foolish':

> *Berowne*   Your capacity
>   Is of that nature that to your huge store
>   Wise things seem foolish, and rich things but poor.
> *Rosaline* This proves you wise and rich, for in my eye –

Berowne I am a fool, and full of poverty.

V ii 376–80

Shakespeare could have remained at the level of simple rhyme, Rosaline countering –

This proves you wise and rich, for in my eye
You are a fool, and full of poverty.

But when Berowne, anticipating the tempo, takes that second line out of her mouth, a tenser sense of space is immediately created between the characters – a force-field which in its turn helps to create the characters themselves as at once the more separate and the more thereby attracted:

Rosaline But that you take what doth to you belong,
It were a fault to snatch words from my tongue.
Berowne O, I am yours, and all that I possess.
Rosaline All the fool mine?
Berowne   I cannot give you less.

V ii 381–4

In the give and take, the to and fro here, there is in every sense a cross-couple: 'You take from me – but only the sense of your own folly.' 'But I give myself back to you.' 'What you give back to me is a fool then. You mean you're trying to make a fool of me?' In the strength of wit improvisedly defending the weakness of love, the cheek and the charm are alike still precariously serious and vulnerable and moving: 'I cannot give you less.' The more you go up in wit, the more you come down in love. There are laws to the tightly rebounding forces in Shakespeare's crowded worlds.

Although Ruskin said that 'Shakespeare was forbidden of Heaven to make any *plans*',[10] the very way that Shakespeare avoids the appearance of mere rigidity of predetermined intention is precisely by the creation of a firm matrix which itself allows improvisations through a process of attraction as spontaneous as that of the finding and fitting of rhymes.

In these improvised rebounds then, the lines from *Love's Labour's Lost* are like lovers' eyebeams continuously crossing, at once yielding and resisting accordingly to the laws of love and of rhyme. Berowne magnificently puts it another way: 'Those

heavenly eyes, that look into these faults,/Suggested us to make'
(V ii 757–8). In such rebounds there is something in between
either complete mastery or utter servitude. And that is why
Samuel Daniel loved the technique of rhyme for the strength
that might be borrowed from its very constraint. He relished
the movement and transformation from passive to active, from a
sense of imposition to a delight in improvisation: 'So that if our
labours have wrought out a manumission from bondage, and that
wee goe at libertie, notwithstanding these ties, wee are no longer
the slaves of Ryme, but we make it a most excellent instrument to
serve us.'[11] What is interesting to Shakespeare, however, is not the
final victory so much as the space to be found and used in between
bondage and liberty.

That space, moreover, literally *exists* in the plays: in the
immediacy of the theatre you can almost see words, thoughts,
acts, people coming into being within the bounding space which
an established situation allows them. As Tommaso Campanella put
it in his *Del senso delle cose e della magia* (1620): 'It is not bodies that
give unity to the world, since the world is composed of contraries,
but rather space, which interposes itself even between separate
bodies and ties the world together.'[12] Shakespeare in our example
interposes between Berowne and Rosaline a loving space, taut with
rhyme: a space of linkage and separation which is half created by
them, but half the creator of them.

But the deployment of space in Shakespeare is not just a set of
verbal responses to the force-field created by *rhyme*: there are
further dimensions that develop out of that initial cast of mind.

For there is never anywhere a vacuum in Shakespeare, even
the gaps and empty spaces in between people are filled; and like
Campanella he endows space in his world with sense and feeling,
with appetite and resistance. 'The air surrounding a body plays the
role of a vase.'[13] In the old visual illusion when two profiles face
each other there is a space between them: when that space is looked
at not just as background but in its own right, it takes the emergent
form of a Grecian urn. 'A natural perspective, that is and is not'
(*Twelfth Night*, V i 215). I shall argue that Shakespeare does not start
with characters so much as with the spatial situation in between
them, or rather creates urn and profiles in so fast a reaction between
the two as to make almost a simultaneous realization of both.

2   ON PERSON AS PLACE WITHIN SPACE

> *John Barton* I'm not saying that the character or the intention
> isn't important, only that occasionally it's valuable to start with
> the text and the language only.
> *Ben Kingsley* Oh, for me it's the right and the only way.
> Otherwise I impose.

What Ben Kingsley is opposing here is the imposition of a kind of
paraphrase – an actor's character-study taken from an impression
of the psychological novel allegedly implicit within or behind the
play. Speaking of the temptation of trying to understand Brutus as
a whole, as a consistent character, *before* knowing how to speak his
lines at any given moment, Kingsley goes on:

> Brutus's inconsistencies are only a microcosm of the whole play.
> If you try and iron out these inconsistencies in order to make
> the play playable, you will in fact anaesthetise the energy within
> the lines. The energy of the character and the predicament of
> the character are only available to the audience if the tension
> between the opposing forces is observed, relished and played.
> But of course that's all theory. It's very difficult to spread-eagle
> oneself inside the giant silhouette of Brutus and remain faithful
> to all these seemingly contradictory elements. Each has to be
> played to the full.[14]

'For the eye sees not itself/But by reflection, by some other things'
(*Julius Caesar*, I ii 54–5). Ben Kingsley seeks not to *impose* himself
upon the play from within outwards, but on the contrary to
fit in to the space and shape, the silhouette, the predicament
and the linguistic situation of the character, 'but by reflection'
outside-in. It is wise counsel not only for playing Shakespeare but
also for reproducing in oneself through technical means something
of Shakespeare's own understanding of the very formation of
human being. In bringing things to *life*, the rule is: as actor to
the shape of character, so Shakespearian character to space within
the play's world.

Let me give an example of that last sudden animation. In *Antony
and Cleopatra* the soothsayer warns Antony of Octavius Caesar:
'Make space enough between you' (II iii 23). The two men must

not overlap or there will be an explosion as of two contrary forces. But on the other hand because there has been too much space between the two, the marriage of Antony to Octavius's sister has been proposed: 'Her love to both/Would each to other' (II ii 143–4). As Octavia herself says, 'Wars 'twixt you twain would be/As if the world should cleave' (III iv 30–1). They could tear the world apart. Thus Octavia is to occupy and reconcile the space between Antony and Octavius in a sort of middle ground at the relatively simple level of mere plot. But it is then that Octavia – already registered as insipidly two-dimensional in comparison with Cleopatra ('She shows a body rather than a life', III iii 20) – suddenly in just a few words to Antony becomes emotionally important, giving an instantaneous *human* feel to the strained space between the two leaders. It is a typically abrupt and improvised transformation on Shakespeare's part, adding a dimension. For Octavia ceases to be merely the space between the two opposing profiles but makes that space over into a form and character in her own pained right:

> A more unhappy lady,
> If this division chance, ne'er stood between,
> Praying for both parts.
> The good gods will mock me presently,
> When I shall pray, 'O, bless my lord and husband!',
> Undo that prayer by crying out as loud,
> 'O, bless my brother!' Husband win, win brother,
> Prays and destroys the prayer; no midway
> 'Twixt these extremes at all.

III iv 12–20

As Ben Kingsley tries to lay his body within the silhouette left by Brutus, so Octavia defines and is defined by the space left between brother and husband. 'Place is as it were a sort of outline . . . a mould into which the thing must fit, if it is to lie properly and not be diffused'; 'Shakespeare's characters live in the moment they speak'.[15] The space and time Octavia must occupy have moulded her, implicating her in the political world; but she then also changes the temporal space, makes it feelingly aware of itself 'as if the world should cleave' here at its stress-point. In the words of 'The Phoenix and Turtle', 'Neither two nor one was called' (line 40).

'Husband win, win brother': chiasmus on the page, a key trope for
Shakespeare's turn of mind, suddenly creates a person on the stage
– someone who, through uncertainty and conflict, has to possess
that extra dimension of inner being precisely because outwardly
she can no longer simply be *either* wife *or* sister but must feel like
both in turn and yet neither completely. If Octavia is the name
for humanly feeling the space between Antony and Octavius, so
more aggressively Kent, in *King Lear*, becomes a character the very
moment he tries to come between the king's words and the king's
actions and make room there: 'Peace Kent!/Come not between
the Dragon and his wrath', 'thou hast sought . . . To come betwixt
our sentence and our power' (I i 120–1, 167–9).

In the situation of Octavia, as in Shakespeare's own development, what we see, I suggest, is comedy reversed, comedy
transformed – for in *Twelfth Night* the space between characters
is itself likewise made over into a character in the person of Viola
going between Orsino and Olivia:

> How will this fadge? My master loves her dearly,
> And I, poor monster, fond as much on him,
> And she, mistaken, seems to dote on me:
> What will become of this? As I am man,
> My state is desperate for my master's love:
> As I am woman (now alas the day!)
> What thriftless sighs shall poor Olivia breathe?
> O time, thou must untangle this, not I,
> It is too hard a knot for me t'untie.
>
> II ii 32–40

Viola's whole speech, like that of a more knowing Helena, is
saying: will this complete mess work out after all as genuine rhyme,
in internal sense and feeling as well as external shape and sound? But
when Octavia occupies that mid-point between extremes which
she herself says cannot exist in *Antony and Cleopatra* –

> When I shall pray 'O, bless my lord and husband!',
> Undo that prayer by crying out as loud,
> 'O, bless my brother!' Husband win, win brother,
> Prays and destroys the prayer

– then it is as if the very nature of the world-space has altered in
this play, in comparison with that in the comedies, and is instead
closer to the physics of *Coriolanus*:

> One fire drives out one fire; one nail, one nail.
>
> IV vii 54

One prayer drives out another:

> A more unhappy lady,
> If this division chance, ne'er stood between,
> Praying for both parts.

In Campanella's terms, 'just as our body, by nature, abhors any
division and yet can be made to suffer such division by violence,
so it is with the body of the world'.[16] Octavia here embodies
that tearing apart. 'Praying for both parts' is not a full line
metrically, although it occupies a whole line: it is left hanging
and unintegrated, the silent horror of its felt impossibility rushing
in to fill the vacuum.

Like nature according to Aristotle, Shakespeare abhors a vacuum.
In *Antony and Cleopatra* even in moments of love the world cannot
finally be either emptied or fulfilled, desire must keep rushing in
and yet it cannot be fully slaked:

> From the barge
> A strange invisible perfume hits the sense
> Of the adjacent wharf. The city cast
> Her people out upon her; and Antony,
> Enthroned i'th'market-place, did sit alone,
> Whistling to th'air, which, but for vacancy,
> Had gone to gaze on Cleopatra too,
> And made a gap in nature.
>
> II ii 221–8

There is no such mention in Plutarch of any danger of a vacuum
resulting from natural forces wanting to go off to admire Cleopatra.
It is pure Shakespeare. For Campanella, in contrast, such a moment
would be testimony to the world's fecundity and plenitude:

> we may conjecture further that since the air hurries in order to
> prohibit a vacuum, there is joy felt in filling a void; and that the

rush is not so much to prohibit the vacuum as it is to spread out in space; for the love of expanding oneself, multiplying oneself, and living full lives in spacious existence obtains in all things that multiply themselves, generate, and expand.[17]

But over Cleopatra the eager air cannot leave a vacuum behind it and there is as a result an exquisitely painful frustration,[18] deriving from a sense not of too little but of too much – too much in Cleopatra's drawing power ever to be wholly consummated:

> his ego non viris arsi – quid fiet ab ipsis?
> in flammam flammas, in mare fundis aquas.
> Ovid, Amores, III ii 33–4

My blood was on fire before: what are you doing now? Pouring flames into the flame; flooding the sea itself with further waves. How can it come to an end? It would take a Lear's sexual violence and ejaculated disgust to tear this massed world apart: 'There is the sulphurous pit – burning, scalding,/Stench, consumption; fie, fie, fie! pah, pah!' (IV vi 127–8).

Indeed, in the plays of violent competition for limited space, the older Aristotelian laws of mechanical force, displacement, resistance, repulsion and re-action replace what we considered earlier – namely, the loving space, the kiss of rhyme, indeed all that rhyme stands for at higher levels:

> Duke And since you call'd me master for so long,
>   Here is my hand; you shall from this time be
>   Your master's mistress.
> Olivia   A sister! you are she.
> Twelfth Night, V i 323–5

There, as Daniel might say, mastery and service are married; there too in Campanella's phrase we feel 'pleasure in the contact between bodies and space, because of that desire and love for expanded existence of which I spoke'.[19] You are she; this fits here; the space offered and the body occupying it interpenetrate and are at one.

But in later Shakespeare a loving space, a kiss, a rhyme end up being more like what is registered in Othello's terrible final couplet:

I kissed thee ere I killed thee: no way but this,
Killing myself, to die upon a kiss.

He [falls on the bed and] dies.
Othello, V ii 354–5

Chiasmus is now closer to synoeciosis, a composition of contraries
which does not ring but jar; the dying kiss is closer to necrophilia
than to marriage. Violence makes 'a breach in nature/For ruin's
wasteful entrance' (*Macbeth*, II iii 113–14).

This change that takes place in the very texture and architecture
of the world may be expressed even thus in a shorthand formulation from *Antony and Cleopatra* – albeit expressed in the Roman
style of Octavius's forebodings, as he hands Octavia to Antony:

Most noble Antony,
Let not the piece of virtue which is set
Betwixt us as the cement of our love
To keep it builded, be the ram to batter
The fortress of it.

III ii 27–31

From cement that joins to ram that batters.

The matrix of the comedies, I am saying, is used but transformed. One can see old traces of its underlying code –

Our separation so abides and flies
That thou, residing here, goes yet with me,
And I, hence fleeing, here remain with thee.

Antony and Cleopatra, I iii 103–5

Queen Hamlet, thou hast thy father much offended.
Hamlet Mother, you have my father much offended.
Queen Come, come, you answer with an idle tongue.
Hamlet Go, go, you question with a wicked tongue.

Hamlet, III iv 8–11

But now there is an increase in the sheer pressure of circumstance
that acts on people, even as rhyme-pressure had acted upon the
very choice and frame of words. It is more tense now; a different
time-pressure works harder upon space than the rhymes of poetic
timing ever did. So at its most extreme with Lear:

O Lear, Lear, Lear!
Beat at this gate, that let thy folly in, [*Striking his head*]
And thy dear judgement out!

I iv 268–70

There is now no room for two opposites in the same place: folly coming in, means judgement goes out. It is as if the tendency to expansion is held in compressed form in Shakespeare's implosive tragedies. Lear's head contains thoughts increasingly too big for it.

In *All's Well That Ends Well*, the ailing King of France when told how much he is beloved by his country, simply replies: 'I fill a place, I know't' (I ii 69). In *As You Like It* Orlando, the displaced younger son, had said: 'only in the world I fill up a place which may be better supplied when I have made it empty' (I ii 180–2). But increasingly, as we move beyond the early comedies, Shakespeare's people may be either forced out of one place or forced back into another – whether it is Kent trying to make room for goodness, or Hamlet claustrophobically struggling to fulfil the role bequeathed to him. There is increasingly a moral or historical space that somebody – some body – must *fill*. And with these differing pressures one feels a tightening of Shakespeare's grip on the world and a temporal acceleration of his imagination – as when, even earlier on in Shakespeare's career, Prince Hal by horrific mistake first took the crown of succession from Henry IV, even before the king was quite dead:

Prince I never thought to hear you speak again.
King Thy wish was father, Harry, to that thought;
      I stay too long by thee, I weary thee.
      Dost thou so hunger for mine empty chair . . .

2 Henry IV, IV v 91–4

The transitional space involved in due succession is swallowed up. Time and the world are compressed. The empty throne seems to call for filling, and in grotesque overlap father and son try as it were to sit down in the same seat at the same time. Just as the external need for rhyme and the internal demand of thought struggle to fulfil each other in a sonnet, or seek to marry in a comedy, so in Shakespeare's darker histories of the world the demands of a felt gap

mine empty chair

shape the man even as he tries to fill that space in his own way.

In such a world characters begin to trust no more, as did Viola, the space offered them. Lady Macbeth's reproach to her husband, who wanted the crown when he could not get it but who when he could get it was frightened to want it, belongs to the physics of displacement and resistance rather than rhyme:

> Art thou afeard
> To be the same in thine own act and valour,
> As thou art in desire? . . .
>   Nor time, nor place,
> Did then adhere, and yet you would make both:
> They have made themselves, and that their fitness now
> Does unmake you.
>
> *Macbeth*, I vii 39–41, 51–4

You would make them both but now handy-dandy they, presenting themselves, do unmake you, says Lady Macbeth – as if you resented the ease; as if you thought that only to resist was to exist; or as if you feared that the world's outer echoing of your own inner fantasy was a way of your being not so much fulfilled as overtaken. It is almost as if not-doing creates space for a sort of equivocal and hamstrung inner individuality simply by withdrawal. And when there is too much time and too much space around, there is of course Hamlet. 'I do not know/Why yet I live to say this thing's to do' (IV iv 43–4): the man thus separated by inner dimension from the matrix, the nutshell, which even so is still all around him.

Macbeth, Hamlet, Coriolanus – each may be thought resistant, even perverse. 'Let it be virtuous to be obstinate' (*Coriolanus*, V iii 26). For in contrast a Machiavellian would be untroubled by a chameleon-like adaptation to the shape suggested by surrounding circumstances. Edmund rhymes easily:

> Let me, if not by birth, have lands by wit:
> All's with me meet that I can fashion fit.
>
> *King Lear*, I iii 180–1

And Machiavelli says simply, 'If it happens that time and circumstances are favourable to one who acts with caution and prudence, then he will be successful.' But Shakespeare (in this actually like Machiavelli himself) is much more interested in the next big moment that comes along after the initial success, or even the moment after *that*, when time and circumstances change *again*: when for the most part, that is, the man who was so successful last time is 'ruined because he does not change his mode of procedure'. Why does he not, why can he not, continue to change and change again *ad infinitum*?

> No man is found so prudent as to be able to adapt himself to this, either because he cannot deviate from that to which his nature disposed him, or else because having always prospered by walking in one path, he cannot persuade himself that it is well to leave it.[20]

There is a limit. And in Shakespeare there is also a sort of complex obstinacy: 'I am in blood/Stepp'd in so far, that, should I wade no more,/Returning were as tedious as go o'er' (*Macbeth*, III iv 135–7).

What is 'character' here? It is what results from the fact that a man becomes what he has done, and that he goes on doing what he has done in increasing lack of interchange with the world until he wears himself out to naught. 'This deed *unshapes* me quite', says Angelo: horrifyingly before my own eyes, I see the changing of the old me –

> A deflower'd maid
> And by an eminent body, that enforc'd
> The law against it!
>
> *Measure for Measure*, IV iv 18–21

I, that eminent body, am becoming what I myself have forbidden, am becoming instead what I have now done: the man who traded justice for sex. Increasingly I fit, and take on even in myself, the unshaping new *shape* of my own distorted act. And there is now no going back to the old character of justice without destroying my present self. In such guilt as Angelo's there is also, almost incredibly, a sort of horrified innocence of realization. Look at me! at what I have come to! So Macbeth as if from outside the self he is now trapped within:

How is't with me, when every noise appals me?
What hands are here?

Macbeth, II ii 56–7

'To know my deed, 'twere best not know myself' (II ii 72). As the man becomes his own bad deed, his mind in horrified reaction half separates itself from the man.[21] The amazed self-realizations – 'I *am* Thane of Cawdor' (I iii 133), 'Is this a dagger . . ./Thou marshall'st me the way that I *was* going;/And such an instrument I *was* to use' (II i 33, 42–3) – increasingly become unavailable to the man. He has gone wearily beyond that; despairing even of despair, he just is. 'Returning were as tedious as go o'er.'

Ernst Cassirer is therefore right to point out the existential importance for Shakespeare of the (admittedly partial and uneven) replacement of an old hierarchical system by a more dynamically overbrimming world where

> meaning lies in the *reversal* of the relationship we are accustomed to accepting between *being* and *acting*. The old Scholastic proposition *operari sequitur esse* is valid in the world of things. But it is the nature and the peculiarity of the human world that in it, the opposite is true. It is not being that prescribes once and for all the lasting direction that the mode of action will take; rather, the original direction of action determines and places being.[22]

In Shakespeare's terms, 'I see men's judgements are/A parcel of their fortunes' (*Antony and Cleopatra*, III xiii 31–2). Character is what *happens*: that is why the minds of such as Macbeth or Lear or Angelo are so terrified to see what events apparently prove them antecedently to have been.

It is above all Coriolanus who does not believe that character primarily exists *before* the moment of acting, any more than on the other hand he believes that character is created *by* the moment of acting. But, in between the two, character for him is forged *in* the very heat of action. For then in the very midst of a fight or a test the force of events asks of those it encounters whether there is any equivalent force potentially in them with which to match it. The rest is secondary. Coriolanus is not interested in being a separate thinking thing involved in either anticipation or memory. He 'rewards/His deeds with doing them' (II ii 127–8). There is simply what he does, in a present preferably as physically real as possible. If Hamlet offered himself a disparaging comparison with Fortinbras, it would have been even more challenging for him to have contrasted himself with Coriolanus instead.

Yet Stephen Greenblatt, writing on the dialectics of self-transformation in *Renaissance Self-Fashioning*, seems to believe that the Renaissance is full of figures almost as devious for the sole sake of personal power as is Edmund – albeit perhaps unconsciously so in their improvisations. Greenblatt's Renaissance figures manipulate the external forces that press internal changes upon them, and thus outside-in retain the power to fashion themselves. But my argument here is that in Shakespeare the emergence of the individual within the pressurizing interstices of circumstance and event is active and passive at once – the very proportions of each, being what is tested in each particular instance. The whole process of 'interchange of state' is fundamentally too fast and too intermingled for either fictive control or independent choice by the self in what is after all the very act of its own formation.

It is the Iagos and the Edmunds of the world who best fit Greenblatt's thesis, in their effort to take up the places held by others. Perhaps Hal too is another such manipulator of both self and others. But Coriolanus is more deeply inno-cent in his concern for the primary power of his being than Greenblatt's emphatically political thesis would allow. Coriolanus got made as such 'for what he did before Corioles' (I ix 62). But afterwards he would not be what the tribunes of the people wanted him to be, simply for the name of power; he experi-enced a sort of moral claustrophobia and felt himself not 'other than *one* thing' (IV vii 42). Consequently, he was unmade when he was thrown out of Rome – *unless* he could find within his own rejected resources a nameless, placeless resistance of being. That inner bit of him thinks to join league with Rome's enemy, the Volsces and that Aufidius whom he actually defeated at Corioles, in order to take his revenge on Rome. Handy-dandy in this chemistry, it is as though his enemy's enemy now has to be his friend. The one thing he is will take *that* shape now. And when the old general Cominius goes to the Volsces' camp to try to reclaim Coriolanus, the man will not answer:

I urg'd our old acquaintance, and the drops
That we have bled together. 'Coriolanus'
He would not answer to; forbad all names:
He was a kind of nothing, titleless
Till he had forg'd himself a name o'th'fire
Of burning Rome.

V i 10–15

He will not answer because this is time-out, a mere temporary present in between the Roman past and the Volscian future. This moment's tough refusal proves that he is not of such innerly yielding stuff as is the also silent Octavia, tested in the space between quitting her brother and joining her new husband:

Her tongue will not obey her heart, nor can
Her heart inform her tongue – the swansdown feather,
That stands upon the swell at the full of tide,
And neither way inclines.

Antony and Cleopatra, III ii 47–50

Rather than be a feather, Coriolanus will be a kind of nothing. For he does not think of himself as available or even real between events or outside action, and, as far as he is concerned, is not *there* as a human person while he is waiting between his past life and his future one. He is not only dismissing Cominius by saying 'I am nothing to you', he is at the same time more vulnerably saying to himself 'I am nothing now, nothing yet.'

And yet the kind of nothing which Coriolanus feels himself to be when he is existentially off-duty is still – as the Hamlet part of Shakespeare's twisting and turning mind would be quick to realize – something that does exist:

When I behold *Caesar* and *Alexander* in the thickest of their wondrous great labours, so absolutely to enjoy humane and corporall pleasures, I say not, that they release thereby their minde, but rather strengthen the same; submitting by vigor of courage their violent occupation, and laborious thoughts to the customary use of ordinary life. Wise had they beene, had they beleeved, that that was their ordinary vocation, and this their extraordinary. What egregious fooles are we. Hee hath past his life in idlenesse, say we; alas I have done nothing this day. What? have you not lived?[23]

Consider Alexander or Caesar who would not accept everyday life as their norm save in moments of mere rest and interlude: their dust, mused Hamlet, for all their grand ambitions and grandiose actions in life served finally only to stop a bung-hole. To Coriolanus, as to Alexander or Caesar, Montaigne would say: 'Are you nothing, unless you are doing something and, at that, something extraordinary? Egregious fool!'

For the kind of nothing that Coriolanus thinks he is *is* something – and, indeed, something that interests Shakespeare (though not Coriolanus) more than anything else. Nothing *is* in Shakespeare, there is no time-out. 'The old peripatetick principle, that "Nature abhors a Vacuum",' says Samuel Johnson in *Rambler* 85, 'may be properly applied to the intellect.' Shakespeare's people are not like Montaigne, they cannot do nothing and still be. And Shakespeare himself cannot stop probing and pressurizing them: rather, by a sort of sideways displacement – a nail drives out a nail – he finds the most real test of the essence of Coriolanus at the moment when Coriolanus himself is least prepared to think of it as such. For there are no reliably safe interim times or places or scenes which do not count in Shakespeare – secure one crumbling area and another takes its place: 'It is like the case of matter in which, as one form perishes, another immediately supervenes. So too in this case, the substitution of bodies never leaves the space empty, but as one body departs, another falls into place.'[24]

Thus Shakespeare's sense of form is protean, as a packed content pushes and probes blindly amidst countervailing forces to find shape, name, action and expression for itself.

As thus, finally, in *Antony and Cleopatra*. Antony, that 'man of men' in Cleopatra's phrase, regards his soldiers collectively as a huge other version of himself. Wishing to thank all his men together, Mark Antony would have them all moulded into one Antony and he dispersed into so many men, that he might return their service to him *en masse*:

> I wish I could be made so many men,
> And all of you clapped up together in

An Antony, that I might do you service
So good as you have done.

IV ii 17–20

That, emotionally, is how Antony at that present moment would
have the matrix shaped, the weight and mass of the play distributed.
But instead it must take another form. When Enobarbus deserts
Antony it is, Antony feels, precisely because Enobarbus is something
in Antony: Enobarbus is not just himself but the knock-on effect,
made personal, of something gone wrong with his chief – 'O my
fortunes have/Corrupted honest men' (IV v 16–17). Equally, the
men who are still faithful are to Antony the final lost version of his
old bigger and better self – and he feels that he no longer deserves
them or can live up to them, urging them instead to become as he
now is, by the pattern of what he has done:

Antony   fly,
         And make your peace with Caesar.
All   Fly? Not we.
Antony I have fled myself . . .

I myself have fled; and so, deeper than that, I have fled even from
my (best and former) self. So:

         Let that be left
Which leaves itself.

III xi 5–7, 19–20

Yet when Antony sends back his treasure with bounty overplus in
both thanks and apology, Enobarbus is left both feeling for Antony,
as if Antony's ruin were in himself, and yet also separately blaming
and turning against himself. In the words of 'The Phoenix and the
Turtle', 'Distance and no space was seen' (line 30). Connected *and*
cut off, Enobarbus cries, 'O Antony,/Nobler than my revolt is
infamous' (IV ix 18–19). That comparison is not merely a matter of
external language: it is felt within Enobarbus as if *he* were Antony's
simile, albeit in reverse, and his revolt were precisely a measure, in
inverse proportion, of Antony's nobility.

Meanwhile, from the other side, Octavius orders that the
deserters of Antony should be put in the front line, as the first
to oppose him –

That Antony may seem to spend his fury
Upon himself.

IV vi 10–11

But Antony, urging Eros to kill him rather than that he should be led through Rome a mocked vestige of his former self, speaks thus, conversely:

Thou strik'st not me, 'tis Caesar thou defeat'st.

IV xiv 68

'Bid that welcome/Which comes to punish us, and we punish it,/Seeming to bear it lightly' (IV xiv 141–3).

Struggling amidst such protean shapes, Antony no longer feels that godlike he *is* the world: he now seems shrunk to being only a small part of it, as the world itself draws its life out and away from him. He had felt it going: 'Here I am Antony,/Yet cannot *hold* this visible shape' (IV xiv 13–14). It is as if, as in the vision of a Campanella, the world is full of one whole life-stuff, and people who are to themselves entire are really only bits of that stuff in its working out. For this life-force which gathered itself together in one man, incarnate in an Antony, gradually ebbs away from him as he wastes it, leaving him to thin itself out into replacement vehicles instead, until the next large occasion.

'The nature which comes into things and departs from them is indeed multiple': 'it makes them more rare, more diffuse, more dilated; or more dense, more compressed and restricted.'[25] Even thus the plays expand and contract, subdivide, then find their subdivisions re-forming or overlapping, making parts within wholes and wholes within parts, Lear in the storm and the tempest in his mind, filling in every dimension of being and each square inch of possibility.

3   ON SPACE FOR A WORD

When the space between Antony and Octavius suddenly becomes Octavia, or when Enobarbus becomes at once something both resulting out of and distant from Antony, when thus two things become one or one thing becomes two, an explosive language erupts out of these force-fields of charged and fully laden being.

Thus it is in *2 Henry IV*, when after taking the crown the
prince says, 'I never thought to hear you speak again', the king
his father replies:

Thy wish was father, Harry, to that thought.

In that saturated atmosphere, the word 'father' must strike twice
with violence in that one appearance. For it has been transposed
like a metaphor from outside to in – from the king's relation to
his son, to the son's wish in his precisely *father-replacing* thought.
Shakespeare's language makes his world so powerfully dense; by
metaphor things are taken from one place or locus, and relocated
within another.

What is happening here is kin to something that may be
illustrated in the sonnets. Sonnet 128 opens magnificently:

How oft when thou, my music, music play'st

If we were to thin this out and disperse it into prosaic space, it
would simply be a charming compliment: sitting at the virginal you
play music but even without playing you are yourself my music. So
too in Sonnet 8:

Music to hear, why hear'st thou music sadly?

The line itself says: how *can* this be in the same line, in the same
person – a voice like music from someone whom music does not
gladden, from someone who beautifully scorns my own music in
her praise? In Sonnet 128 the poet similarly hears his beloved
playing something as beautiful to the ear as she herself is to the
eye, at the selfsame time: 'What's so surprising about music is that
it comes from outside. It feels as if it comes from the inside.'[26]

Thus a reader, cottoning on to the metaphor, might say in slow
retrospective description, 'You play music and, now I think of it,
you are my music too'; but poetry says in a flash of mentality, 'thou
my music, music play'st'. The two words 'music' may look as if
they are on the same chronological *line*, but they are not really
so, for the first 'music' (the metaphorical idea) is taken from the
second (the literal sound) even *before* the second is finally put down
on paper. The mind has leapt ahead of itself, producing the future
in the instant; has moved abruptly but invisibly between different
levels or loci of meaning; and has produced a sudden compression

of space in the very midst of thinking lineally: 'music, music'.[27]
In short, the word 'music' has taken the thought that goes with
it into a different *place* of reference. Shakespeare, in his relish of
both speed and density, loves to change places in a second or to
bring together in the same space widespread reference–points.[28]
This process is Shakespeare's mentally imaginative equivalent to
Coriolanus's belief – a belief that acting and being happen virtually
together at the same charged moment in the same packed space:

> In the life of the spirit there is no standing still; therefore, if a
> person does not do what is right at the very second he knows
> it - then, first of all, knowing simmers down. . . . Willing allows
> some time to elapse, an interim called: 'We shall look at it
> tomorrow.' During all this, knowing becomes more and more
> obscure, and the lower nature gains the upper hand more and
> more; alas, for the good must be done immediately, as soon as
> it is known (and that is why in pure ideality the transition from
> thinking to being is so easy, for there everything is at once), but
> the lower nature's power lies in stretching things out.[29]

In a concentrated but pure instant of separation and return,
Shakespeare seizes the idea of music from the word 'music'; or
takes the transferable metaphor of 'father' from the way that the
word allows a tiny *space* for separate thought between itself and
the thing it stands for. Thus, that gap between word and thing is
not something that Shakespeare regrets, as if it disabled language:
on the contrary, it is something he silently but actively *uses* in his
thinking, yielding him as it does invisible room for quick cerebral
movement in the immediate exploration of mental space.

Shakespeare's characteristic procedure thus involves a sheer
speeding up of the process which for once was slowly described
in *A Midsummer Night's Dream*:

> Such tricks hath strong imagination,
> That if it would but apprehend some joy,
> It comprehends some bringer of that joy.

V i 18–20

The mental shift from effect back to cause, from quick apprehending
to steadier comprehension, is more usually done in one fell swoop
in Shakespeare. It is not just knife first, then wound, but something

rather less separated: 'Thou lay'st in every gash that love hath given me/The knife that made it' (*Troilus and Cressida*, I i 62–3)

Yet see Shakespeare's thinking in a larger and more physically immediate context:

> On each side her
> Stood pretty dimpled boys, like smiling Cupids,
> With divers-coloured fans, whose winds did seem
> To glow the delicate cheeks which they did cool
> And what they undid did.
>
> *Antony and Cleopatra*, II ii 211–15

The glow rushes at once to fill the place that the cooling fanned; cause and effect are mutually entrammelled. There is barely time for full comprehension: it is held tight within the immediate apprehension. And thus the condensed immediacy of 'thou my music, music play'st' becomes that superb two-way movement: 'undid did'. There is scarcely a second between the two words, as Shakespeare's mind turns round. With Cleopatra herself he undoes, does:

> I saw her once
> Hop forty paces through the public street,
> And having lost her breath, she spoke, and panted,
> That she did make defect perfection
> And, breathless, power breathe forth.
>
> II ii 238–42

She stops, breathless; but Shakespeare carries on, 'breathless power breathes forth', which in its sheer flowing generosity of being is very like 'Increasing store with loss and loss with store'. For in addition, filling every square inch with meaning, Shakespearian spelling allows the suggestion of 'pour' as well as 'power': 'and breathless pour breath forth'. She in her breathlessness is only thinking of breathing in, but even as she gasps for breath what life she thus breathes out! 'What is yours to bestow is not yours to reserve' (*Twelfth Night*, I v 189–90). Cleopatra often takes advantage of her own beauty but there is too much here for it to be just that. Or rather the result includes and is still more than any (infectiously comic) means of seduction that may have induced it – the girlishness showing the woman through it all, hopping fast, then breathing life, producing even by her very artfulness what is still natural to her; defect made perfect. For in that apprehending instant this is what she is, more than ever can be quite comprehended even by herself. And in the plenitude of the world even this little, finite, anecdotal moment about a beautiful woman being childishly out of breath can become for a second central to the universe's infiniteness:

> For all mobile bodies are equally near to and equally far from the prime and universal motive power. . . . There is in the universe neither centre nor circumference, but, if you will, the whole is central, and every point also may be regarded as part of a circumference in respect to some other central point.[30]

'Find out new heaven, new earth' (I i 17): this is Shakespeare's version of Bruno's infinite and rich relativity. For we find something like Bruno's fullness and overbrimming lack of hierarchy in the packed Shakespearian verse-form which combines so many different levels of being still within its one ongoing line: 'thou, my music, music play'st.' The science of this is not arcane. In their own way, actors, by the very nature of performance, are very good at realizing this instantaneousness of life in Shakespeare which the language of most critics is all too slow to register. As Michael Pennington says, the actor has the advantage 'of having lived with the language for a long time at rehearsals, but he has only one opportunity to convey it to an audience'.[31] One go, and then it is gone again in the breathing instant of sheer life.

I want to conclude that the rule in Shakespeare is this: as in one go character emerges out of spatial situation, so thought and consciousness arise likewise amidst the tight configurations of words.[32] I will explain.

We have already seen how in *A Midsummer Night's Dream* Shakespeare uses technique as a form of detachment, employing numbers in place of persons. But there comes an intuitive danger-point when the distance, threatening to become too great, abruptly provokes a reaction in Shakespeare which returns him to a human sympathy felt then not merely dutifully but as if by sudden necessity and for the first time. The numbers become human, the spaces become characters for an instant. So, when Philostrate urges the

royal company not to hear the play of the rude mechanicals because
it is too crude and too ludicrous

> Which, when I saw rehears'd, I must confess
> Made mine eyes water; but more merry tears
> The passion of loud laughter never shed.

Theseus replies

> What are they that do play it?

and suddenly in Philostrate's reply, despite himself, the distance
from tears of comedy to tears of pathos closes:

> Hard-handed men that work in Athens here,
> Which never labour'd in their minds till now.
>
> V i 68–73

'*Labour'd* in their *minds*' is like the next evolutionary step,
raised upon itself through metaphor, yet metaphor so swiftly
reincorporated within the line as to seem literal again. Played off
against hard hands, that word 'minds' seems to have come from
another place or another dimension of being – and then, finding itself
here, strikes the spectators' 'minds' too, in literal sympathy closing
the gap between audience and actors. These people are like the
peasants that Ruskin in *The Stones of Venice* would educate regardless
of their initial outward mistakes of grammar, or the labourers that
Bartle Massey in George Eliot's *Adam Bede* will teach slowly to
spell out words they know so quickly and intimately as things ('the
c-o-r-n is d-r-y'): they should not be treated *un*kindly as if they had
no 'minds'.

Even so, a word suddenly *comes* in Shakespeare, finding room
as if it were needed – as thus, Ariel reporting to Prospero on the
condition of his enemies:

> *Ariel*   Your charm so strongly works 'em
>   That if you now beheld them, your affections
>   Would become tender.
> *Prospero*   Dost thou think so, spirit?
> *Ariel*   Mine would, sir, were I human.
> *Prospero*   And mine shall.
>
> V i 17–20

It is that word '*human*' – only retrospectively seen as called into being to answer not 'thou' or 'think' but the word 'spirit' – which measures the distance from which Shakespeare travels back. 'Were I – human.' It explodes inwardly in someone who is human. For that is what it feels like – the word 'human' coming back *to* a human for its place of meaning, just as 'never labour'd in their minds till now' comes back inside our minds. It is as if the word 'human' has long been needed – but only discovered to have been so long needed at the very moment of one's being surprisingly relieved to find it. 'We only know, I believe, what we know now: "knowing" no more consists in what we once knew than in what we shall know in the future.'[33]

Therefore the mental journey of Shakespeare's return from outside-in is now almost instantaneous, something thrown back to mind when it has reached that outer point of detachment from the human which seemed figured in the airy spirit Ariel:

Mine would, sir, were I human.
> And mine shall.

Prospero's 'And' means 'at once': 'In pure ideality,' said Kierkegaard, 'the transition from thinking to being is so easy, for there is everything at once. . . . The lower nature's power lies in stretching things out.' But then immediately Prospero has also to catch up with himself, comprehend what has just been apprehended, and – above all – consciously *inhabit* the space which the word has just created for him:

> And mine shall.
Hast thou, which art but air, a touch, a feeling
Of their afflictions, and shall not myself,
One of their kind, that relish all as sharply
Passion as they, be kindlier mov'd than thou art?
> *The Tempest*, V i 20–4

Prospero is like a very good reader of Shakespeare: what was seized (by Ariel) as imagination is picked up (by Prospero) in explosive resonance as sudden memory. The relation between the words 'spirit' and 'human', or between 'thou' and 'myself', or between 'air' and 'touch, feeling' is that of a felt reaction, one word both yielding to and also producing another, as though each thing in the world 'must suffer in acting and act in suffering'.[34]

There is an otherwise *unspeakable* power in Shakespeare which takes off in words and from words – from 'kind' to 'kindlier', from 'thou music play'st' to 'thou, my music'. That is why Shakespeare himself seems so invisible, so hard to make out separately: he is so completely immersed in the words and in the tacit thought-movements between them. Taking off from words, his power raises itself to comparatively higher levels ('kindlier') still by means of words. I have argued that that tacit working-process between words occurs at other levels too: if Shakespeare must work within words and their spreading associations, likewise his characters must remain within dense verbal situations they cannot get out of. For what is 'character' in Shakespeare? – it is in the first instance simply somebody occupying a place *and* being aware *of* it *in* it. 'None of the categories exists without mutual interweaving. You cannot find one category existing without others being interwoven, not even substance itself which is said to be capable of existing on its very own.'[35] No substance without consciousness, no place without mind, no space without time, no words without the maximum of their meaning, no persons without interrelationships. So it is with startling comic beauty in *As You Like It* as each character realizes his or her place in a bafflingly separated relation to others:

Silvius	And so am I for Phebe.
Phebe	And so am I for Ganymede.
Orlando	And so am I for Rosalind.
Rosalind	And so am I for no woman.
Phebe [to Ros.]	If this be so, why blame you me to love you?
Silvius [to Phebe]	If this be so, why blame you me to love you?
Orlando	If this be so, why blame you me to love you?
Rosalind	Who do you speak to 'Why blame you me to love you?'?
Orlando	To her that is not here, nor doth not hear.
Rosalind	Pray you no more of this, 'tis like the howling of the Irish wolves against the moon.

V ii 98–111

In all this interweaving, there is a full minute or two before Rosalind breaks the spell by that final question – which in the

Folio's '*Why* do you speak *too* . . .', includes the liquid movement of 'Why do you speak *to* [the script] "Why blame you me to love you?"?' It is a question which opens a space poor Orlando cannot yet fill – to Rosalind's immediate and barely disguised annoyance: 'Pray you no more of this.' But during that spell it is as though the occupants of Shakespeare's plenteous world – each one pushing out the words of the next one by a sort of sympathetic force of sideways displacement – are at once held together and apart, each one of them paradoxically separated and connected by the same difference. Only, the more a character such as Rosalind knows within the place she occupies, the less she can simply remain in it. And knowing as much as Rosalind does, the reader or the watcher of this grouping has a mind in a spin. It is in the context of this matrix that Orlando's lament is so eruptively powerful:

> But, O, how bitter a thing it is to look into happiness through another man's eyes.
>
> V ii 41–3

For this is what it is like to see more from your place than your place has in it, and yet to have mentally to go back and remain there.[36] So, near the end Lear says, looking at himself so strangely for a bare moment as if from outside, 'I should e'en die with pity/To see another thus' (IV vii 53–4). In another second that 'another' turns back inside again into being, unbearably, himself.

In such a situation – be it comic or tragic – when nothing else can escape confinement, language breaks out of Shakespeare like necessity: for the language is no more merely something freely and leisurely thought out than the characters in the plays may be said deliberately to choose to do things in due course. Lear's madness is the most extreme example of words escaping when, under pressure, nothing else can – as a mind finds itself full of a situation altogether too big for it:

> *Fool* Thou should'st not have been old till thou had'st been wise.
> *Lear* O let me not be mad, not mad, sweet heaven;
> Keep me in temper; I would not be mad.
>
> I v 41–4

There is not due space and time now to become wise *before* being old, any more than later there is time in the play for Cordelia to die *after* Lear instead of before him. 'She should have died hereafter', as Macbeth puts it, 'There would have been a time for such a word' (*Macbeth*, V v 17–18). But the process thus compressed, Lear cannot hold it – cannot hold its bursting meaning in a mind paradoxically thinking of itself as increasingly unable to think: 'not be mad, not mad'. The play drives on past such attempts to halt its momentum, as if the realization within such a plea itself only implosively increased the pace of deterioration. The only way on for the play is Gloucester's:

> henceforth I'll bear
> Affliction till it do cry out itself
> 'Enough, enough,' and die.
>
> IV vi 75–7

It is as if *King Lear*, inseparably struggling against itself, is a play which can only kill the affliction which is hurting it through its very own reluctant deaths: 'Be comforted, good Madam; the great rage,/You see, is kill'd in him' (IV vii 78–9). 'I should e'en die with pity.' There is no way out.

In this chapter I have been arguing that in Shakespeare events call characters into being in order to fill the space they figure out; characters simultaneously create each other through opposing balances. These calls and creations are registered in dynamic words of being which, as Middleton Murry long ago testified, attest to Goethe's saying:

> 'Man is the first speech that Nature holds with God.' In Shakespeare we seem to watch Nature involved in her destiny of self-discovery.[37]

For the sake of such workings-out, Shakespeare continually finds himself a creative pattern of language, a network of modifications and connections, a dynamic situation in space.

When Lear says:

> I know you do not love me; for your sisters
> Have, as I do remember, done me wrong:
> You have some cause, they have not.

Cordelia finds herself (for there is no time or space for deliberation here) saying simply

> No cause, no cause.
>
> IV vii 73–5

It is an answering activity that plucks the word 'cause' out of the wreckage of Lear's voice and mind and pain and puts it at once into her music. It would be contradiction and interruption – 'You have some cause' 'No cause' – did it not immediately turn itself into harmony in its own terms. Is not that why she needs to say 'no cause' twice?

It is repetition and the modification of repetition that is one of the paradigmatic starting-points for this poetry's creation of a second language hidden within language. By repetition Shakespeare establishes for himself a pattern which he can imitate and modify. What is the tacit language-within-language of 'No cause, no cause'? There is the same inner reason for it as for Cordelia's answering by means of repetition a moment before when Lear said:

> Methinks I should know you and know this man;
> Yet I am doubtful: for I am mainly ignorant
> What place this is, and all the skill I have
> Remembers not these garments; nor I know not
> Where I did lodge last night. Do not laugh at me;
> For as I am a man, I think this lady
> To be my child Cordelia.

> And so I am, I am.
>
> IV vii 64–70

Cordelia does not say, 'And so she is: this lady is your child Cordelia.' 'I am' is the direct acknowledgement and the sheer sufficiency. It is spoken only once in the Quarto. But the Folio has it 'And so I am, I am' and not just, as a recent editor suggests, 'to pad out the half-line'.[38] In the Folio it is 'And so I am, I am', because it also is 'No cause, no cause'. These words hold good, in every sense, and Cordelia holds to them again and again, stands by them: faithful, the same, for ever and ever. For by these words Cordelia does not even have to answer Lear's 'I *know* you do not love me' with an explicit 'I do, I do'. This is something deeper, at the level of sheer being, than merely deliberate reassurance or soothingness; for saying the words has actually made them become true:

> And so I am, I am.
> *Lear* Be your tears wet? Yes, faith. I pray, weep not.

Her words wipe all tears from all eyes – but her own, and what provokes her tears begins with 'Do not laugh at me'. This is a man who cannot recognize 'these' garments, who without escape or excuse still is brought back to

> What place this is.

It would not be the same if Cordelia simply said it once, factually: 'I am', 'No cause'. It is as though the situation demands the words: they are picked up from Lear himself. And the words when repeated then come back to make the person – Cordelia, I am, with no cause – who can in turn confirm them. 'Yes, faith.' For the space between their first and second soundings – 'I am I am' 'No cause no cause' – is the space during which the thought finds power to become the thinker of itself. This is crucial in Shakespeare: how words call into being thoughts around and about them, how words find just sufficient space in the inner or outer worlds for feelings, how words themselves become minds and hearts in people. It is like Prospero taking to heart that word 'human' and thus being it. 'I am, I am.'

Yet it is a bitter thought that Lear's final 'Thou'lt come no more' in itself remembers how things like that 'And so I am, I am' were precisely that coming once more, once again. 'No cause' becomes 'no more', becomes the crying repetition 'No, no, no life!', just as Lear's maddened 'Then, kill, kill, kill, kill, kill, kill' (IV vi 185) becomes 'Never, never, never, never, never!':

> No, no, no life!
> Why should a dog, a horse, a rat, have life,
> And thou no breath at all? Thou'lt come no more,
> Never, never, never, never, never!

> V iii 304–7

Again the Folio is better at reproducing the play's pattern, sounding the word 'never' five times, to the Quarto's three. For what is so implosively terrible about that long repetition of the word 'never' is the implicit acknowledgement that Lear cannot *ever* get over it or fully realize it. The death of Cordelia is the most sudden thing of all in Shakespeare. 'Never': a word saying simply again and again, and bitterly for ever and ever, that this life won't be repeated and is not eternal. The repetitive form is played off against the meaning of its very own content. 'Thou'lt come no more': a life unbelievably both finished and incomplete. The power that rises each time from these words and then is *reimmersed* in them – 'Never, never, never, never, never!' – cannot find space to free itself from the situation in which it finds itself, only increases the realization of its own defeat.

So I say that although Shakespeare's power takes off from words and raises itself by words, it can never visibly transcend the verbal world it works in. 'Never, never, never, never, never.' It can only silently return itself, and the meanings it has found, to more words within the human space. 'Not mad, not mad.' Shakespeare's is never, finally, like Dante's a freely transcendent power.[39] It is something only 'mirror'd there/Where it may see itself': 'The eye sees not itself/But by reflection, by some other things' (*Julius Caesar*, I ii 54–5). So the word 'human' came back upon Prospero, even as the word 'mad' to Lear. But we can no more see to the bottom of our acts than we can with our own eyes see our own faces. The law of gravity in Shakespeare's world of contained compression says this: howsoever a creature can momentarily, 'by reflection', see above itself even through having seen itself among others, still it must return to itself and remain within the physical world in which it is placed:

> If it be now, 'tis not to come; if it be not to come, it will be now; if it be not now, yet it will come.

> *Hamlet*, V ii 216–18

One could put it almost any way round, the verbal world is full of possibilities which seem endless. But there is after all only ever a finite now to which one keeps being returned. Hamlet's lines beautifully register that one truth, however many ways there are for it to be true.

The creative power in Shakespeare can never be stably abstracted from what it makes – can never be abstracted into lasting and final explanation, say. As though abhorring a vacuum, the power works both to separate elements out of solution and to immerse them back into it almost at once. It is a creative principle which can only be briefly glimpsed, or transiently inferred, in its very act of creation.

Chapter 2

'Compounded of Many Simples': Shakespeare's Compositions

'People talk about producing the definitive Shakespeare performance', said the actor and director, Lee Beagley, talking quite casually in the course of a workshop. 'Who do they think they are? God? In Shakespeare's language there are too many overlapping possibilities. And simultaneously they lead you in different directions. Mere mortals can only choose a few of them, suggesting *something* of the complexity.'

Writing about Shakespeare is probably no easier than performing him. For what pushes critic, actor, or director to what seem to be the very limits of human thinking, is something that Dr Johnson described in the Preface to his *Dictionary*, on the difficulty of dealing with the complexities of language itself. Johnson says that when kindred meanings are so interwoven, when so much is suggested all at once, 'when the radical idea branches out into so many parallel ramifications', how can a 'consecutive' account be given of meanings that are almost simultaneously 'collateral'?

This chapter must be a complicated one, precisely because it tries to deal with these overlapping considerations as they go on in Shakespeare. The first three sections are devoted to examining particular Shakespearian techniques hinted at in Chapter One. The longer fourth section then shows how these techniques, of themselves, create meanings for Shakespeare, the importance of which again goes beyond mere technique itself.

My first section is about the use of 'overlap', a means by which Shakespeare produces that sense of so much going on at the same time in the plays.

The second concerns something almost opposite – Shakespeare's deployment of 'separation', with particular reference to the creation of that sense of separatedness out of which comes the consciousness of individuality as an inward dimension.

Section three shows how the technique of overlap occurs not only across a whole play between different characters, as shown in section one, but also in the overlaying of one consideration upon another within individual characters themselves.

Where Chapter One dealt mainly with plenitude in space, Chapter Two is concerned with the complementary dimension of time. The more use there is made of overlap in space, the more that in itself forces out an awareness of the temporal pressure of existence.

The first three sections deal with technical matters and increasingly, throughout them, I make use of Shakespeare's great French contemporary, Montaigne, for purposes of comparison and contrast; only in the fourth and final section, in relation to *Hamlet* and *Coriolanus*, will the reader see the full implications of the use of Montaigne in studying Shakespeare.

1   THE USE OF OVERLAP, CONVENIENT AND INCONVENIENT

Shakespeare's, of course, was an age much concerned with the creation of multiple, three-dimensional perspectives of life. In painting, the aim, as Gombrich has shown, was the representation of the simultaneous existence of different planes and dimensions in time and space:

Pliny has preserved for us the remark of a Hellenistic critic who praised the skill of the famous painter Parrhasios in creating the illusion of roundness by the outlines of his figures. This, we read, is the most subtle part of painting, 'for the outline must go round and so end, that it promises something else to lie behind and thereby shows even what it obscures'. . . . [The figures of Parrhasios] suggest what they can no longer show. We feel the presence of the features we do not see, and so he can show us a dancing maiden turning *into* the picture, an image that would have appeared senseless to any pre-Greek artist . . . a figure with only one arm, or a head without eyes. . . .
    The device of *overlap* caused similar admiration. In his description of a real or imaginary painting Philostratus commends the trick of the artist who surrounds the walls of Thebes with armed men 'so that some are seen in full figure, others with the legs hidden, others from the waist up, then only the busts of some,

heads only, helmets only, and finally just spearpoints. All that, my boy, is analogy, for the eyes must be deceived as they travel back along the relevant zones of the picture.'

It must have been this passage which inspired Shakespeare to describe in *The Rape of Lucrece* a painting of the fall of Troy:

> For much imaginary work was there, -
> Conceit deceitful, so compact, so kind,
> That for Achilles' image stood his spear
> Grip'd in an armed hand; himself behind
> Was left unseen, save to the eye of mind:
> A hand, a foot, a face, a leg, a head
> Stood for the whole to be imagined.[1]

It is with this particular key shape of thought, in the underlying geometry of Shakespeare art, that I want to start this chapter: the overlay or overlap, as the technical means of suggesting to the eye of the *mind* an extra inferable dimension of life and meaning.

The eighteenth-century critic Maurice Morgann said that there was something in the composition of Shakespeare's characters which made them different from those drawn by other writers – 'The characters of every drama must indeed be grouped; but in groups of other poets the parts which are not seen do not in fact exist.' There was an extra dimension in Shakespeare:

> there is a certain roundness and integrity in the forms of Shakespeare, which give them an independence as well as a relation. . . . We often meet with passages which, tho' perfectly felt, cannot be sufficiently explained in words, without unfolding the whole character of the speaker . . . every part being in fact relative and inferring all the rest.[2]

Morgann is right: the parts which are not seen *do* in fact seem to exist in Shakespeare. The power of his language leaves behind a resonant third dimension, a brief space found for sudden inference even as the words disappear and the scene moves on in time:

> *Orsino* And what's her history?
> *Viola* A blank, my lord: she never told her love.
> *Twelfth Night*, II iv 110–11

To quote Morgann, it feels as if, under pressure of time, there is something left 'latent', 'in the back ground', a whole 'history' beneath the silence. For the words they speak are not just the characters' externalized communication; the words themselves help to create the inside of the characters who speak them.

Thus it is not difficult to see in Shakespeare an equivalent use of perspective and overlap in language rather than in paint. Consider Shakespeare's unfolding of multiple perspectives in an early comic example of that grouping of characters which Morgann describes.

In the opening of act IV scene iii of *Love's Labour's Lost* Berowne is stricken with love, despite the earlier compact he has reluctantly made with his fellows to eschew women for the sake of academic study. But, he says,

I would not care a pin if the other three were in.

At once the young King of Navarre comes in. Berowne hides; the king reads aloud a love-sonnet he has himself just written, then stops and hides, like Berowne, because Longaville enters. Now Longaville, like the King, is reading aloud a love-sonnet of his own composition. Then, in turn, he too suddenly hears someone coming and hides. Enter Dumain, the last of the company of young scholars, sonnet again absurdly to the ready, the artifice so natural to these young men. This – 1 Berowne, 2 King, 3 Longaville, 4 Dumain – completes level one of the flat pattern. There are four young men of the court of Navarre and four young ladies visiting from the court of France: by comically lucky chance each man has, independently, picked a different lady. It is all simple and successive and incremental, one lover coming on after another. But still, for all the movement, this repetitive plotting works in a relatively static, two-dimensional way because all differences from lover to lover are, unbeknownst to them, comically so similar.

But level two is where what we may call the overlap begins to take place. Longaville breaks cover to catch Dumain breaking his word, but no sooner does Longaville do this, than of course the King in turn reveals himself to expose Longaville:

Come, Sir, you blush; as his your case is such;
You chide at him, offending twice as much.
                                        Love's Labour's Lost, IV iii 128–9

And then what else but that, in the same way, Berowne should jump out to accuse the King – now guilty as it were three times over. So the pattern has simply been played back in reverse order, rhyming no less by symmetry of situation than by word, but with the added dimension of each lover trying to get one over on the other, in respect of obtaining an 'over-view'. 'Are we betray'd thus to thy over-view?' (line 172). Thus Berowne crows:

All three of you, to be thus much o'ershot?
You found his mote; the king your mote did see;
But I a beam do find in each of three.
                                        IV iii 157–9

The first on the scene is now fourth in the sequence but also top of the tree. And yet there is also a fifth over-hearer: Shakespeare complicit with ourselves his audience. The very form now begins to say, tacitly, to Berowne: 'And why beholdest thou the mote that is in thy brother's eye, but considerest not the beam that is in thine own eye?' (Matthew 7.3). Measure for measure begins here.

Level three in the number-pattern takes us one dimension further, into further interior depth. Now enter Costard bringing back, unknowingly, Berowne's own misdirected letter to his beloved. What is this letter, Berowne? Read it to us, says the King innocently. Berowne knows that now he too is caught. There is a longish pause in the theatre: the pause for inference, as Morgann might put it, for the eye of the mind to do its seeing. A thought, held by the audience, is now getting back on stage.

The pause involves the recognition of the pattern even by one who is a member of it: indeed a member who had hoped to remain above it all – but just as all the others had too. In the continuing knock-on effect of the scene from lover to lover which stops only with Berowne, this is the reflexive point at which, to use Russell Hoban's phrase, 'pattern becomes consciousness'.[3] The whole static scene is now set moving even within the head of one of its very own participants.

Thus Berowne to the King:

> Guilty, my lord, guilty! I confess, I confess.
> *King* What?
> *Berowne*   That you three fools lack'd me, fool, to make up
> the mess;
>   He, he, and you, my liege, and I,
>   Are pick-purses in love, and we deserve to die.
>   O! dismiss this audience, and I shall tell you more.
> *Dumain* Now the number is even.
> *Berowne*   True, true; we are four.
>
> IV iii 202–7

Here Berowne's individual consciousness is not only a consciousness *of* the pattern but becomes consciousness *in* the pattern,
returning to it – in a way that Hamlet (as we shall soon see)
cannot. 'He, he, and you, my liege, and I' becomes 'we'. 'We
are four.' The comic rule of life in the very structure of this
play is that no one can singly presume to an over-view – for as
Montaigne puts it:

> Our eyes see nothing backward. A hundred times a day we
> mocke our selves, upon our neighbours subject, and detest some
> defects in others, that are much more apparent in us; yea and
> admire them with a strange impudency and unheedinesse.[4]

But the rhyme in *Love's Labour's Lost* only has to imply all this
– none odd, all even, all fitting – and implies it with more ease,
more swiftness, and (above all) with more sheer *sociability* than a
more separated moral consciousness, such as even Montaigne's, can
manage.

T.R. Langley calls just such a structure in Shakespearian comedy,
typified as it is by rhyme's work in knitting all things together,
'convenient'. For that is the word Sir Philip Sidney uses in *An
Apology for Poetry* to distinguish profound comedy from superficial
laughter: 'for delight we scarcely doe but in things that have a
conveniencie to our selves or to the generall nature; laughter
almost ever commeth of things most disproportioned to our selves
and nature.'[5]

Berowne's is a sort of crestfallen version of Castiglione's courtly *sprezzatura*, that nonchalant capacity for improvisation, called also 'a good grace'.[6] He speaks with good grace in every sense: 'to make up the mess' he lays a place at dinner for himself even when pulled in for questioning; he improvises rhyme itself as if cheekily to turn uncovered hypocrisy into an act of generous pity: 'you three fools lack'd me.' But then at once he adds, more vulnerably, 'lack'd me, fool' – implicitly saying in the group code: 'Please, it is humiliating enough, let Costard and Jaquenetta go and hear no more – it is all something to be shared amongst us who share the weakness.' This utterly relative perspective is now complete. *Love's Labour's Lost* does not require Berowne to go further in isolation but almost immediately upon second thought returns him to the ordinary ongoing social world. At such comic moments more could be thought and said, and thought and said indeed more explicitly and seriously; but the satisfying creation of a secondary, albeit fallen, pattern means that temporarily at least it does not need to be.[7] It is in Langley's terms profoundly 'convenient'.

Yet what develops in Shakespeare after the cohering patternings of early comedy is, as we shall see, something in a deep sense *inconvenient*: unlaughably disproportioned and unfitting, lacking in confident trust, increasingly separated out, and consisting above all of more and more awkwardly overlapping considerations. After all, in the Elizabethan age the word 'conveniencie' was not just applicable to matters of comedy. It was also taken seriously in Hooker's concern with the making of 'convenient' arrangements in a state – with especial regard to the particular discretionary implementation of general laws:

> As the generality is natural, *Virtue rewardable and vice punishable*: so the particular determination of the reward or punishment belongeth unto them by whom the laws are made. Theft is naturally punishable, but the kind of punishment is positive, and such lawful as men shall think with discretion convenient by law to appoint. In laws that which is natural bindeth universally, that which is positive not so. . . . Laws do not only teach what is good but they enjoin it, they have in them a certain constraining force. And to constrain men unto anything inconvenient doth seem unreasonable. Most requisite therefore it is that to devise

laws which all men shall be forced to obey none but wise men be admitted.[8]

'Positive' laws deal with just that area of subtlety which fascinates Shakespeare – where the customary, the arbitrary, the discretionary and the fortuitous negotiate a particular shake-down for problems bearing a general weight.

In such a area, 'Distinguo is', says Montaigne, 'the most universall part of my logike' (vol. II, p.12). In this chapter I shall place against Hooker's belief in the need for one law and one whole world-order Montaigne's more sceptical and inconvenient sense of dissimilar and distinct particulars: that the contrast may show what is at stake in Shakespeare's own experimental positionings.

This chapter will be partly concerned with three contemporaneously 'inconvenient' plays which struggle to implement laws. The framing of appropriate penalties is the very subject-matter of *Measure for Measure*, where Angelo decides to revive the old law ('not dead, though it hath slept') whereby fornication is punishable by death. He sees it as precisely the role of positive law to be *in*convenient to Vienna's citizens as a form of restraint and re-education: but the degree of tolerable strain is precisely what the idea of conveniencie (as something deeper than pragmatism) takes into account. In *Hamlet* this language of discretion is taken over by Claudius and merged with pragmatism from the very start: 'Yet so far hath discretion fought with nature . . .' (I ii 5); precisely how Hamlet meanwhile will implement the mandate of the ghost without the tainting of his mind is very much his tactical problem. In *All's Well That Ends Well* Shakespeare deals in the more informal laws of life, at that local level of snags and anomalies where the satisfactoriness of remedy by discretion and even pragmatism is to be tested. So much of Shakespeare's mature work, I shall argue, including the later writing of *Coriolanus*, is about finding variations upon or alternatives to the experimental case of *Hamlet*. For Hamlet's is the most inconvenient case of all.

But it is to *Measure for Measure* that I first of all turn for an extended demonstration of the sheer use of overlap as a form of thinking in shape and time. For in *Measure for Measure*, in comparison with *Love's Labour's Lost*, the competition of persons trying to occupy the same space at the same time in their different ways, charging that space with their different purposes, has become far greater. Indeed, the overlapping considerations are so complex that overlap itself becomes a technique of substitution that has to work across the whole play.

Measure for Measure is a play dominated by the idea of one person taking the *place* of another. In the first instance, the duke's place – meaning, his very position in the world – is taken by his deputy Angelo:

> I have deliver'd to Lord Angelo –
> A man of stricture and firm abstinence –
> My absolute power and place here in Vienna.

I iii 11–13

Angelo is to impose a greater strictness by putting fresh life into the very 'shape' of the law and preventing it from any longer inertly rigidifying:

> We must not make a scarecrow of the law,
> Setting it up to fear the birds of prey,
> And let it keep one shape till custom make it
> Their perch, and not their terror.

II i 1–4

His person is to bring that stuffed shape back to life. He begins with an effectively lapsed law against fornication as punishable by death.

Hooker, so concerned to find the fitness of things, reports as follows on an analogous apparently arbitrary local law, a positive law established 'amongst the Grecians':

> it was agreed, that he which being overcome with drink did then strike any man, should suffer punishment double as much as if he had done the same being sober. No man could ever have thought this reasonable that had intended thereby only to punish the injury committed, according to the gravity of the fact. For who knoweth not, that harm advisedly done is naturally less pardonable, and therefore worthy of the sharper punishment?

But in that country at that time, violence was mostly committed by those who succumbed to drink. Drunkenness was then the current social evil to be combated. Thus concludes Hooker:

Lawmakers must have an eye to the place where, and to the men amongst whom.

Hooker, p.94 (book I, ch.10.9)

That is what is crucial about the specific implementation of general laws and principles – the overlapping considerations that make up their context. Conveniency at this level is not a matter of something being merely either expedient or decorous: it is about something *fitting* into space and time.

What Angelo seeks to do at any rate is narrow the 'scope' which the duke's former laxness allowed in Vienna (I iii 35) - the very room for manoeuvre contracts in the play:

So every scope by the immoderate use
Turns to restraint.

I ii 119–20

Claudio, the test case on whom that strictness first falls for the sin of fornication, says that he does not know of Angelo

Whether the tyranny be in his place,
Or in his eminence that fills it up.

I ii 152–3

It is precisely that richly confused area of overlap between a person and the person's place – be it place as office or place as situation – which is full of thought to Shakespeare.[9] So Angelo, seeking clarity, will try to say to Isabella: 'It is the law, not I, condemn your brother' (II ii 80). Yet it is also true that the 'I', though not itself the same as the law, should lead 'a life *parallel'd*/Even with the stroke and line of his great justice' (IV ii 77–8). But of course in *Measure for Measure* the shape soon ceases to be measured in terms of such undeviating parallels. It is typical of Shakespeare to be interested in plausibly right thoughts existing in what is increasingly a wrong person – Angelo – or right thoughts coming in the wrong place or at the wrong time. Such are the ironic overlaps.

Moreover, the very meanings of the word 'place' in this play change with the persons who use it. Strict Angelo tells the provost who must execute Claudio for fornication, 'Do you your office,

or give up your place' (II ii 13). In the meantime the real low-life
villains rely on dodging the meaning: 'though you change your
place, you need not change your trade' (I ii 99–100); while of
the comic version of the law called Constable Elbow, with his
malapropisms, it is said: 'Do you hear how he misplaces?' (II i 87).

But most seriously, when first Escalus and then Isabella plead to
Angelo for Claudio's life, the argument is that Angelo should put
himself in Claudio's place – 'Had time coher'd with place, or place
with wishing', says Escalus (II i 11); while Isabella seeks room for
complex turns of thought:

> If he had been as you, and you as he,
> You would have slipp'd like him, but he like you
> Would not have been so stern.
>
> II ii 64–6

But Angelo has already said to Escalus, ''Tis one thing to be
tempted . . . Another thing to fall':

> You may not so extenuate his offence
> For I have had such faults; but rather tell me
> When I that censure him do so offend,
> Let mine own judgement pattern out my death
> And nothing come in partial.
>
> II i 17–18, 27–31

Which way round is it all to be? This is the play's central image
of one thought overlapping upon another, each having the same
components but in opposite positions.

Angelo cannot put himself in Claudio's position so long as he is
more aware of himself as in the duke's place. But if Angelo is where
he is in memory of the duke's failings as judge and lawgiver and
protector of public morals, it is for Isabella to try to make Angelo
now occupy her point of view, as that of Mercy, rather than Justice.
Or conversely:

> I would to heaven I had your potency,
> And you were Isabel! Should it then be thus?
>
> II ii 67–8

'It is the law, not I.' I am in the place of the Law, says Angelo.
It is necessary for me to be its impersonal instrument in place of
being a mere frail person. But put yourself in Claudio's place, says
Isabella. Or, she adds, let me put myself in yours. Put new grace
and forgiveness in place of old law and morality, put Heaven in
place of Earth. It is as though Angelo and Isabella stand before
each other as from different world-views, indeed as though from
different worlds existing none the less at the same time in the same
world. Nothing makes more evident the utter need that Hooker
felt for an integrated order of *law* in the widest possible meaning
of that word – religious, natural, biological, social and individual:

> The good which is proper unto each man belongeth to the
> common good of all as a part of the whole's perfection.
> But yet these two are things different; for men by that
> which is proper are severed, united they are by that which
> is common. Wherefore besides that which moveth each man
> in particular to seek his private, there must of necessity in
> all public societies be also a general mover, directing unto
> the common good and framing every man's particular to it.
> . . . Such as in one public state have agreed that the supreme
> charge of all things should be committed unto one, they I
> say considering what inconveniences may grow where states
> are subject under sundry supreme authorities were for fear of
> those inconveniences withdrawn from liking to establish many.
> . . . The multitude of supreme commanders is troublesome. *No
> man* (saith our *Saviour*) *can serve Two Masters.* . . . . Suppose that
> tomorrow the power which hath dominion in justice require
> thee at the *Court*, that which in war at the field, that which in
> religion at the *Temple*. All have equal authority over thee and
> impossible it is that thou shouldst be in such case obedient to
> all. By choosing any one whom thou wilt obey, certain thou art
> for thy disobedience to incur the displeasure of the other two.
>
> Hooker, p.152 (book VIII, ch.3.4)

Angelo is meant to be that one unifying authority, trying to
re-establish a hierarchy of priorities. Spare Claudio, he thinks, and
spoil the state. What looks like grace in one context is a return to
sheer laxness in another more earthly one, where fallen men take

advantage of what they see as weakness. 'Show pity', says Isabella. 'I show it most of all when I show justice', he replies (II ii 100–1). For as Escalus says in Angelo's place, 'Mercy is not itself, that oft looks so' (II i 280). Mercy and pity lose what they depend upon – lose their very status as mitigation – if they entirely replace or undermine the law's *primary* act of judgement. 'Those many had not dar'd to do that evil/If the *first* that did th' edict infringe/Had answer'd for his deed' (II ii 92–4).

The problem is 'how laws inferior are derived from that supreme or highest law' (Hooker, p.122, book I, ch.16.2). For whatever the immediate local priorities in Vienna, Justice and Mercy still need each other. And indeed, at another level, for all their opposition, it is also as though Isabella and Angelo themselves are in some way alike – each absolute. Shouldn't you, a would-be nun, be on my side, Angelo asks her, seeing your brother's act as vice not merriment? 'O pardon me, my lord', cries Isabella, pulling herself up short, out of the pattern and context established by her argument's sheer momentum, in order to relocate the place of her own self:

> it oft falls out
> To have what we would have, we speak not what we mean.
> I something do excuse the thing I hate
> For his advantage that I dearly love.
>
> II v 117–120

'Having' and 'meaning', loving and hating, specific persons and general 'things' have become horribly confused.

Isabella, a novice, fundamentally accepts Angelo's view of Claudio's impregnating Juliet: 'a vice that most I do abhor,/And most desire should meet the blow of justice':

> For which I would not plead but that I must;
> For which I must not plead but that I am
> At war 'twixt will and will not.
>
> II ii 29–33

But her inner division is subsumed in the conflict between herself as 'will' and Angelo as 'will not', when Angelo's strictness takes the place of her own inner qualms.

A fornicator is like a murderer, says Angelo, the one takes life, the other sinfully brings it into being – to which Isabella replies "Tis set down so in heaven, but not in earth' (II iv 50). Yet from Angelo's point of view, her plea for mercy itself belongs more to heaven than to earth. Moreover, in further overlap, even whilst she speaks of Heaven, she gives him earthy thoughts. Opposites attract. Angelo finds himself feeling sexual desire for Claudio's sister even as he condemns the brother for fornication. Her body for her brother's life is what Angelo demands, her self in place of Juliet: 'Give up your body to such sweet uncleanness/As she that he hath stain'd' (II iv 53–4).

Yet 'O place, O form', cries Angelo, horrified at the power which rank gives him to hide personal offences within public offices and replace justice with sexual favour (II iv 12). 'This deed unshapes me quite' (IV iv 18): he no longer fits, inside him, the place he continues to occupy without. He cannot deceive himself as Lear can, saying, 'Thou shalt find/That I'll resume the shape which thou dost think/I have cast off for ever' (*King Lear*, I iv 306–8). There is no resuming. Instead Angelo replaces his fight against sexual sin, 'like a good thing being often read/Grown sere and tedious' (II iv 8–9), with sexual sin itself, again as if there is an underlying likeness between opposites. Moreover, it is as if his horror at what he is doing is not only that of his original self but also itself Isabella's. For the things that 'make her good' are precisely what seem to make him 'desire her foully' (II ii 174–5). Yet when she expresses *her* horror at his proposed deal, he does not feel his own any longer. If she exposes the deal, 'Who will believe thee, Isabel?' – he defends himself and the state, as if they were one:

> my place i'th'state
> Will so your accusation overweigh
> That you shall stifle in your own report
> And smell of calumny. . . . As for you
> Say what you can: my false o'erweighs your true.
>
> II iv 155–8, 168–9

His measure weighs more than hers in this context, even though 'my false . . . your true' is at another level created out of this strangely symbiotic relationship. Still, who can she tell? She will say to the duke that if a bad man 'may seem' as grave as Angelo, then 'so may Angelo' be an arch-villain: 'O that it were as like as it is true' (V i 55–60, 107). Here is Shakespeare setting the world adrift amidst what to a Montaigne would be dissimilar particulars rather than Hooker's integrations.

'Place draws bodies together, and arranges them, as time arranges events'[10]: in this play the more people try to occupy the same place as each other and change that place by their very presence, the more the overlap in space forces out further displacedly related events in time.

Thus, Isabella turns from Angelo at the end of act II to Claudio at the beginning of act III in the name of integrity and belief.

Yet when Claudio himself, in his desperation for life, urges the sexual sacrifice upon Isabella, as if for moral and religious reasons, Isabella becomes to Claudio like the original Angelo, condemning him to death. She says:

> Is't not a kind of incest, to take life
> From thine own sister's shame?

III i 138–9

And why? Because Isabella has just seen Claudio becoming like the second Angelo, the seducer. Yet Claudio's thought, in so far as it is expressive of a deep need to live, is also a right thought. But coming where and when it does, to Isabella, it is a right thought somehow without a right place for itself. For as with Angelo and Isabella, Isabella and Claudio seem to be from different worlds while within this same one. The relativism of the perspective, in holding together two opposing absolutes within it, is dizzying in that to-and-fro of sympathies which it demands.

And all the time, displaced and disguised, there is the Duke like an audience to his own testing experiment. When Lucio lyingly says that not he but the friar spoke of the Duke as a fleshmonger, fool and coward, then the Duke in disguise as that friar replies, 'You must, sir, change places with me, ere you make that my report' (V i 334–5).

But changing places has been going on continually in this play. When the Duke thinks Angelo will thus trade mercy for sex, then the Duke himself speaks Angelo's earlier language of strictness, as if to show why he needed Angelo in the first place:

> When vice makes mercy, mercy's so extended
> That for the fault's love is th'offender friended.
>
> IV ii 110–11

Indeed, it is only when the displaced Duke sends Mariana to Angelo instead of Isabella – 'we shall advise this wronged maid to stead up your appointment, go in your place' (II i 250–1) – and himself returns to take Angelo's seat – 'We'll borrow place of him' (V i 361) – that the situation begins to be resolved. For then Angelo finds it incredible, beyond his belief, that Isabella should plead for Angelo to the duke, even as she pleaded for Claudio to Angelo:

> Look, if it please you, on this man condemn'd
> As if my brother liv'd.
>
> V i 442–3

It is at once consistent and amazing – for as the Duke says to Mariana of her entreaty that Isabella should take Angelo's part even for Mariana's sake:

> Against all sense you do importune her.
> Should she kneel down in mercy of this fact,
> Her brother's ghost his paved bed would break,
> And take her hence in horror.
>
> V i 431–4

Rather, he urges: 'An Angelo for Claudio, death for death' (V i 407). But Isabella does for Angelo what she did for Claudio, despite what she thinks Angelo did to Claudio. She absorbs the reactive impulse to achieve balance by revenge. It could have gone either way: the very structures of revenge and forgiveness are so near together as form, as well as so far apart in feeling and outcome. Do unto others, go in their place. This act of Isabella's spontaneously re-creates the pattern which derives from 'the greatest of all examples of substitution for others'[11]:

Why, all the souls that were, were forfeit once,
And He that might the vantage best have took
Found out the remedy.

                                                    II ii 73–5

Christ Himself took the part and place of all sinners. By virtue of
what Isabella does, under the Duke's renewed authority, Angelo
does not receive as a criminal that sentence of death which his
own judgement patterned out and which he would now willingly
receive with all the speed that despair and shame would urge:

But let my trial be mine own confession.
Immediate sentence, then, and sequent death
Is all the grace I beg.

                                                    V i 370–2

'I crave death more willingly than mercy' (V i 474). But the very
shape and pattern is turned another way:

It lies not in the offender to cause himselfe to be whipped, how
and when he list, but in the judge, who . . . cannot impute
that unto punishment, which is the free choice of him that
suffereth. The divine vengeance presupposeth our full dissent,
for his justice and our paine.

                                      Montaigne, vol.II, p.227
                          (ch.xii, 'An Apologie of Raymond Sebond')

For Shakespeare what comes first theologically or ontologically
does not come first chronologically and (the experiment of *Measure
for Measure* shows) cannot be set up to do so, as Angelo initially
tries to do. Only as part of an unanticipatable process fraught with
'dissent', only in the very experience of time sorting itself out, may
the right thing come in the right way at the right time – be it
justice or grace. So in Hooker's terms, positive law, dependent on
contingency, may be the way in which absolute justice has to seek
to reveal itself. The higher law is not revealed to men simply as in
the beholding of it in a book, but the copy of it 'worketh *in* them,
because it discovereth and (as it were) readeth itself to the world
by them when the laws which they make are righteous' (Hooker,

p.122, book I, ch.16.2). And the continuing overlapping possibility of the presence of the wrong thing is there too: for as the Duke discloses Claudio unharmed there is still room for him to see and catch a naturally relieved 'quickening' in Angelo's eye (V i 493).

2　FROM INCONVENIENCY TO INDIVIDUAL SEPARATION

Let me offer an arrested image of Shakespearian overlap at its most extreme – what Leontes calls *co-joining* (*The Winter's Tale*, I ii 143), held at the very moment of inner and outer worlds becoming terrifyingly intermingled.

Leontes stares at his wife in converse with his best friend:

> 　　　　　　This entertainment
> May a free face put on, derive a liberty
> From heartiness, from bounty, fertile bosom,
> And well become the agent: 't may, I grant:
> But to be paddling palms, and pinching fingers,
> As now they are, and making practis'd smiles
> As in a looking-glass . . .
>
> 　　　　　　　　*The Winter's Tale*, I ii 111–17

The essential movement is 'may . . . may . . . But'. The last production of *The Winter's Tale* I saw froze the action at this point. Whilst Leontes was thus innerly thinking, the suspects, physically alongside him, to whom his thoughts referred remained momentarily caught in their positions. The simultaneity between one person's thinking of others and those others themselves going on living was temporarily suspended. It was as if Hermione and Polixenes were for the moment represented on stage as what they were in Leontes's mind, his thoughts overlapping their persons, his mind turned inside-out. Look at those two: I see it may all be innocent, it *may*, but.

This is like Othello thinking he now finds Cassio's kisses on Desdemona's lips. Othello wishes he did not know it; while he had not known it, then subjectively at any rate it had been as if it had not happened:

> What sense had I of her stolen hours of lust?
> I saw't not, thought it not, it harmed not me.
> I slept the next night well, fed well, was free and merry;

I found not Cassio's kisses on her lips.
He that is robbed, not wanting what is stolen,
Let him not know't and he's not robbed at all.

Othello, III iii 339–44

Like Leontes, Othello has begun to know too much about his own subjectivism.

That thinking and believing and trusting could be *separate* from the objective reality to which they refer is itself hardly a bearable thought to have to think. Would I declare myself a cuckold, or my son a bastard, Leontes asks Camillo:

Without ripe moving to it? Would I do this?

I ii 332

Terrifyingly, it is as though Leontes's very anticipation of the danger of delusion safeguards his delusion and, worse, is part of it. So Macbeth is most mad not when he most fears it –

Whence is that knocking? –

How is't with me, when every noise appals me?

Macbeth, II ii 56–7

– but when he ceases to seem so to himself:

I have almost forgot the taste of fears.
The time has been, my senses would have cool'd
To hear a night-shriek; and my fell of hair
Would at a dismal treatise rouse, and stir,
As life were in't. I have supp'd full with horrors:
Direness, familiar to my slaughterous thoughts,
Cannot once start me.

Macbeth, V v 9–15

In their different ways men such as Macbeth and Othello and Leontes have put something mental (be it delusion or defiance of guilt and fear) *in place of* the external world, even by referring to it. They are no longer *one*: doubling back upon themselves, they have begun to think about their own thinking. 'In the reflected act of the intelligent and the intelligible', says Giordano Bruno, of the attempt of a person to understand himself, 'that which is discerned and contemplated becomes one thing and another.'[12] It is this emergence of an individual consciousness no longer at home in the world, and equally ill at ease with itself, that produces partially separate character in these plays and disturbs the shape of the plays accordingly.

Separation is another key experimental technique with Shakespeare. As so often, the simpler clues to the interest of a major concern are to be found in minor places – as in the challenge Malvolio offers Sir Toby: 'If you can separate yourself and your misdemeanours, you are welcome to the house, if not . . .' (*Twelfth Night*, II iii 98–9). 'If . . . ' But can it be done? And if so, how far can it be done? How far can an act of separation be performed before there is within the tight Shakespearian matrix a corresponding reaction against it?

Shakespeare sceptically relishes the sight of his several characters all living in their own worlds, while all simultaneously still held within the one world. He relishes it all the more when they themselves then begin to feel pulled between views from inside and out. For then individualism is no more than a *half*-separated mental territory. And once people are drawn into that ambiguous realm between inner and outer worlds, where what is plausible is also what is suspect, nothing goes right. When Hermione declares her complete innocence, Leontes replies:

> I ne'er heard yet
> That any of these bolder vices wanted
> Less impudence to gainsay what they did
> Than to perform it first.

> > *The Winter's Tale*, III ii 54–7

Of course he is right – the guilty are often the first to declare themselves innocent too. But again, like Hamlet, this is a man who now knows too much. And in the face of this fundamental loss of belief Hermione herself can only say:

> That's true enough

adding, in the face of that general plausibility, what is still the specific (but unverifiable) truth in this particular case:

> Though 'tis a saying, sir, not due to me.

> > III ii 57–8

'Reason', says Montaigne, 'hath so many shapes, that wee know not which to take hold of. Experience hath as many.' One case is never quite the same as another, no one thing fits entirely and conveniently with any other: 'The consequence we seeke to drawe from the *conference* of events, is unsure, because they are ever *dissemblable*' (vol.III, p.322, ch.xiii, 'Of Experience'). It is not congruence but dissimilarity which provides the rule.[13] In contrast to system-makers such as Hooker or the Neo-Platonists, I shall be using Montaigne throughout this chapter as a further spokesman for this perception of the inconvenient unfittedness of things; and as a supreme contemporary example of how far individual separation and detachment may be taken.

For as Shakespeare's greatest contemporary, Montaigne is like Shakespeare in seeing unfittingness far more than he sees system. And by 'Montaigne' here I mean no more and no less than that distinctly separate *person* which the writer autobiographically created for himself in the composition of the *Essais*. Montaigne is sceptical about concepts. But a person may do what a concept cannot: hold together contradictions and complexities without logical resolution, and survive by the sheer determination of separated being.

In contrast to me, claims Montaigne, most men say: Forget oneself for the sake of your neighbour, put the general and universal before the particular. 'Most of the world's rules and precepts hold this traine, to drive us out of our selves into the wide world, to the use of publike society' (vol.III, p.256, ch.x, 'How One Ought to Governe His Will'). But Montaigne sceptically stays himself instead.

Warily personal, to Montaigne our categories of judgement are mere general plausibilities. I am not greatly pleased, says Montaigne, by the man who, seeking to legislate away the need for the difficult, particular judgement of individual cases, then supposed

> by the multitude of lawes, to curbe the authority of judges, in cutting out their morsels. He perceived not, that there is as much liberty and extension in the interpretation of lawes, as in their fashion.
> Montaigne, vol.III, pp.322–3 (ch.xiii, 'Of Experience')

'The multiplying of our inventions shall never come to the variation of examples.' As Terence Cave has shown, Montaigne's sense
of a cornucopia of rich meanings goes hand in hand with a sceptical
sense of ultimate vanity.[14] With Montaigne, you can never catch
up with the complexity of life. The more laws you make, in the
attempt to cover everything, the more interpretations you still have
to make, in the midst of a mass of overlapping considerations, that
you may judge how general laws fit each particular case. In *Macbeth*
Malcolm is left saying to Macduff, 'Let not my jealousies be your
dishonours,/But mine own safeties', as if in haplessly concessive
reply to what there is in himself of tragic suspicion:

> Though all things foul would wear the brows of grace,
> Yet Grace must still look so.
>
> > *Macbeth*, IV iii 23–4, 29–30

'All's true that is mistrusted', says Leontes (*The Winter's Tale*,
II i 48). But, as Othello and Leontes are to find, distrust is no
more secure than trust itself was in the first place. The painful
insufficiency of comic pattern in later Shakespeare results above
all in the loss of trust and the misplacement of belief. Montaigne
is one example of how to survive, sometimes almost gleefully, in
such a situation.

A state of partial separation and resulting inconveniency is what
Shakespeare's tragic protagonists must inhabit. 'All Shakespeare's
great tragic heroes are *unfitted* for their roles. . . . [Shakespeare
follows] his instinct of making his hero *incongruous* with the
situation. As Macbeth is not the man for murder, so Othello is
not the man for suspicion and intrigue.'[15] But it is with Hamlet
above all that a sense of the inconvenient and the ill-fitting comes
most formidably into Shakespeare's writing.

Hamlet is the great turning-point, not least because the play could
almost have been a comedy. Its protagonist has that Shakespearian
capacity to turn witty improvisation, quickly finding space within
a tight corner, into a means of singly sustaining himself:

> *Horatio* My lord, I came to see your father's funeral.
> *Hamlet* I prithee, do not mock me, fellow student.
>   I think it was to see my mother's wedding.
> *Horatio* Indeed, my lord, it follow'd hard upon.

Hamlet Thrift, thrift, Horatio. The funeral bak'd meats
            Did coldly furnish forth the marriage tables.

                                                    I ii 176–81

Queen Hamlet, thou hast thy father much offended.
Hamlet Mother, you have my father much offended.
Queen Come, come, you answer with an idle tongue.
Hamlet Go, go, you question with a wicked tongue.

                                                    III iv 8–11

Polonius My lord, I will take my leave of you.
Hamlet You cannot, sir, take from me anything that I will more
willingly part withal – except my life, except my life, except
my life.

                                                    II ii 213–17

But what prevents *Hamlet* from remaining essentially comic is a
now different relation of mind to the pattern surrounding it. One
mind, Hamlet's, cannot stay in the pattern or is forced out of it (the
mind itself cannot quite tell which). For it is the repetition at the
end of my third quotation – 'except my life, except my life, except
my life' – that stands for everything in Hamlet that cannot remain
inside the scope of a surrounding pattern, yet does not know what
to do with itself when left outside it. The binding function of
repetition, examined in Chapter One, changes here to something
surviving and going on only as left over, and its music gives way to
sheer tone of voice as a more separate thing, 'except my life, except
my life', in a mind so consciously hearing itself. Hamlet *is* the point
at which a sense of pattern yields consciousness but a consciousness
which cannot return to the pattern again:

> *Queen* Thou know'st 'tis common: all that lives must die,
>   Passing through nature to eternity.
> *Hamlet* Ay, madam, it is common.
> *Queen*   If it be,
>   Why seems it so particular with thee?
>   *Hamlet*, I ii 72–5

In his response, Hamlet picks up the word 'seems' not the word
'particular': for what is particularly experienced is already felt as a
thing repressed within the 'common' pattern in this play.

To Hamlet, the conventional 'shapes of grief' cannot any longer simply 'denote me truly':

> These indeed seem,
> For they are actions that a man might play;
> But I have that within which passes show,
> These but the trappings and the suits of woe.
>
> I ii 83–6

Here is Leontes's 'may' again: a man 'might' play at such things. If hypocrites may put on suits of woe, what am I to wear who feel woe truly? The trappings no longer fit a mind which, before it can use them, has *already* seen how they can be misused and misinterpreted. Yet Hamlet has no other forms of expression, no other clothes to wear. No longer trusting in appearances, Hamlet instead develops 'within' him an alternative capacity – a faculty for mental extrapolation, mental anticipation, mental replacement. That is to say, he uses inner thought to take the very things which that thought represents *out* of the ongoing common run, *out* of the regardless sequence of time. Hamlet, says Robert A. Johnson in *Transformations* (New York, 1991), represents the first transforming separation of man into a deeply three-dimensional being. In Shakespeare from *Hamlet* onwards, individual character is increasingly present in the plays, but present as increasingly either separated out from or felt as entrapped within the pattern of the play.

As we shall see, a reading of Montaigne is crucial to a study of Hamlet. How to survive, stoically self-balanced, in that space where one is situated when neither a part of the pattern nor wholly apart from it, is also Montaigne's subject-matter.

For Montaigne represents something in autobiography's version of life that the characters in Shakespeare's plays sometimes seem to want or need – something which is to do with detached self-preservation. In epicurean mood Montaigne has that large insouciance – the dazzling shrug of *sprezzatura* as Castiglione called it – which was almost a possibility in Hamlet himself:

> Our life is composed, as is the harmony of the world, of contrary things; so of diverse tunes, some pleasant, some harsh, some

sharpe, some flat, some low and some high: What would that Musition say, that should love but some one of them? He ought to know how to use them severally and how to entermingle them. So should we of goods and evils, which are consubstantiall to our life. Our being cannot subsist without this commixture, whereto one side is no lesse necessary than the other.

Montaigne, vol.III, pp.352–3 (ch.xiii, 'Of Experience')

Montaigne loves the sheer tone of questions implicit with their own answers: 'What would that Musician say?' A man makes experiential moan: 'Alas I have done nothing this day', and Montaigne replies: 'What? have you not lived?' (vol.III, p.376, ch.xiii, 'Of Experience'). It is as though, in a later comedy *All's Well That Ends Well*, where comedy has now had to go through the writing of *Hamlet*, Shakespeare is asking himself why Hamlet could not have more of that individual musical tone of a Montaigne:

The web of our life is of a mingled yarn, good and ill together; our virtues would be proud, if our faults whipped them not, and our crimes would despair, if they were not cherished by our virtues.

All's Well That Ends Well, IV iii 60–4

It is in the very overlap of those two inseparable clauses, alike and yet different – 'our virtues would, if our faults not', 'our crimes would, if not by our virtues' – that the music of a sort of ruefully witty freedom plucked from the very midst of helpless limitation is so remarkably found. For freedom of that compromised kind, rather than imprisonment within tragic paradox, is precisely Montaigne's aim. Crucially, he does not want to get locked into a process, as Hamlet is when so unhappily committed to revenge. He wishes to keep his own quite separate shape, to preserve a space for inner consciousness within a more fixed sense of boundaries. He hates a situation where once he has started he cannot stop; where, like Macbeth, he might be overtaken even by his own overcommitted emotions. Montaigne lived for a long time amidst civil war, trying to find ways to maintain himself inside as well as out. As we shall see, it is not by chance that Montaigne reconstructs himself in 'essais' rather than immerse himself in the creation of dramas. In marked contrast to a protagonist in a Shakespearian drama, Montaigne presents himself as a man who wants essentially *un*dramatic time and space in which to pause and be free, in which to have psychological room to see changes dispassionately. Otherwise there are terrible mental distortions under the force of circumstances.

Sceptical, quietist, moderate, mobile, uncommitted and witty, Montaigne is radically unlike tragic Shakespeare. For Montaigne puts his own character first, detachedly established in its own terms and in its own separated time and space, with his own normalizing sanity of rhythm, tone and language. 'Mine opinion is, that one should lend himselfe to others, and not give himself but to himselfe' (vol.III, p.252, ch.x, 'How One Ought to Governe his Will'). Too often, to a mind bent upon self-preservation as is Montaigne's, it must seem that Shakespeare's men recklessly give themselves away.

And yet Montaigne is also kin to that more casual part of Shakespeare which continues to seek comic denial of tragedy's necessity and experiments with alternatives to Hamlet's imprisonment in a defeated absolutism. It horrifies Hamlet, as if it bespoke the Fall itself, that Claudius could smile, and smile, and be a villian.

Yet consider, says Montaigne, how once people conceive a hatred against a celebrated orator or an advocate, then the very next day they find in the light of their very own oversimplifying desires that 'he becommeth barbarous and uneloquent' (vol.III, p.264, ch.x, 'How One Ought to Governe his Will'). What Montaigne wants to be able to say about the orator is that 'he does this thing wickedly, that thing virtuously', and thus not take an obsessively fixed and general view tainted by locked-in emotions, but remain open to the mobility of particulars in free time. 'Our being cannot subsist without this commixture' – one day in one respect a man is wicked, another day in another way virtuous. There is no fixed pattern; there is rather a rich, intermingled and essentially transient world.

> As no event or forme doth wholly resemble another, so doth it not altogether differ one from another.
> Montaigne, vol.III, p.328 (ch.xiii, 'Of Experience')

There is here a space, neither entirely like everything else nor entirely different from everything else, which with all its untidiness and imprecision becomes the very ground of Montaigne's equivocal individualism.

3 THE OVERLAP AND THE INDIVIDUAL IDENTIKIT

In *Measure for Measure* we saw how different people try to take up the same place. As inner separatist, Montaigne may now help us see how, conversely, different times and different possibilities overlap and come together in the same person. Montaigne loves to consider how a man gets put together and made up. It is that sense of the identifiable individual emerging from heterogeneity which makes Montaigne, even in his differences, so consistently an analogy for Shakespeare's sense of character.

Taking himself for example, Montaigne was astonished to find that, in a sense, the individual could be said to be made up of barely compatible philosophies, of different thoughts which had already *been* thought by different people in different ages before him:

> I suffer my humours or caprices more freely to passe in publike; Forasmuch as though they are borne with, and of me, and without any patterne; well I wot, they will be found to have some relation to some ancient humour, and some shall be found, that will both know and tell whence, and of whom I borrowed them. My customes are naturall; when I contrived them, I called not for the help of any discipline: And weake and faint as they were, when I have had a desire to expresse them, and to make them appeare to the world a little more comely and decent, I have somewhat indevoured to aide them with discourse, and assist them with examples. I have wondred at my selfe, that by meere chance I have met with them, agreeing and sutable to so many ancient examples and Philosophicall discourses. What regiment my life was of, I never knew nor learned but after it was much worne and spent. A new figure: an unpremeditated Philosopher and a casuall.
>
> Montaigne, vol.II, p.256
> (ch.xii, 'An Apologie of Raymond Sebond')

Stoic Montaigne? Epicurean Montaigne? Schools become in Montaigne moods in time, parts of a personal whole itself far smaller in a way than those very schools which partly comprise it. It is no more true that Montaigne in writing stole his thoughts from ancient philosophers, than that in living he had already modelled himself upon their precepts. Everything that makes Montaigne's life a real *life* is, as he sees it, such as is not planned in advance but is accidentally 'natural' and 'unpremeditated' rather than deliberately 'borrowed'. It is, above all, 'without any patterne', where pattern for Montaigne always means deliberate imitation of a tradition or convention. Montaigne only learns what philosophies governed his life '*after*' he had settled it:

> This also hapneth unto me, that where I seeke my selfe, I finde not my selfe: I find my selfe more by chance, than by the searche of mine owne judgement.
>
>   vol.I, p.51 (ch.x, 'Of Readie or Slow Speeche')

Yet what he freely finds, 'by meere chance', is not only that what he thinks comes from what he is, but also that what he *is* turns out to be a chance amalgam of, say, a thousand different thoughts thought by a hundred different men, in many different systems or societies hundreds of years ago. It is a matter not so much of 'patterne' as 'commixture'.

'My customes are naturall.' What Montaigne offers is not Stoic or Epicurean but Natural Montaigne. As Terence Cave puts it, 'He speaks of "naturalizing" art where others "artificialize" nature' – he elaborates models of a quasi-natural text; he writes as if he were speaking; he writes as if he were improvising (Cave, p.300). Yet in his very claim for naturalness there is of course also something of hidden artifice, in Montaigne's creation of a version of himself through the very act of writing. Self-sceptical, Montaigne is unafraid of any artificial help he can exploit in his quest for personal peace and survival. For even if in Natural Montaigne there was also something of an Artificial Montaigne, still what Montaigne points to is Commixed Montaigne. Commixed, because if a man cannot be wholly natural, no more has he such power over himself as to be wholly artificial either:

> Even if for a thousand years one [individual] strove to imitate another in any given respect, he would never attain precision (though perceptible differences sometimes remain unperceived). Even art imitates nature as best it can; but it can never arrive at reproducing it perfectly.[16]

There is the mix. What we celebrate as uniqueness could equally well be seen before that as incoherence and imprecision, a mortal pattern of ever shifting defects. I shall want to say that Shakespeare, as so often, makes us feel as if he is one of the first to make character out of seeing it at once both ways.

But so too did Commixed Montaigne. For in Montaigne's view what a *mixed* piece of likeness and difference is any so-called individual: no more and no less than made up of one thought or disposition overlaid with another and another and another, in all the blurred confusion of fact and fantasy, art and nature. The resulting man comes into focus through lens over lens, with no thought uniquely his, with each thought traceable back perhaps to some different time or place, yet with all these elements of being compounded in a slightly new, unpremeditated and emphatically untidy way.

In Montaigne indeterminate shades of difference are part of all that free and rich imprecision of human life: 'As no event or forme doth wholly resemble another, so doth it not altogether differ one from another.' Montaigne can never wholly say anything definitive: only the experience of shifting time itself, in its sanction of a consciously limited, relative attempt called an 'essay', enables him to write from a temporary and partial point of view amidst the very commixture of things:

> I take my first Argument of fortune: All are alike unto me: And I never purpose to handle them throughly: For there is nothing wherein I can perceive the full perfection. . . . Of a hundred parts and visages that everything hath, I take one.
>
> vol.I, p.342 (ch.l, 'Of Democritus and Heraclitus')

For Montaigne finds in the essay a relaxed temporal form by which to say, as a licence for his own content: I can only be taken as thinking of this as I do now, from this particular perspective. There are other perspectives even in me at other times, let alone in other people.

This whole way of thinking about what makes up a particular person - the varying overlap of one trait or considera-tion or occasional context upon another – is deeply congen-ial to Shakespeare's turn of mind. It is rooted in the very

traditions of Renaissance rhetoric. Marion Trousdale invokes
Rudolph Agricola's late fifteenth-century neo-Aristotelian work
on invention:

> Definition, Aristotle points out, is by words, and words to
> be intelligible must be general. That is to say, they must be
> common to each of a number of things. Even in combination
> such words do not belong only to the thing described, for a
> two-footed animal belongs to animal and two-footed. Nothing,
> in other words, can be known singly. 'Whatever needs to be
> established,' Agricola says in explanation of the places, 'must
> acquire credibility from something else.' This means that the
> only way in which one can responsibly know about things is by
> knowing the categories to which they belong. We learn about
> Othello by searching out all the common places by means of
> which Othello can be defined.[17]

In this identikit, nothing can be known singly. 'Had time coher'd
with place, or place with wishing' (*Measure for Measure*, II i
11) is always the Shakespearian hypothesis: how many of these
– time, place, wish – shall I bring together or keep apart? 'What
convenience both of time and means/May fit us to our shape'
(*Hamlet*, IV vii 148–9)?

Like Jaques with a melancholy all of his own, we are 'compounded of many simples' (*As You Like It*, IV i 16). And
again we can see in Shakespeare the simple template that itself
generates complexity. For example: in *Coriolanus* Shakespeare gives
to Aufidius a verbal equivalent of the device of perspectival overlap
or compounding. It is a way of thinking about Coriolanus which,
inside the play, matches the means by which in the first place
Shakespeare himself must have tried out his work's shape in
his mind:

>   Whether 'twas pride
> Which out of daily fortune ever taints
> The happy man; whether defect of judgement,
> To fail in the disposing of those chances
> Which he was lord of; or whether nature,
> Not to be other than one thing, not moving

From th'casque to th'cushion, but commanding peace
Even with the austerity and garb
As he controll'd the war; but one of these –
As he hath spices of them all, not all,
For I dare so far free him – made him fear'd,
So hated, and so banish'd.

Coriolanus, IV iii 37–48

Slow the blur of Coriolanus down. Stop for a second and ask in the play's midst: what was *behind* it all? Pride? Lack of judgement? Integrity? If only one of them, and not all three of them, then which one of them? Or are they 'spices' of – or even just different names for – each other? The tools used are those of conventional rhetorical disputation, presenting a particular case from many plausible sides, in terms of perhaps overlapping general considerations.[18] But what is remarkable here is that Aufidius, as he himself partially recognizes, is trying to separate out what is inseparable in a man who is 'not to be other than one thing'. Of such attempts as Aufidius's to find a single answer, Montaigne might recall this:

> *Socrates* demanded of *Memnon* what vertue was; There is, answered *Memnon*, the vertue of a Man, of a Woman, of a Magistrate, of a private Man, of a Childe, of an old Man: What vertue meane you? Yea marry, this is very well, quoth *Socrates*; we were in search of one vertue, and thou bringest me a whole swarme.
>
> Montaigne, vol.III, p.328 (ch.xiii, 'Of Experience')

We propose one question, and we get a whole huddle of further questions back again. The more you seek one thing, the more you find many things. To Montaigne this is a rueful comic truth that makes him let go of single-mindedness. To Shakespeare, more tensely, it is a creative tool – that the more you ask 'Is it this thing or that thing or this?', the more difficult the different things themselves become to separate. Shakespeare loves to work back-to-front: the more he cannot disentangle, the more he is also making up and putting together. 'I know to divide him inventorially would dozy th'arithmetic of memory' (*Hamlet*, V ii 113–5). Like Cleopatra, who 'did make defect perfection' and what she undid did, that which Shakespeare cannot do becomes what he can.

For by the time a play reaches its middle, Shakespeare's own initial questions and starting-points in the depiction of his characters return to baffle (and thus add further internal dimensions to) the characters themselves. 'Whether . . . or . . . or whether': the very syntax suggests that what Aufidius tries to do with regard to Coriolanus is what Hamlet tried to do in relation to himself – divide and conquer:

> Now whether it be
> Bestial oblivion, or some craven scruple
> Of thinking too precisely on th'event –
> A thought which, quarter'd, hath but one part wisdom
> And ever three parts coward – I do not know
> Why yet I live to say this thing's to do
> Sith I have cause, and will, and strength, and means
> To do't.
>
> *Hamlet*, IV iv 39–46

Not only is the explanation here divided between forgetfulness on the one hand and too much thinking on the other, but too much thinking is itself subdivided between one part wisdom and three parts cowardice. It is as if a sort of stationary thinking is trying to establish itself here in the midst of a drama which, even so, runs on counter to it. For 'whether . . . or' initially becomes only 'I do not know [which]'. And then 'I do not know' fluidly runs on over the line-ending not simply to end the 'whether . . . or' construction but, 'looking before and after', to begin its own:

> I do not know
> Why yet I live to say this thing's to do
> Sith I have cause, and will, and strength, and means
> To do't.

Whether it was one thing or another did not really matter: the thing is anyway still to do. The curve of these lines, made so relative in time, differs from the stationing effect attempted by division. For the effect is 'even while I speak of not knowing why I do not do it, I *do* not do it'.

The movement is kin, I think, to that described in particular in the last two lines of the following period:

> Who would fardels bear,
> To grunt and sweat under a weary life,
> But that the dread of something after death,
> The undiscovered country from whose bourn
> No traveller returns, puzzles the will,
> And makes us rather bear those ills we have
> Than fly to others that we know not of?
>
> *Hamlet*, III i 76–82

The very syntax acknowledges that, for all the desire to quit it, we are held within the realm of the transient by 'But that' then becoming 'rather . . . Than'. Indeed, the very desire to quit time is held within time, as within the sentence itself. For these are sentences of character, where character in this context means: human thought separate from a world whose defects or obstacles none the less provoke it. And the only place for such thinking, bespeaking what a character would if he could, is in isolated soliloquy when 'if onlys' exist outside the pattern of the world.

What allows Hamlet mental space for all these overlapping considerations in the play is what Hooker, seeking to find the right subordination between them, calls our very largeness of speech:

> Our largeness of speech how men do find out what things reason bindeth them of necessity to observe, and what it guideth them to choose in things which are left as arbitrary; the care we have had to declare the different nature of laws which severally concern all men, from such as belong unto men either civilly or spiritually associated, such as pertain to the fellowship which nations, or which Christian nations have amongst themselves, and in the last place such as concerning every or any of these, God himself hath revealed by his holy word; all serveth but to make manifest that as the actions of men are of sundry distinct kinds, so the laws thereof must accordingly be distinguished.
>
> Hooker, pp.123-4 (book I, Conclusion)

Shakespeare brings together words and clauses just as he brings together differing considerations, jostling for space, overlapping with and modifying each other's meaning. The figure of metaphor, or 'transport' as Puttenham calls it, means taking a word from one place and putting it into another 'not so naturall, but yet of some affinitie or conueniencie with it' (quoted Trousdale, p.84). That love of transport and overlap is why oxymoron – Gloucester's 'Burst smilingly', Prospero's 'did us but loving harm' - is a model figure for Shakespeare. But *Hamlet* is the point at which a desire for an order such as Hooker's, at once so unified and yet so diverse in the name of Law, meets the separating and particularizing force of Montaigne's scepticism: 'The multiplying of our inventions shall never come to the variation of examples.' To the mind that wrote *Hamlet* there is always a grey area between what is unique in a situation and what is not; there is no clear comfort either way, things are neither wholly integrated nor completely separate and unconnected. *Hamlet* marks the point at which the very largeness of our speech creates as many problems as solutions. In all that confused overlapping of past and present, responsibility and freedom, religion and superstition, revenge and morality, particular and general, finite and infinite, Hamlet finds himself continually asking: *What* category, framework, or word can define his current situation.

Although Hamlet's thoughts can find space for themselves, such speeches cannot get outside time. They are still relative, as characters are. 'I do not know/Why yet I live to say this thing's to do/Sith I have cause, and will, and strength, and means/To do't'; 'And makes us rather bear those ills we have/Than fly to others that we know not of'. For all the temporarily attempted distinctions in these lines, one thing blurs into another: 'I yet still speak, only because I don't yet do', 'All that makes me seem to stay and bear is the continually not being able to fly while still wanting to'. There is a built-in evanescence to Shakespeare's curving sentences.

I am saying that what relates these sentences is their being–in–time. Even as they are spoken, in an attempt to comprehend a situation, drama takes over and the temporal situation keeps going on, relativizing, beneath and within them. If they were shorter sentences – if life were simple enough to be contained in short sentences which even so were still long enough to hold their place in the world and not become mere exclamations – then perhaps, just perhaps, there would be time for them to get spoken as an intact whole. But howsoever it be, the long sentences lose their power of stationing and of finalizing; time has got into their very utterance:

> Not all the parts exist at once, but some must come as others go, and this way together they make up the whole of which they are parts. Our speech follows the same rule, using sounds to signify a meaning. For a sentence is not complete unless each word, once its syllables have been pronounced, gives way to make room for the next. . . . In these things there is no place to rest, because they do not last.[19]

'But thought's the slave of life, and life time's fool' (*1 Henry IV*, V iv 81). It is like that marvellous line near the end of *Hamlet* that has so bothered editors:

> Since no man of aught he leaves knows, what is't to leave betimes?
> > *Hamlet*, V ii 195–6 (New Cambridge edition after Q2)

'Knows' and 'leaves' each govern 'of aught': no man of aught he leaves knows aught – so that instead of being separate, the two verbs run into one another ('leaves-knows'), as if there is barely time to separate knowing from leaving. 'Each word gives way to make room for the next', the whole cannot hold on to itself in time. As with the perspective painter of the Renaissance, there is no longer the absolute and abstract view of a two-dimensional plane: 'Not so much a place as a moment is fixed for us, and a fleeting moment: a point of view in time more than in space.'[20]

The final overlapping consideration in Shakespearian drama is always, inescapably, Time. Just as characters are made out of the overlay of different factors, one upon another, so time is made up of different scenes, one after another, which contrapuntally test the composition of those characters. And this idea of time as the final element in life's technical experiment with man is again one that Montaigne shares with Shakespeare.

Take a single man, says Montaigne, and place him in different contexts. Put the man in battle and he may charge forward bravely; put the same man in court and he breaks down in tears at the loss of a law suit. He can bear poverty but he cannot stand slander. One moment he can be courageous, the next a coward. This is an experiment, an assay or essay, to use Montaigne's word: here is a man, here is a context, they overlap like two slide-pictures, change the context, do you change the man?

Therefore may not a couragious act conclude a man to be valiant. He that is so, when just occasion serveth, shall ever be so, and upon all occasions. If it were an habitude of vertue, and not a sudden humour, it would make a man equally resolute at all assayes, in all accidents: Such alone, as in company; such in a single combat, as in a set battel; For, whatsoever some say, valour is all alike, and not one in the street or towne, and another in the campe or field. As couragiously should a man bear a sicknesse in his bed, as a hurt in the field and feare death no more at home in his house, than abroad in an assault. . . . If he be timorously-fearefull at sight of a Barbers razor, and afterward stowtly-undismayed against his enemies swords: The action is commendable, but not the man.

> Montaigne, vol.II, p.12
> (ch.i, 'Of the Inconstancie of our Actions')

Unless the man is always courageous in each different scene and context, his courage in any one particular occasion is probably as much a product of the occasion as of the man. 'Distinguo is the most universall part of my logike' (vol.II, p.12). Sceptical Montaigne knows well enough that he cannot precisely isolate and calculate the separate factors that make up the human commixture. But he is sure that there are always at least two things to be distinguished, rather than simply one to be taken at face value. In any overlap, there is always a commixture of the man and the circumstances outside him, and there is always an agent distinct from the action he carries out. We forget ourselves when the two come together in time. Renaissance analysts, in contrast, remember to take apart what in time runs together:

For men change with the actions; and whiles they are in pursuit they are one, and when they return to their nature they are another.[21]

There is a man and there is also the temporal world – the one goes into the other, comes out again, and the degree to which action is derived more from the one than the other is always the crucial degree to be measured.

Authors go wrong, says Montaigne, in 'framing a constant and solide contexture of us. They chuse an universall ayre, and following that image, range and interpret all a mans actions.' They choose a once-and-for-all account. The better way, in the light of man's inconsistency, is 'distinctly and part by part, judge of him' (vol.II, p.8). Plutarch in his parallel lives of the Greeks and Romans did not weigh the two races in the lump but 'compareth the parts and the circumstances, one after another, and severally judgeth of them' (vol.II, p.455, ch.xxxii, 'A Defence of Seneca and Plutarke'). This method of successive contextual experiment is also adopted by that other great reader of Plutarch, Shakespeare.

For Shakespeare takes a dramatis persona through scene after scene, leaving behind, or creating ahead, all the questions about the relation of one moment in a life to the next, even as he goes along. Is there such a thing as consistency of character? What if any is the right view to be taken of this character here? With Shakespeare's experiments we seem to be in at the very beginning of such questions. Working from bottom up rather than top down, Shakespeare will simply get himself and his language into a spatial situation which almost of itself will then go on in time to produce those thoughts and feelings even as the life-process itself does.

Thus consider the figures of Coriolanus and Hamlet as two contrasting experiments.

Coriolanus, said Aufidius, commanded peace just as he controlled war. Menenius tries to excuse Coriolanus before the common people by saying, 'Consider this':

> he has been bred i'th'wars
> Since a could draw a sword, and is ill school'd
> In bolted language; meal and bran together

He throws without distinction.

Coriolanus, III i 317–20

'Consider further':

> That when he speaks not like a citizen,
> You find him like a soldier.

III iii 52–4

He is 'one thing', through all the scenes: 'Yet will I still/Be thus to
them' (III ii 5–6). Machiavelli tells the story of Manlius who was
brave, honourable, irreproachable, and ascetic. But when Manlius
tried to make all these qualities of his into the norm for others, he
necessarily turned into a tyrant: 'When, therefore, a man of this
kind obtains the rank of commander he expects to find everyone
else like himself, and the boldness which characterizes him makes
him order bold actions.'[22] Is Coriolanus like Manlius, projecting
himself, unthinkingly and misplacedly, upon his whole world?

The play's persistent experiment forces out of itself this question:
can he who almost *is* Rome maintain his oneness even in turning
against Rome? For Shakespeare is obsessed with these configurations when different versions of the same thing face each other,
turning inside-out, outside-in, simultaneously. Thus the force of
this paradoxical pattern is passed on, in terms sufficiently reduced
as to be articulatable, to those closest to Coriolanus:

> For his best friends, if they
> Should say, 'Be good to Rome', they charg'd him even
> As those should do that had deserv'd his hate,
> And therein show'd like enemies.

IV vi 112–15

As the symbiosis comes undone, Coriolanus's mother, caught in
the new space between Coriolanus and the Rome she has taught
him to embody, finds herself saying to her son:

> If it were so that our request did tend
> To save the Romans, thereby to destroy
> The Volsces whom you serve, you might condemn us

As poisonous of your honour. No . . .

V iii 132–5

But hers is Coriolanus's situation as passed on outside of himself, a mirror wherein we see that the two forces in opposition to each other are really one whole, split into opposition even with itself:

> for how can we
> Alas! how can we for our country pray,
> Whereto we are bound, together with thy victory,
> Whereto we are bound?

V iii 106–9

Crucially these splits seem to be happening *at the same time*, as if time pushes on in plays such as this, until too much is brought together and contained in all too small a space, 'mature for the violent breaking out' (IV iii 26).

At the end of *Coriolanus*, there is no longer any *one* thing. Violently in conflict, we do want *and* we do not want Coriolanus to be broken by his own humanness and ungodded. Save for the love of wife which he cherishes silently as a weakness that she bears on his behalf, Coriolanus until now has not known love separate from his public function. His whole function was his mother's private love made public service and, equally, the public love of the country made deeply private, in the complete overlap of personal and impersonal in one. Now at the end love is separate, unintegrated, in a way that a man such as Hooker could not have imagined when he saw an edifice of laws to hold the biological, individual, familial, social, political and religious in shape all together. Coriolanus's world collapses: 'O mother, mother!/What have you done?' (V iii 183–4). At some level if he could not win it all, and all together, then indeed Coriolanus wanted to lose, wanted to be defeated by the claims of mother, wife and child. But he could not do anything himself, for it was himself that would have to be undone: so he could only wait to hear the words that would undo him. Coriolanus is the opposite of what Keats, in a letter of 22 November 1817, said Shakespeare himself was: Coriolanus is a man of power, of determined character, rather than a man of genius operating anonymously like certain ethereal

chemicals in the mass of neural intellect. And to be selfless is for
the man of power to be no doer, to have no self, and to be dead.
Coriolanus lets that happen to him.

In *Hamlet*, in contrast, the same scenic method is used, through the
consciousness of Hamlet himself, for different purposes. For it is as
though Hamlet asks *whether* indeed there is any one thing in him
that can maintain itself through all the changes. Thus, for example:
Hamlet in act III scene i goes straight from his 'To be or not to be'
speech back into the world to encounter Ophelia:

> And enterprises of great pitch and moment
> With this regard their currents turn awry
> And lose the name of action. Soft you now,
> The fair Ophelia! Nymph, in thy orisons
> Be all my sins remembered.
>
> III i 86–90

There is, disturbingly, barely a moment for separate transition in
this stifling world. No wonder one moment runs over into a quite
different one. The 'Get thee to a nunnery' dialogue that follows is
then overheard by Claudius and Polonius as if they were watching a
play, and ends with Claudius and Polonius discussing Hamlet even
as it began with Claudius, Polonius, the Queen, and Rosencrantz
and Guildenstern doing the like. Stepping out of that frame and
turning the tables, Hamlet himself in act III scene ii sets up the
play within a play that torments Claudius, and then finally turns
on Rosencrantz and Guildenstern for trying to play upon him
as upon a pipe. In scene iii, Hamlet on his way to confront his
mother in scene iv overhears Claudius's speech of guilty despair
en route.[23] 'When sorrows come,' in this play of overlaps, 'they
come not single spies/But in battalions' (IV v 78–9). Time and
again, one person suffers from what really belongs to another:
'So full of artless jealousy is guilt,/It spills itself in fearing to
be spilt' (IV v 19–20). Indeed, one representative measure of
the complex series of overlaps, the turn-arounds, the various
mirrorings and spilt contagions here is the point at which Hamlet
turns from his mother ('Come hither, my dear Hamlet, sit by me')
to Ophelia:

Nay, good mother, here's metal more attractive

III ii 108

only to bring before Ophelia, still, thoughts that belong more aptly with his mother:

Ophelia You are merry, my lord.
Hamlet Who, I?
Ophelia Ay, my lord.
Hamlet O God, your only jig-maker. What should a man do but be merry? For look how cheerfully my mother looks and my father died within's two hours.
Ophelia Nay, 'tis twice two months, my lord.
Hamlet So long? Nay then, let the devil wear black, for I'll have a suit of sables. O heavens, die two months ago and not forgotten yet! Then there's hope a great man's memory may outlive his life half a year.

III ii 120–30

He is talking to Ophelia but doing so in order to be overheard by the King and Queen, as if he were in two different places at once. If Hamlet is right to wish to punish Claudius, it is *how* he does it that becomes the problem – as though this were like Hooker's account of laws which 'we term *mixed*': 'because the *matter* whereunto it bindeth, is the same which reason necessarily doth require at our hands, and from the law of reason differeth in the *manner* of binding only' (Hooker, pp.95–6, book I, ch.10.10; my emphases). How to do it? 'The mind', agrees Montaigne, 'must have it's motion with discretion' (vol.III, p.258, ch.x, 'How One Ought to Governe His Will'): it may make more or less of what the body has to bear in any physical situation. But Hamlet fears what Claudius calls 'discretion'; in its complication he fears an apparent opposition to the straightforward claims of 'nature'. Thus as Hamlet double-talks to Ophelia, the play, terrifyingly, goes on inside his head even as he remains still a part of it. This is why for much of the time his tone is so literally unplaceable, for so often even as he speaks out, he almost simultaneously hears within him a hollow echo of what he just now was saying: 'except my life, except my life, except my life'. Character here is almost defined by being the result of a man overhearing himself:

> This is most brave,
> That I, the son of a dear father murder'd,
> Prompted to my revenge by heaven and hell,
> Must like a whore unpack my heart with words.
>
> II ii 578–81

Yet though he can thus look at himself as if from outside the play
itself and his own part in it, he himself does not know whether
'get thee to a nunnery' is more to save Hamlet from Ophelia or
Ophelia from Hamlet. He cannot separate his apology to her from
his disgust at her: 'I did love you once. . . . You should not have
believed me. . . . We are arrant knaves all, believe none of us . . .
wise men know enough what monsters you make of them' (III
i 115, 117, 129–30, 140–1). He cannot talk to her in particular
without thinking of women in general; one thing is no sooner
itself than it also begins to stand for another. In this confusion all
is connected separation, separated connection.

When the Russian director Meyerhold 'wanted Hamlet to be
played by two actors, perhaps a man and a woman, and for one
Hamlet to read the tragic monologues and the other to bother him.
The second Hamlet would be comic', he was exactly reversing the
very process of character creation in Shakespeare which begins, so
to speak, in the overlap of two lenses.[24]

> Are not the horse and the ass two distinct species? Certainly, and
> yet of the two is made a third, the mule which is neither one nor
> the other. . . . Bronze is made of copper and tin.[25]

In Hamlet Shakespeare could make of the two a third, even by
the very consciousness of the mixed man wondering whether
this amalgam of himself could hold together. Shakespeare could
make two into one, one into two. So Freud suspected when he
called Macbeth and Lady Macbeth two disunited parts of a single
psychical individuality, as though they had been copied from a
single prototype. No wonder Hamlet seems to become so many
different people at different times in the play:

> Was't Hamlet wrong'd Laertes? Never Hamlet.
> If Hamlet from himself be ta'en away,

And when he's not himself does wrong Laertes,
Then Hamlet does it not, Hamlet denies it.

V ii 229–32

'Who does it then?' Nothing is quite definitely or resolvably
particular, everything is haunted by general plausibilities, other
considerations and possibilities. For Hamlet already knows what
I tried to establish as Shakespeare's working method in Chapter
One – that a man could take a thousand different shapes in a
thousand different situations. There are more things here than 'I
have thoughts to put them in, imagination to give them shape,
or time to act them in' (III i 126–7). No wonder Hamlet seems
to be so many different ages, from eighteen to thirty. The play is
more about 'assuming' positions rather than fully being or believing
in them in fixed time, space, or shape. No wonder too that the
play itself is thus full of so many versions and additions, so many
variations and revisions and afterthoughts, such that the whole text
may hardly ever have been able to be performed at once.[26] For
Hamlet shows Shakespeare's method of creation by ever-increasing
overlaps taken to its most extreme.

4 SHAPES AND TECHNIQUES BECOMING MEANINGS AND BELIEFS:
MONTAIGNE AND SHAKESPEARE

Montaigne would not allow himself to become so entrapped as
Hamlet or to be so wholly committed as Coriolanus. In saying that,
we can now begin to draw together the human meaning that results
from the different uses of the same techniques in Shakespeare and
Montaigne. Nothing is more important in Shakespeare than the
fact that finally he cannot be Montaigne.

The man that Montaigne creates as himself in his writings is, I
have shown, one that always makes for himself *extra space*: 'a man
that by no meanes would be enthronged' (vol.III, p.210, ch.ix,
'Of Vanitie'). Montaigne is like a critic of Shakespeare's people,
in their crowdedness. It is as though he would say of them: their
consciousness is always elsewhere, it constantly drives them out of
themselves. But against this life-dynamic Montaigne tries to live by
pulling back inward and recalling himself, by making reservations
and separations, by lending himself rather than giving himself to
the world. 'The minde . . . must have it's motion with discretion'

(vol.III, p.258, ch.x, 'How One Ought to Governe His Will') –
discretion: the very aspect of consciousness that disturbs Hamlet.
Montaigne separates himself from his actions in the belief that his
actions belong to external fortune, whereas his real self is registered
only in his thoughts and writings:

> Some may peradventure suppose that by deeds and effects, and
> not simply by words, I witnesse of my selfe. I principally set
> forth my cogitations; a shapelesse subject, and which cannot
> fall within the compasse of a worke-manlike production; with
> much adoe can I set it downe in the ayrie body of the voice.
> . . . Effects would speake more of fortune, than of me. They
> witnesse their part, and not mine.
>   vol.II, p.60 (ch.vi, 'Of Exercise or Practice')

Writing lent Montaigne a mental space, providing artificial defence
against the world's encroachments. For experience of civil war led
Montaigne to preserve himself by lodging inside him the thought
of the separation of the private and the political. Thereon in his
emphasis is always on the more non-dramatic private context:
the sheer basic ordinariness of the bed of sickness says more than
the field of battle. In the more temporally extended humdrum
situation the external excitements, which may momentarily take
a man beyond himself in an extraordinary situation, are taken away
and he is left more at the mercy of his own natural devices. Let
us not look just for the extraordinary short sprint in life: 'he
that seeth [the soule] march her naturall and simple pace, doth
peradventure observe her best' (vol.I, p.342, ch.l, 'Of Democritus
and Heraclitus'). Montaigne never did great deeds: 'I can keepe no
register of my life by my actions; fortune placeth them too lowe'
(vol.III, p.183, ch.ix, 'Of Vanitie'). It is the indefinite thoughts in
himself, not the gross actions in fortune's realm, which show his life
most truly.

It was, says Montaigne, the death of his bosom-friend, La
Boetie, who knew Montaigne better than Montaigne knew
himself, that turned him in his bereavement to autobiographical writing as an act of no more than partial replacement.
The relationship with La Boetie had been one of sheer 'commixture':

In the amitie I speake of, they entermixe and confound themselves one on the other, with so universall a commixture, that
they weare out, and can no more finde the seame that hath
conjoyned them together. If a man urge me to tell wherefore
I loved him, I feele it cannot be expressed, but by answering;
Because it was he, because it was my selfe.

That is to say, it had not been a relationship according to deliberate
'pattern':

It was not to bee modelled or directed by the paterne of regular
and remisse friendship, wherein so many precautions of a long
and preallable conversation are required. This hath no other *Idea*
than of it selfe, and can have no reference but to it selfe. It is not
one especiall consideration, nor two, nor three, nor foure, nor a
thousand: It is I wot not what kinde of quintessence, of all this
commixture, which having seized my will, induced the same to
plunge and lose it selfe in his, which likewise having seized all
his will, brought it to lose and plunge it selfe in mine.
                    vol.I, pp.201-2 (ch.xxvii, 'Of Friendship')

It was as though all the single overlapping considerations had
merged beyond separately computable numbers to produce what
can only be registered as 'himself' and 'myself' and the friendship
'itself'. That was over now. After the loss of such friendship, all
Montaigne could do was be one who had now separated himself
out and tried to find a room and a home inside.

Montaigne's is a language that reaps the benefit of going through
the point of tiredness, in becoming a man beginning the final
second half of a life. 'We have lived long enough for others':

live we the remainder of life for our selves: let us bring home our
cogitations and inventions unto our selves, and unto our ease.
. . . Shake we off these violent hold-fasts, which else-where
engage us, and estrange us from our selves. . . . The greatest
thing of the world, is for a man to know how to be his owne.
                    vol.I, p.256 (ch.xxxviii, 'Of Solitarinesse')

It speaks for an age's whole way of thinking that ourselves used
to be written as 'our selves': amidst tempting attractions and

distractions, that is the challenge – namely, knowing how to become one's own – which Montaigne's autobiographical essays stand for. 'Every man runneth out and unto what is to come, because no man is yet come into himselfe' (vol.III, p.300, ch.xii, 'Of Phisiognomy'). This is where Montaigne's sheer quietist sanity is so much the achievement of a particular conception of *character*: a present voice speaking easily and casually out of now settled past experience, a living tone of reasoned aplomb, 'in the ayrie body of the voice'. We should not rely on the extraordinary just because we cannot live with what is ordinary; we should not be looking outside ourselves simply because we cannot abide inside; we should not be thinking about how to die a good death when we should be learning how to live a good life. Montaigne turns on the human tendency to be always elsewhere and tries to return it home:

> Every man lookes before himselfe, I looke within my selfe . . . other men goe ever else-where, if they thinke well on it: they goe ever foreward . . . as for me I roule me into my selfe.
>
> vol.II, p.385 (ch.xvii, 'Of Presumption')

This is that old unabashed pride that Lawrence wished to recall to modern life in *Aaron's Rod*: 'Give thyself, but give thyself not away'; 'Everybody ought to stand by themselves in the first place. . . . They can come together, in the second place, if they like.'[27]

But if the Montaigne depicted in the *Essais* had his 'Distinguo', in contrast Shakespeare's Coriolanus, as we have seen, throws meal and bran together 'without distinction'. Coriolanus is not a separate man. In his own mind, I have argued, he stands *for* Rome. He *is* the Roman world striking 'Corioles like a planet' (II ii 114). 'O me alone!' he cries in a speech which I think the Folio is right to ascribe to him, rather than to his soldier-followers: 'Make you a sword of me' (I vi 76). Spearheading the attack, he feels himself to be like a sword in the hand of a giant collective being called Rome itself.

Moreover, Coriolanus 'rewards his deeds with doing them' (II ii 127–8). If in the moment of acting he is Rome, and if Rome stands and falls with him and in him, then in the aftermath of action he cannot bear the separation of being rewarded by Rome. 'I have done/As you have done', he tells his soldiers:

that's what I can, induc'd
As you have been, that's for my country.

I ix 15–17

Deeds are done *and* done with for Coriolanus as they are not in
Macbeth. Now when all is done, he is just a common soldier again
as each has been, the god of war in him no longer called out into
being. That mode of being which consists in 'afterwards' makes no
other sense to Coriolanus, and is unreal. He does not want his
deeds detached from himself and the time of their doing, even
by the 'addition' of the name Coriolanus from defeat of Corioli.
The present, the real present of action, is all that there is, apart
from a restful recess in time on his return to those for whom
he fought.

Unreality in Coriolanus is described as play-acting – show the
people your wounds, ask them to give their voices to make
you consul:

It is a part
That I shall blush in acting.

II ii 144–5

– if you try to do it something revolts in you, you do it wrong. You
can't do it. Or you won't do it, not can't: so your own mother says.
Compromise: you use policy in war so use it in peace; go to them
again, she says. And he replies:

Why did you wish me milder? Would you have me
False to my own nature? Rather say I play
The man I am.

III ii 14–16

You try again to do what she urges:

To th'market-place!
You have put me now to such a part which never
I shall discharge to th'life.

III ii 104–6

It still does not work. For when Cominius seeks to 'frame'
Coriolanus's spirit that he may show himself to the populace in

the market-place, and when Volumnia thus says 'He must, and will', Coriolanus begins to find his will – 'I will not do't' – for the first time separating itself from his sense of duty: 'Well, I must do't.' The 'must' and the 'will' are no longer his own, incarnate together as one, but have become his mother's recipe: 'He must, and will' (lines 97, 101, 110). When his 'I must do't' then reactively becomes 'I will not do't' again (at line 120), Volumnia bitterly taunts her son with 'Do as thou list' (128). But nothing now is as he lists, either way, because of the very split between desire and duty. When, self-defeated, he finally replies like a childish puppet, 'Look I am going', she responds only with:

> Do your will.
>
> III ii 138

As if it were! Once split, he cannot be constant to what is only half himself. In the next scene he will have to turn round again upon his new resolve: a logic which he cannot control in himself thus goes outside him into the twist and turn of serial events.

His political enemies, the tribunes, knew he could not go through with the play-acting, significantly knew it better than did his allies, better than anyone, save perhaps Coriolanus: 'He cannot temp'rately *transport* his honours' (II i 222). For his enemies are specialists, they can separate out the political from the human, the external effects and accidents from the internal causes. They know what Coriolanus is like and can exploit that knowledge from without in a way that is freer than is the man himself within: they are second-order people parasitically able to see and thence manipulate what, being primary, is more involuntary. Coriolanus is at least as much innocent as proud. In the theatre in such a play as this, the audience ought to be no longer in *social* relation to what is on the stage, as in comedy. Instead the audience sees an image of another social community misinterpreting the play's isolated protagonist, a society between which and the protagonist the audience must mentally place itself. And yet at the same time, Rome does not so totally misinterpret Coriolanus as to allow the audience simply to dismiss the thought that Coriolanus is also obstinately proud. His pride overlaps with his integrity.

Thus Shakespeare carries out his experiment, the same man,

a different context. Coriolanus is unable to carry over into the political world what in him *is* him, without leaving his deeper self unfittingly stranded there, angry and embarrassed, not adapted or adapting. 'His heart's his mouth:/ What his breast forges, that his tongue must vent' (III i 255–6). If he cannot stop himself, nor will Shakespeare.

Yet when Menenius says in explanation that Coriolanus is basically a soldier whose words need to be translated for him, not taken literally from outside and used against him, this politic defence is still something less than the complete truth. For Coriolanus is not simply a specialist soldier as the tribunes are specialist politicians: what he does is 'what I can' (I ix 16) – and all he can is make a whole vision of Rome incarnate in his particular soldiership. From outside, this can seem just one view of Rome made in a soldier's personal, even egotistical image. But inside it feels like something to which a life is dedicated. For Coriolanus is a believer, not an actor; a believer in what he can hardly believe he *cannot* see around about him in Rome. Indeed, he says of the common people in language which if it wounds does so out of its own hurt:

> I would they were barbarians – as they are,
> Though in Rome litter'd; not Romans – as they are not.
>
> III i 236–7

'His attitude to the citizens', claims the actor Alan Howard, 'is "If only they would hate me as much as I hated them, out of that purity of conflict and engagement something productive might come . . . instead of everybody going behind doors and working out little deals".'[28] But Coriolanus cannot be his own mediator and thus explain his belief; he *is* his belief, even though he cannot bear to see his belief as no more than his, personally alone.

But what the theatre audience sees is that his belief is a belief in Rome itself which no one else there in Rome seems to share. Unbelievably to Coriolanus the nobles let themselves down, sacrificing reality itself to the compromises of politics: 'Purpose so barr'd, it follows/Nothing is done to purpose' (III i 147–8). Rome cannot seem to accept the image of itself that Coriolanus embodyingly offers it, until all he can offer it instead is his impassioned insults – be what you should be or see what you are:

> let them
> Regard me as I do not flatter, and
> Therein behold themselves.

III i 65–7

– until, in turn, all Rome can do is banish *him* – banish him? Unbelievable to him:

> I banish you . . .
> There is a world elsewhere.

III iii 123, 135

It is a wonderfully large saying, as grand as Coriolanus himself – and yet, especially for Coriolanus, there *is* no world elsewhere. Coriolanus was the Roman world: when he separates from Rome, the overlap or match between within and without is coming apart. In leaving Rome, Coriolanus has both taken something away and left something behind. What can he then do, save turn back against the Rome that banished him? But in turning back against Rome, his occupation's gone, the conflicts and contradictions are too great to be contained in 'one thing'. His family kneel before him, he stands: his mother urges him, puts his wife before him. There *is* a difference between those beliefs of his mother's which have long become Coriolanus's own inside him, and that mother herself outside trying everything to coerce him. But there is no point in speaking of the distinction, when finally he must act the part of seeming to yield to her, even in truly loving both her and his wife. The very determination to hold to his revenge, despite the pleas of mother, wife and child, has become the thing he most loathed of all – a bit of acting:

> Like a dull actor now
> I have forgot my part and I am out,
> Even to a full disgrace.

V iii 40–2

If he has become an actor, he is finished. In turning on Rome, he has also been going to war with himself.

Coriolanus is a believer not an actor. A believer from so far deep inside that, in the words of Cominius, 'If I should tell thee o'er this

thy day's work,/Thou'ldst not *believe* thy deeds' (I ix 1–2). So deep
does it go with him that he does not even see himself as a believer.
But he knows he is not an actor from without. He cannot do as the
Montaigne depicted in the *Essais* might have had such a one do:

> I am ready to finish this man, not to make another. . . . The more
> we amplifie our neede and possession, the more we engage our
> selves to the crosses of fortune and adversities. The cariere of
> our desires must be circumscribed, and tied to strict bounds of
> neerest and contiguous commodities. Moreover, their course
> should be managed, not in a straight line, having another
> end, but round, whose two points hold together, and end in
> ourselves with a short compasse. The actions governed without
> this reflection, I meane a neere and essentiall reflection, as those
> of the covetous, of the ambitious and so many others, that runne
> directly point-blancke, the course of which carrieth them away
> before them, are erroneous and crazed actions. Most of our
> vacations are like playes. *Mundus universus excercet histrionam.*
> *All the world doth practise stage-playing.* Wee must play our parts
> duly, but as the part of a borrowed personage. Of a visard and
> apparence, wee should not make a real essence. . . . It is sufficient
> to disguise the face, without deforming the breast.
>
> vol.III, pp.262–3
> (ch.x, 'How One Ought to Governe His Will')

Montaigne hates the paradox of a man being driven out of himself
even by the demands of his very self. He hates it 'whenever
the individual abandons himself so completely . . . that his
present consciousness of his own existence in its entirety, his
full consciousness of a life distinctively his own, melts away in
the process'.[29] Consciousness is the stay by which to shake off
violent hold-fasts; consciousness is the defence and the essence of
separate individuality.

Coriolanus 'cannot temp'rately transport his honours/ From
where he should begin and end' (II i 222–3). He wants and
knows no boundaries. He goes forward into the world not
round inside himself. But Montaigne turns the straight line of
action into the reflective circle of his *Essais*, finishing the man,
even as Samuel Daniel in his sonnets turned chaos into a round
orb of order.

This is where the difference between Montaigne and Shakespeare becomes decisive. For Shakespeare, a play means something quite other than it does for Montaigne: it means the sheer drama of time in the movement of one human being through shifting scenes and versions of him- or herself.

It precisely does not mean the sort of conscious play-acting that Coriolanus in Shakespeare's own play puts by. 'All the world doth practise stage-playing': for Montaigne public life means acting a part as 'of a borrowed personage'. Montaigne keeps the essential self apart from the roles played by it, even by consciousness of the temporary necessity of its own disguises. 'Being unable to direct events', says Montaigne in that need of his to find some space by whatsoever improvisation, 'I governe my selfe; and if they apply not themselves to me, I apply my selfe to them' (vol.II, p.369, ch.xvii, 'Of Presumption'). Shakespeare knows all about those flexibly potential turn-arounds. But for Coriolanus it is as though, for all his personal pride, he has no separately detached 'real essence' at the conscious level at which Montaigne means it. 'You are too absolute' (III ii 39): Coriolanus wants precisely that absorption of himself into the world that Montaigne most abhors. Reality for Coriolanus is action, where 'there is no distinction between . . . the agent and his operation, since this is an immanent act whereby things keep themselves in existence'.[30] The thought is Campanella's – *operari est esse*:

> 'Action,' he says, 'is the act of the agent insofar as it *extends itself* into the recipient.' ('Actusque extensus in patiens est actio.') It consists properly speaking in the effusion of the agent's likeness into something that is either contrary to, or different from, itself; for no passion, and therefore no action, is possible between two things which are absolutely the same ('Actio est effusio similitudinis agentis in patiens, quod oportet ergo illi esse contrarium aut diversum. Si enim simile est omnino, non patitur ab eo; quoniam agere est quoddam assimilare sibi quod est dissimile.') To act is to communicate the likeness of the active cause to something else precisely because it is something else.
>
> Campanella, pp.152–3

Such is Coriolanus: he cannot see himself, he will not wholly reflect upon himself; but rather by acts of imposition, he *makes* what he also depends upon believing in, actually come to *be* in front of his very eyes. To make a thing happen or come to be in the outside world is to create from inside yourself what the world beyond yourself either resists or accepts, and, if accepts, then confirms as real. Coriolanus has made even Aufidius bear the inward as well as outward marks of Coriolanus. For Coriolanus, banished from Rome, goes to offer himself to the one man whom Coriolanus himself ('were I anything but what I am') would wish himself to be (I i 230–1). And then Aufidius embraces his one-time opponent as though Coriolanus had long been the same thing as he, only in greater degree and in different form:

> and do contest
> As hotly and as nobly with thy love
> As ever in ambitious strength I did
> Contend against thy valour.
>
> IV v 111–14

That is in Aufidius the mark of Coriolanus's effusion of 'the agent's likeness into something that is either contrary to, or different from, itself; for no passion, and therefore no action, is possible between two things which are absolutely the same'.

Coriolanus is an instinctive believer – even Othello in his very wrongness is just such a believer. It makes them extend themselves, their visionary thoughts covering their world like beams from out of their eyes, crossing and intersecting those thrown out by others. But Montaigne is not a believer in that actively dynamic sense; he is not so 'absolute' in the present as to forget the relative:

How diversly judge we of things? How often change we our phantasies? What I hold and beleeve this day, I beleeve and hold with all my beleefe: all my implements, springs and motions, embrace and claspe this opinion, and to the utmost of their power warrant the same: I could not possibly embrace any verity, nor with more assurance keepe it, then I doe this. I am wholy and absolutely given to it: but hath it not beene my fortune, not once, but a hundred, nay a thousand times, my daily, to have embraced some other thing, with the very same instruments and condition, which upon better advise

I have afterward judged false? A man should at the least become wise, at his owne cost, and learne by others harmes. If under this colour I have often founde my selfe deceived, if my Touch-stone be commonly found false and my balance un-even and unjust; What assurance may I more take of it at this time, then at others?

vol.II, pp.276-7 (ch.xii, 'An Apologie of Raymond Sebond')

Have I not been wrong, when I thought myself so right, hundreds of times before now? If so, why trust myself so much now? Moreover, we are often just as foolish when correcting ourselves as we were in making the original mistake. Wise men, hundreds of men, the whole human race has got things wrong for centuries, 'man's nature either in one thing or other, hath for many ages together mistaken her selfe':

What assurance have we that at any time she leaveth her mistaking, and that she continueth not even at this day, in her error?

vol.II, p.293 (ch.xii, 'An Apologie of Raymond Sebond')

Montaigne tells the story of a blind nobleman who pretends he isn't blind, goes shooting, aims hopelessly wide but is satisfied if his servants tell him he was close – well, what if, all along, we too are like this in our own equivalent dark:

Who knowes whether mankind commit as great a folly, for want of some sense, and that by this default, the greater part of the visage of things be concealed from us?

vol.II, p.309 (ch.xii, 'An Apologie of Raymond Sebond')

In each of these examples what is so remarkable is the sheer tone of mind that is able to release the question with a rueful shrug: 'Hath it not beene a hundred, nay a thousand times . . . ?' 'What assurance may I . . . ? What assurance have we?' 'Who knowes but . . . ?' Montaigne trusts nothing, but turns the lack of certain knowledge and trust, the sheer force of indeterminacy, into a form of mental freedom.

Securing himself within himself at just those limits where desired knowledge emphatically runs out, Montaigne is content to be just one person within the wide universe, without deceiving himself into seeing less than he does or should. Thus he is able to use the highest of all perspectives:

> whosoever shall present unto his inward eyes . . . the Idea of the great image of our universall mother Nature, attired in her richest robes, sitting in the throne of her Majestie, and in her visage shall read, so generall, and so constant a varietie; he that therein shall view himselfe, not himselfe alone, but a whole Kingdome, to be in respect of a great circle but the smallest point that can be imagined, he onely can value things according to their essentiall greatnesse and proportion. This great universe . . . is the true looking-glasse wherin we must looke, if we will know whether we be of a good stampe, or in the right byase.
>
> vol.I, p.165
> (ch.xxv, 'Of the Institution and Education of Children')

– and uses this height precisely to secure that sense of proportion which returns him to a lower, smaller level of being, as the proper human norm:

> We hinder our thoughts from the generall and maine point, and from the causes and universall conducts: which are very well directed without us, and omit our owne businesse: and *Michael*, who concernes us neerer than man.
>
> vol.III, p.191 (ch.ix 'Of Vanitie')

Unlike Hooker, Michel de Montaigne refuses to let his relation to the world force him into an anxiety about the overall Law. To Montaigne, concern for knowing and then implementing the Law grants too much status to the finality of action. Outcomes are often merely forced, are often only chance. The 'essay' is thus the form and size of belief or unbelief with which Montaigne is most happy, sheerly as 'Michel'. What Montaigne has is the essentially comic resolve to *be secondary*, in the sense that, finally leaving the primacies of the great universe to itself, he finds in that a licence to keep the range of his thoughts within those of one creature in the whole creation.

Having read Montaigne,[31] Shakespeare could not but have seen the achievement of the man, precisely in thus *making* himself a man, Michael, single and particular. For Shakespeare well knew

the problems involved in so doing, in particular in *Hamlet*: 'Hamlet
cannot adjust the infinite part of him to the finite'; his 'long course
of thinking, apart from action, has destroyed Hamlet's capacity for
belief'.³² It is to *Hamlet* that I finally return in this chapter.

Himself so unlike Coriolanus (or even that smaller man of action
Fortinbras), Hamlet is equally unable to be like Montaigne. Larger
and freer than Horatio, Montaigne is more truly 'the man who is
not passion's slave' (III ii 72) – but Hamlet cannot even be Horatio.
For Hamlet is not just ruefully sceptical like Montaigne: rather,
'like a neutral' (II ii 477), he believes in *nothing*, and what is more,
finds it intolerable to do so. 'You should not have *believed* me', he
says to Ophelia, his own dismayed disgust at the failure of fidelity
and belief in the world of Claudius and Gertrude characteristically
first incorporated in himself and then turned inside-out again.
Consciousness is a problem, not a defence.

For all his failure to find one thing in which to believe, Hamlet
cannot let go of infinite concerns, as can Montaigne, and keep his
thoughts within the physical being of a single limited person. Nor
can he be like Helena in *All's Well* who finds in limitation a sheer
freedom to be what she can, and will not make herself a victim of
her own abilities:

> Our remedies oft in ourselves do lie,
> Which we ascribe to heaven. The fated sky
> Gives us free scope; only doth backward pull
> Our slow designs when we ourselves are dull.
> What power is it which mounts my love so high?
> That makes me see, and cannot feed mine eye?
> The mightiest space in fortune nature brings
> To join like likes, and kiss like native things.
> Impossible be strange attempts to those
> That weigh their pains in sense, and do suppose
> What hath been cannot be.
>
> *All's Well That Ends Well*, I i 187–97

Hamlet cannot break free, either from the ghost or from himself,
and cannot think like this: 'let us take no more excuses from
externall qualities of things. To us it belongeth to give our selves
accoumpt of it. Our good, and our evill hath no dependency, but

from our selves' (Montaigne, vol.I, p.343, ch.l, 'Of Democritus and
Heraclitus'). 'In ourselves; we ourselves' says Helena too: all along
whatever 'hath been' in this world, always *could be* in potential,
before ever it came to be in fact – while, all the time, others
denied the very possibility in self-fulfilling prophecies of doom.
There is pessimism of the intellect, said Gramsci, but there is
also optimism of the will. With that will, Helena's desperation
still demands a comic mode where Hamlet for all his jesting will
never find one to fit. If Hamlet is one sort of outsider, Helena is
another, for throughout *All's Well* no place at all in the play is
easily given to her. She *makes* her place and does so without being
able to congratulate herself on using the means of male heroism.
Like Rosalind in *As You Like It*, she is one of Shakespeare's brave,
active women. She wins Bertram but, hating her for it, he will not
consummate the marriage. She takes Diana's place, as Mariana takes
Isabella's in *Measure for Measure*, and, tricking her own husband into
making love to her when he supposes her Diana, she finds herself
thinking afterwards:

> But O, strange men,
> That can such sweet use make of what they hate,
> When saucy trusting of the cozened thoughts
> Defiles the pitchy night; so lust doth play
> With what it loathes for that which is away.
>
> IV iv 21–5

It is as if she were momentarily an anonymous somebody else,
partly because she thinks, floatingly: he enjoyed me, but would
not have enjoyed it if he had known that it was me. But she is
also impersonal at this point because no view, however personally
unaccommodatable it at first may seem, is denied room in this
play. There is a moral vocabulary here ('trusting/cozened', 'defiles'
'hate, lust, loathes') without a moral sentence to contain it properly.
For the sexual act was here a 'making use' and a 'playing with',
even whilst his loving unknowingly took the place of loathing and
hating, through lust on his side and cozening on hers. And yet it
was also 'sweet' and 'strange' in mutual love enacted as mutual
betrayal. The fact is that the thought 'if he had only known' is also
now irrelevant: the sexual act happened in the dark there between

the bodies and whatever either mind thinks afterwards, the couple
must simply go along with the fact. The pragmatism of acts has ever
been Helena's way as soon as she eschewed mere pining for love.

An Isabella, in contrast, has to *justify* forgiving Angelo, on the
grounds that he did not actually sleep with her – despite his intent
to do so and belief he had done so:

> His act did not o'ertake his bad intent,
> And must be buried but as an intent
> That perish'd by the way. Thoughts are no subjects;
> Intents but merely thoughts.
>
> *Measure for Measure*, V i 449–52

It is an extraordinarily interesting and elaborate argument for one
who is steeped in a Christian morality where intent is vital. But
to the more secular Helena, thoughts are indeed no subjects, no
extra justifications are necessary – as they always are for Hamlet.
The deceits that the Duke has cumbersomely to incorporate within
a moral scheme in *Measure for Measure* ('the doubleness of the
benefit defends the deceit from reproof', 'the justice of your title
to him/Doth flourish the deceit': II i 258–9, IV i 74–5) – these
expediencies are simply accepted by Helena on the basis of sheer
desired outcome, rather than made into something like Hooker's
positive laws. Indeed, were Angelo like Helena, he would not
think he did desire Isabella 'foully' for those things that made her
'good': the desire could be good too. For Helena has felt in the
very place of neglect a licence for 'free scope' - the size of what one
can do being determined, pragmatically, only after one has tried to
do it, and not by self-diminishing doubt beforehand. Our business
is with Michael not Man; with Helena not the Universe. Fate
'only doth backward pull/Our slow designs when we ourselves
are dull'.

Poor dull-feeling Hamlet then: 'how weary, stale, flat, and
unprofitable/Seem to me all the uses of this world' (I ii 133–4),
'This goodly frame the earth seems to me a sterile promontory'
(II ii 298–9) - and this from a man who has told his mother that
he knows not 'seems' (I ii 76). But 'seems' and 'seem to me', in
their very admission of the part he plays in what he sees, are the
very mark of the punitive self-consciousness of his depression.

Yet if in the public realm Hamlet can become an actor and a seemer, as a Montaigne can and a Coriolanus cannot, it is never wholly or easily pragmatic for Hamlet. Rather, he dissimulates in defence of his recognition that the whole public world is itself secretly acting:

> O villain, villain, smiling damned villain!
> My tables. Meet it is I set it down
> That one may smile, and smile and be a villain –
> At least I am sure it may be so in Denmark.
>
> I v 106–9

He can write down the fact of the deceit, for writing seems to create a place in which to think such a thing sanely, objectively and permanently. But very soon he will again have to speak and move and be himself within this world. And then he cannot find the comically incredulous tone of *All's Well That Ends Well* – as when a lord, overhearing Parolles thinking over what deceptions he will need to carry out in order desperately to preserve his reputation, says:

> Is it possible he should know what he is, and be that he is?
>
> *All's Well That Ends Well*, IV i 35

It is a great question. But the answer in *All's Well* is still comic: yes, we do that, are like that, all the time.

Instead, Hamlet almost immediately improvises the thought that if Claudius is in disguise, so must Hamlet be:

> Here, as before, never so help you mercy,
> How strange or odd some'er I bear myself –
> As I perchance hereafter shall think meet
> To put an antic disposition on –
> That you, at such time seeing me, never shall,
> With arms encumber'd thus, or this head-shake,
> Or by pronouncing of some doubtful phrase,
> As 'Well, we know', or 'We could and if we would',
> Or 'If we list to speak', or 'There be and if they might',

Or such ambiguous giving out, to note
That you know aught of me – this do swear.

I v 177–87

But look how obliquely that thought about disguise has expressed
itself in parenthesis. This isn't just Hamlet's caution; there is
something in Hamlet already compulsively parodic of the human
hollowness surrounding him that causes him an inner loss of
trust:

As 'Well, we know', or 'We could and if we would',
Or 'If we list to speak', or 'There be and if they might'.

It is as though Hamlet becomes a disturbed version of the Fool
– seriously disturbed because he is not licens'd. I think Claudius
evil, but he smiles, and nobody knows, and the ghost's absolutes
do not stay: so is 'nothing either good or bad but thinking
makes it so' (II ii 249–50)? All that Hamlet can produce as
Fool-to-relativism is a sort of parodic unreality, having to act
mad because the world *is* maddening while not acknowledging
itself to be other than quite sane and normal. The parodic unreality
goes like this:

Polonius What do you read, my lord?
Hamlet Words, words, words.
Polonius What is the matter, my lord?
Hamlet Between who?

II ii 191–4

It is a performance which, however bravely witty, is finally
destructive of the whole pretence of meaning.

Hamlet can find temporary comic relief in that more solid
version of his own playfulness which is expressed in the Grave-
digger: 'How absolute the knave is. We must speak by the card
or equivocation will undo us' (V i 133–4). But with Hamlet
himself, the parodying of unreality increasingly becomes his only
reality: indeed, the pretence of madness is useful precisely in so far
as it blurs even to Hamlet himself the degree to which what you
are pretending to be is also becoming what you are. The playing

can take over, overlap, till acting becomes real to Hamlet and he hardly knows a danger from a safety-valve. Thus when the King says, 'How fares our cousin Hamlet?' Hamlet answers as if he belonged in another half-separated world by taking 'fares' to mean 'eats' not 'does':

> *King* I have nothing with this answer, Hamlet. These words are not mine.
> *Hamlet* No, nor mine now.
>
> III ii 95–7

Hamlet *evacuates* his place, leaves the words behind to play upon Claudius as nothing. But to do so leaves *him* hollow, for it is also as if in this social context his words are never really 'mine now'. The satiric parodies begin to externalize in an alien comic mode the alienation he is seriously but incommunicably suffering from inside. It is as much a danger sign to Hamlet as to his mother if Gertrude should indeed think it is not her 'trespass' but his 'madness' that in him 'speaks' (III iv 148). For the madness put on in order to expose the trespass is no longer consistently distinguishable from a madness that still suffers from the sins and crimes. They overlap.

That is how time is oscillatingly registered in *Hamlet*: something from inside emerges for a moment in the midst of what seemed externally directed; or, something at one moment feigned, at another seems the expression of what's real. It was going to be like this from the moment that Hamlet felt that 'I have that within which passes show'. 'That within' which cannot be properly shown is thereafter only ever called 'something' in this play: 'There's something in his soul' (III i 166), 'Yet have I in me something dangerous' (V i 255), a thing related to that sense in him of 'something in this more than natural' (II ii 363–4), of 'something rotten in the state of Denmark' (I iv 90), and to his fear of 'something after death' (III i 78). For this consciousness that will not simply clothe itself in the shows of grief, and thus will not let Hamlet be part of the customary shape and pattern of life in Denmark, is emphatically not itself called into being in this play as in so

many others, is not (as we saw so often in Chapter One) the
emergent temporal product of the pressures of space around
it. On the contrary, it exists as a result of a person *not* feeling himself as called into being. It is just 'something', almost
unnamed. We do not see Hamlet getting made. For Hamlet's problem is that he does not really start, but bears a consciousness that, not having been created by what he has done,
exists only negatively by dint of his not fitting in with all
around him. He is out of joint: for he has become a consciousness *before* ever he has encountered a concrete, visible
situation in which actively and positively to create and shape
himself. There was no specific or natural or given moment in
which simply and unthinkingly to revenge himself on Claudius.
The crime itself was only revealed in a way that created a
backdated shock. So much in the play and in the protagonist
cannot now find itself expressible within the terms of the particular;
it seems too late to be thus confined; too much has or has not
happened.

But if, as we have seen, Hamlet does not fit the clothes set
out for him, he has no other clothes or forms of expression
in the world. He can only silently refuse to seem – in a
version of integrity oddly comparable with Coriolanus's. Or
alternatively he can try to use playing sheerly for his *own* ends.
Thus, Hamlet goes into the world's secret mode of play-acting in
order to know what is going on there even from inside it: then,
without losing himself, he seeks from within it to dominate its
processes. Yet, without losing himself *is* the question. 'We must
often deceive others, lest we beguile ourselves', warns Montaigne
(vol.III, p.257, ch.x, 'How One Ought to Governe His Will');
but Hamlet is his father's son, he cannot separate himself as can
Montaigne, and thus he is in danger of beguiling himself even
while deceiving others. The trouble is, as Montaigne put it, when
I play with my cat, am I sure I am playing with it or is it playing
with me?

Campanella says 'cognoscere est esse', or to know is also to be,
and 'cognoscere est fieri rem cognitam', to know a thing is also (in
part) to become the thing known. Thus, in the act of seeking to
know what it is that is going on in Denmark, is Hamlet mastering
it or becoming like it?

We do not perceive anything by which we are not affected and by which we are not changed. I feel warmth when I become warm; I perceive sound when a sound strikes my ear; I see color when a color affects my eye. So every sensation is through assimilation. The agent makes a passive subject similar to itself through assimilation. . . . When we perceive something, we are in some way alienated and changed into something else, so that we know when we become something else.

Campanella, p.52

Campanella thought this way of knowing might result in self-alienation and a loss of one's self even to the point of insanity. 'But howsomever thou pursuest this act,/Taint not thy mind', urged the ghost (I v 84–5). Shakespeare himself must have known of the dangers of infected imagination. 'It is not necessary that the whole spirit be transformed, but only a part of it; and even this part does not have to be transformed entirely, but only to the extent that from the little that is affected, it can infer the rest of the power of the object acting upon itself' (Campanella, p.101). 'That one may smile . . . .' What is terrifying here is that Hamlet's very separation, so painfully felt by him in Denmark, so unhappily unlike Montaigne's detachment, is itself still part of, and even half-created by, all that surrounds him. All that vengeful witty playing with Rosencrantz and Guildenstern still centres around the more vulnerable plea to 'be even and direct with me' (II ii 287).

In the confusion of boundaries in this play there are moments when neither Hamlet nor we know whether he is safely behind his defences or whether, without even moving save mentally and emotionally, he has unwittingly and involuntarily extended and exposed himself beyond them. 'I never gave you aught', Hamlet says to Ophelia (III i 96), and an actor can hardly decide how far this is denial, how far guilt as well, or how he can convey something of both at the same time without ignoring either. 'But yet I could accuse me of such things . . .' says Hamlet to Ophelia (III i 123), where surely the externally directed punishment and warning and disgust are also internally felt, simultaneously, as guilt. How to register thus simultaneously the mix, the doubt as to mind and voice's emphasis? There is not time. Whether it be this, or this, or that. Too much has overlapped by now to be able to tell. We may conclude thus: that the sheer accumulated context in which by now he speaks overwhelms any clear intent of the speaker.

'Words, words, words' so promptly give Hamlet thoughts, so many thoughts – too many thoughts crossing over each other for any to be singled out. There are brief runs of rhythm when, like some jazz-player, Hamlet gets his timing together, as when telling Polonius to look after the players:

> *Polonius* My lord, I will use them according to their desert.
> *Hamlet* God's bodkin, man, much better. Use every man after his desert, and who shall scape a whipping?
>
> > II ii 523–5

Grace and shrug are together at once. If it could have been sustained, 'Use every man after his desert, and who shall scape a whipping?' might have incorporated both *All's Well*'s

> our virtues would be proud, if our faults whipped them not, and our crimes would despair, if they were not cherished by our virtues
>
> > IV iii 61–4

and *Measure for Measure*'s

> > How would you be
> If He, which is the top of judgement, should
> But judge you as you are?
>
> > II ii 75–7

– the two plays and their attitudes, pagan and Christian, displaced on either side of Hamlet's central problem of unification. But with Hamlet's saying, the rhythm runs out again a second later, and there seems to be no more time for stabilizing the clue of sudden reactive thought into the more continuing attitude of stable character. And if thoughts cannot be thus singled out and stabilized, they are denied that realm of present trial in life that is another way of seeing their real meaning. They perish by the way.

The Helena of *All's Well* intuitively knew this when she believed in simply seeing what worked, whatsoever our thoughts and feelings about it. As she tells the King who judges himself medically a hopeless case:

Oft expectation fails, and most oft there
Where most it promises; and oft it hits
Where hope is coldest, and despair most shifts.

II i 138–40

The more we hope, the more we are often disappointed. But Helena also knows that the opposite is not thereby more true: viz. that the less we hope, the more likely it is to come out right. Shrug. Trust. Or just try and see:

The consequence we seeke to draw from the conference of events is unsure, because they are dissemblable. No quality is so universall in this surface of things, as variety and diversity. . . . Dissimilitude doth of it selfe insinuate into our workes. . . . Resemblance doth not so much make one as difference maketh another. Nature hath bound herselfe to make nothing that may not be dissemblable.

Montaigne, vol.III, p.322 (ch.xiii, 'Of Experience')

Que sais-je, who knows? There are no certain precedents and patterns. There is what there is, is all we can say.

Shakespeare himself kept trying things out, going with what the shapes before him suggested, varying the overlaps. *Measure for Measure* in one way, followed by *All's Well That Ends Well* in another, each managed resolutions for what was so mixed-up: they are different assays at the *Hamlet* problem. And yet just as Shakespeare in *Coriolanus* will never let us be completely free of the overlap of primary belief and secondary pride in the protagonist himself, so in *Measure for Measure* there is never a pure certainty that morality would not involve a certain manipulativeness for which (to the potential amusement of a Helena) it felt obliged to apologize. So too in *All's Well That Ends Well* there is never a complete assurance that pragmatism may not become involved in cynicism. One consideration is never quite free of another. In *All's Well*, all that Parolles can say when he is caught out is, 'Who cannot be crushed with a plot?' (IV iii 272) – yet, deflated as he is by his own exposure as a liar and a boaster, who would have thought Parolles could have found the heart or nerve to say as much? It is a marvellously tart leveller from one still alive and kicking. Yet inconveniently it is also *at the same time* a later, darker, lonelier version of that comic forgiveness we saw Berowne find. Even so, by going with any mood or turn of life in 'assay', Shakespeare celebrates something that toughly comes out of cynicism and defeat in Parolles: 'Simply the thing I am/Shall make me live' (IV iv 280–1). I have to live. Hamlet will not say that, will not become that simply secondary thing called, as it were, Michael, not Man.

But Hamlet is no Hercules, no Alexander. In his mind even real godlike men such as these or Coriolanus turn to dust. Yet he still feels himself rebuked by them as by a first generation of primal models and kings and fathers whose gifts were still their strengths. In this later evolution, Hamlet's very gifts of mind have become weaknesses. What Hamlet needs, if he is to get out of this coil by some means other than suicide, is the old lost belief. But compare the two following passages. Here is Hamlet, moved at one remove by the emotion of the actor at his own part:

> And all for nothing!
> For Hecuba!
> What's Hecuba to him, or he to her,
> That he should weep for her? What would he do
> Had he the motive and the cue for passion
> That I have?
>
> II ii 551–6

It is both so near and so far from the language of this ancient believer:

> I learned to lament the death of Dido, who killed herself for love, while all the time, in the midst of these things, I was dying, separated from you, my God and my Life, and I shed no tears for my own plight.
>   What can be more pitiful than an unhappy wretch unaware of his own sorry state, bewailing the fate of Dido, who died for love of Aeneas, yet shedding no tears for himself as he dies for want of loving you?[33]

Augustine wept neither for himself nor for Christ: 'instead I wept for Dido.' Yet for Hamlet the trouble is that he was *not* 'unaware of his own sorry state' at the time. Hamlet's awareness is already in place of belief. And likewise what he, an actor in real life, sees outside him in the emotion of the player, is something that takes the place of what (he only feels) he *should* feel inside. That is to say, Hamlet already knows too much to break down as did Augustine. He knows too much about 'nothing': Pyrrhus 'Did nothing', the player's tears were 'all for nothing'. But Augustine can live a life that has a narrative in time because for him there is some relation between time and truth. For Augustine, if there is something basically wrong in one's initial position eventually it will have to make itself known in time itself. The truth will out, with increasing directness, after he has found himself weeping (why?) for the fiction of Dido. But Hamlet already has everything at his finger-tips, has nothing that he has not thought of. Yet, having consciousness always as a form of anticipation, he has accordingly no sequence of time to unfold his thoughts and lead him through the living-out of his own story.

Instead the play begins to take on a shape of its own and form the strange pattern of 'something', *almost* mentally deducible, working itself out in odd connections in space. The mousetrap is as a mirror for Claudius to see himself; Hamlet sets up 'a glass' made of his own words wherein his mother 'may see the inmost part of you' (III iv 18–19), turning her eyes into her very soul. Hamlet sees versions of or alternatives to himself everywhere. 'For by the image of my cause I see', he says of Laertes, 'The portraiture of his' (V ii 77–8). Something drives Ophelia, 'divided from herself' (IV v 85), to take over Hamlet's mixed tone of madness both for real and for ever: 'Thought and affliction, passion, hell itself/She turns to favour and to prettiness' (IV vi 185–6). 'Thought and affliction, passion, hell itself' are almost names for Hamlet himself, his madness turned into hers.

In *Hamlet* it is not as though space creates such pressure on the play that its matter bursts out into time as time's events, but rather that time itself, unable to relieve the pressure, becomes reinvolved in a quasi-spatial configuration across the play as a whole. 'All through the play there is the uneasiness of something trying to get done, something from outside life trying to get into life, but baffled always because the instrument chosen is, himself, a little outside life.'[34] As with Ophelia in her madness, there are 'unshaped' thoughts throughout this play trying distortedly to find

a shape or language or medium (IV v 8). It feels like such a slow play
in action because it brings so many of its heavy burdens, continually
unexorcized, to each and every moment, seeking expression. In
just a single scene, even as Claudius remorsefully prays, Hamlet
separately contemplates immediate revenge; and it seems incredible
that these two people could be said to be in the same place when
really they are in such different time-bands, such different internal
worlds. Yet often these different worlds, these different people, also
seem lodged within Hamlet himself. 'Something' as well as nothing
in the play is going on, something which Hamlet himself is and is
also infected by, which he suffers from and causes others too to
suffer from in turn – something which moves around so much,
inhabiting one body then another:

> Nature is fine in love, and where 'tis fine
> It sends some precious instance of itself
> After the thing it loves.

IV v 161–3

It is love that is spoken of here – the love of Ophelia for her dead
father. But 'something' that is not quite love is, to use Campanella's
word, *assimilating* others to it, sending instances of itself into human
characters in this play till, overlapping, they become part of its
configuration:

> It is part of the play's ironic teaching that life must not be baffled;
> but that, when she has been wrenched from her course, she must
> either be wrenched back to it or kept violently in the channel to
> which she has been forced.[35]

The neo-Platonist Ficino, turning difference into coherence,
says that under the optimum balance of pressures of space in the
world, all its parts are in loving harmony with each other. And even
without that optimum state, no part hates another even if that other
is its own opposite:

> For fire does not flee out of hatred of water; but out of love for
> itself, lest it be extinguished by the coldness of the water. Nor
> does water extinguish fire out of hatred of fire; but it is led out of
> certain natural desire for multiplying its own cold to create water
> like itself out of the body of the fire.[36]

Apparent hate is love back-to-front – if not love gone wrong, at least love unable to go as right as in spirit it would. Shakespeare was always fascinated by the overlap of the right thing coming from the wrong person – from Iago, for example, who is as aware of the anomaly as is Shakespeare himself:

> And what's he then that says I play the villain,
> When this advice is free I give, and honest,
> Probal to thinking, and indeed the course
> To win the Moor again? . . .
> > How am I then a villain
> To counsel Cassio to this parallel course
> Directly to his good? Divinity of Hell!
> > > *Othello*, II iii 303–6, 315–17

But *Hamlet* goes even further, cosmically. In its own connected separations the world of *Hamlet* is like a fallen version of the neo-Platonic divine comedy, is like the back-to-front or nightmare side of the neo-Platonic dream of universally related innocence:

> Thus Campanella declares that to know is to become what is known, and Patrizzi says that to know is to be united with what one knows, there being a mystical play on the notion of union – *coitus* - in *cognoscere*: 'co-knowing' is being made one with the thing known. This stems, perhaps, from the ancient metaphysical (and mystical) doctrine, of which Plato's Symposium contains the most memorable vision, that in the beginning, subject and object, man and nature, sensation and thought, were one; then a great catastrophe divided them; since when they everlastingly seek reunion – re-integration - which can be achieved in 're'-cognition. Hence the belief in magic, as the acquisition of power by the subject over the object, by re-entering it, immersing oneself in it, and so reassimilating it to oneself, a notion which is at the heart of much Renaissance natural philosophy.[37]

Hamlet represents not only the great catastrophe but a distorted memory of all the old original connections and forces and dynamics and shapes still working in the same way but, like love turned into hate, working now either the wrong way round or in strange compounds of itself.[38] 'I must be cruel only to be kind', says Hamlet to his mother (III iv 180), or, almost twisted by circumstances, 'Forgive me this my virtue' (III iv 154). It is as though the play contains both that fundamental breach between knower and known that creates the protagonist and, across that breach and between all the characters, an older force of being still trying to send 'some precious instance of itself/After the thing it loves'.

Chapter 3
'And What's Her History?':
Shakespeare's Histories and Late Plays

1 OF SEQUENCE AND SUCCESSION

For all the force of York's protest to Richard II –

> Take Herford's rights away and take from time
> His charters and his customary rights.
> Let not tomorrow then ensue today.
> Be not thyself. For how art thou a king
> But by fair sequence and succession?
>
> *Richard II*, II i 195–9

there is something in Shakespeare which is bored by mere sequence and succession – in the broadest sense of those terms – *if* they come easily. If the sequence is complex or, alternatively, if its sheer linear simplicity is unbearably imprisoning, then Shakespeare is interested. But easy wins, success by simple succession (or, in Macbeth's terms, 'surcease . . . success') – these are uninteresting to Shakespeare: 'lest too light winning/Make the prize light' (*The Tempest*, I ii 452–3).

The Oxford English Dictionary (OED) gives as the first definition of succession 'the action of a person or thing following or succeeding to *the place* of another', hence 'the coming of one person or thing *after* another'. But Shakespeare is emphatically more interested in 'in place of' rather than merely 'after':

> Alack, why am I sent for to a king
> Before I have shook off the regal thoughts
> Wherewith I reigned?
>
> *Richard II*, IV i 162–4

That 'before' in Richard's mind exists none the less *after* he has been physically deposed. It takes time for what he now is to sink in, even whilst Richard, displaced from his role, asks himself what if anything there is inside him but the behaviour and the memory of what he has been in the outside world. Shakespeare is concerned more with what goes on *in between* what the OED calls 'the passing from one act or state to another' than with the mundane temporal order of one thing simply coming after another, like today, tomorrow:

> Between the acting of a dreadful thing
> And the first motion, all the interim is
> Like a phantasma . . .
>
> *Julius Caesar*, II i 63–5

He will not even put it the simpler way round: 'between the first motion and the acting of a dreadful thing'. Brutus's mind exists in the present interim only by first going forward to the future and then back again. Thus Shakespeare is more interested in history as a prompting to look at the way characters inhabit *time* than as a sequence of causes and effects.

Shakespeare loves it when we can barely keep up with him – and when even his own characters can barely do so, it offers us a dynamic image of life. For it is a matter of tender relish to Shakespeare when Helena in act III of *A Midsummer Night's Dream* cannot believe in Lysander and Demetrius's sudden profession of love. The play has moved on, but Helena, in thinking the men mock her, is still behaving as if she were in act I or the first scene of act II. In his twists and turns of time and place, Shakespeare loves to make a development in act II turn back upon a person still thinking herself in act I, precisely in order that he might create act III itself; likewise Falstaff at the end of act V of *2 Henry IV*, still belatedly claiming that the king will send for him in private; or Romeo in act III scene ii telling the mortally wounded Mercutio 'the hurt cannot be much'. When Helena cries to the others, 'I am sure you hate me with your hearts' (*A Midsummer Night's Dream*, III ii 154), she has not yet caught up with Shakespeare. And it is precisely this displacing time-lag which ensures, with all of comedy's trustingness, that a character is most deeply herself when least secure in being so.

Yet perhaps Shakespeare sometimes thought his boredom with

simple sequence – 'tomorrow and tomorrow and tomorrow' – a fault. For certainly it is an impatience which finds expression as mocking cruelty in the deposers Sebastian and Antonio in *The Tempest*, as they listen to the attempts of Gonzalo and Adrian to comfort the King:

> *Alonso [to Gonzalo]* I prithee, spare.
> *Gonzalo* Well, I have done. But yet –
> *Sebastian* He will be talking.
> *Antonio* Which, of he or Adrian, for a good wager, first begins to crow?
> *Sebastian* The old cock.
> *Antonio* The cockerel.
> *Sebastian* Done. The wager?
> *Antonio* A laughter.
> *Sebastian* A match!
> *Adrian* Though this island seem to be desert –
> *Antonio* Ha, ha, ha!
> *Sebastian* So, you're paid!
> *Adrian* Uninhabitable, and almost inaccessible –
> *Sebastian* Yet –
> *Adrian* Yet –
> *Antonio* He could not miss't . . .
>
> > *The Tempest*, II i 26–42

Done . . . But yet. Though . . . Yet. It is cruel mockery, but Shakespeare himself is no respecter of such long-winded slowness of the will in lieu of wit, such knowingly predetermined compensations, or such obviously predictable turns of thought. He needs real obstacles. When Shakespeare uses 'yet' with his own power it is more as it is with Prospero here – suddenly realizing that he must prepare himself, as well as Ariel, in order to set Ariel free:

> Why, that's my dainty Ariel! I shall miss thee,
> But yet thou shalt have freedom.
>
> > *The Tempest*, V i 95–6

It would not be so subtly good were it more opened out: 'Thou shalt have freedom, dainty Ariel, Yet I shall miss thee.' That would give the feeling a wrong place, releasing it as if it were a thing more for Ariel to feel outside than Prospero within. Consider again Shakespeare's musical movement, albeit here in small: it is 'my' Ariel, through affection now as well as power; but it will not be my Ariel much longer, 'I shall miss thee'; 'but yet' (severely and neither predictably nor consolingly) I return to and I keep my previous promise. The regretful, potentially final goodbye of 'I shall miss thee' is held instead within an instinctively registered and then determinedly reaffirmed order of life. The emotion in between is not so much repressed as summoned by the very resolve that ignores it. 'Thou shalt have freedom.'

The sort of 'sequence' Shakespeare relished is such as makes thought overtake time rather than laboriously follow it. The tediousness of good Adrian is as nothing compared with the improvisatory skill of a liar like Falstaff – and Shakespeare's history plays are full of improvisers: Richard of Gloucester, Antony, the tribunes in *Coriolanus*, even Bolingbroke in *Richard II*. Thus, for example, in two moments from act II scene iv of *1 Henry IV* Falstaff himself is suddenly forced to show how to turn time into timing. As Hal corners him about the robbery at Gadshill, Poins, like a taunting schoolboy, slyly seconds the prince:

Prince These lies are like their father that begets them, gross as a mountain, open, palpable. . . . Well, how couldst thou know these men in Kendal green when it was so dark thou couldst not see thy hand? Come, tell us your reason. What sayest thou to this?
Poins Come, your reason, Jack, your reason.

Prince What a slave art thou to hack thy sword as thou hast done, and then say it was in fight! What trick, what device, what starting-hole canst thou find out, to hide thee from this open and apparent shame?
Poins Come, let's hear, Jack, what trick hast thou now?
                    1 Henry IV, II iv 220–1, 226–30, 257–62

At such moments Falstaff, if he cannot answer, is liable to be as stranded as is the Fool in *Twelfth Night* according to Malvolio's description:

I saw him put down the other day with an ordinary fool, that
has no more brain than a stone. Look you now, he's out of his
guard already: unless you laugh and minister occasion to him, he
is gagged.

Twelfth Night, I v 81–6

If a fool can say nothing in reply, he *is* nothing. He cannot keep
the game going, he cannot fight back, he cannot return the ball,
but is like one lost for a rhyme. An underlying black sadness or
seriousness breaks into life's game; a silence opens around him.
Humiliatedly diminished and isolated, the fool dies a little. This
silence is a vacuum, and, says Campanella, things in nature would
rather face destruction by their very opposites than face a vacuum:

> The vacuum represented a greater threat to the body than even
> its contrary. Fire, for example, agrees with earth in that, at least,
> both are corporeal and have agent forms, while the vacuum is
> neither corporeal nor has it a form. Thus feeling or sensing
> the vacuum between them, contraries become sad, almost
> anticipating their annihilation, because a vacuum, as compared
> to a body, is a nothing.[1]

Those contemporaries of Shakespeare who think about the construction of the mind, like Montaigne, or of matter itself, like
Campanella, provide, as I have assumed throughout, closer analo-
gies with what is going on in the plays than do the chroniclers or
the social historians.

The rule is: flee even the thought of a vacuum. 'Do not bid
me remember mine end', says Falstaff (*2 Henry IV*, II iv 232) - an
end eventually executed by Hal's response on becoming Henry V:
'Reply not to me with a fool-born jest' (*2 Henry IV*, V v 55). So
here after Gadshill, under pressure of anticipating his annihilation,
momentarily hesitant and lost, Falstaff must make space for his
bulky self, must find some room in time:

> *Prince* Come, tell us your reason. What sayest thou to this?
> *Poins* Come, your reason, Jack, your reason.
> *Falstaff* What, upon compulsion? 'Zounds, and I were at the
> strappado, or all the racks in the world, I would not tell you on

compulsion. Give you a reason on compulsion? If reasons were
as plentiful as blackberries, I would give no man a reason upon
compulsion, I.

1 Henry IV, II iv 228–36

With Poins echoing the prince, it is two against one, and the one
must then repeat himself within his own terms to hold them off.
Falstaff needs his repetition – compulsion! reason! I! – to establish
his own rhythm of being in this world of sound, holding off the
horizontal run of the sequence by inserting a principle ('I would
not tell you on compulsion') from a different, as it were vertical,
dimension.

> *Prince* What trick, what device, what starting-hole canst thou
> find out, to hide thee from this open and apparent shame?
> *Poins* Come, let's hear, Jack, what trick hast thou now?
> *Falstaff* By the Lord, I knew ye as well as he that made ye. Why,
> hear you, my masters, was it for me to kill the heir-apparent?
> should I turn upon the true prince? Why, thou knowest I am as
> valiant as Hercules: but beware instinct – the lion will not touch
> the true prince; instinct is a great matter. I was now a coward on
> instinct . . .
>
> *1 Henry IV*, II iv 259–70

Now it is not 'compulsion' but 'instinct' that saves the day.
Cowardice is here converted, just as before the very compulsion
from without was dispersed even by naming it: even thus 'a man
at the nipping talke of his fellow, taketh the verie same words and
returneth them back againe, pricking him with his owne weapon'.[2]
Exit Falstaff.

Yet all these little verbal runs and moments are bound back
together again when minutes later Falstaff, re-entering in a sudden
change of mood, tells Hal how Sir John Bracy is come 'from
your father' to summon the Prince to court tomorrow in order
to prepare for civil war:

> But tell me, Hal, art not horrible afeard? Thou being heir
> apparent, could the world pick thee out three such enemies
> again, as that fiend Douglas, that spirit Percy, and that devil
> Glendower?

Falstaff repeats:

> Art thou not horribly afraid? Doth not thy blood thrill at it?

– to which the voluntarily displaced Prince makes return as from a higher level:

> Not a whit, i'faith, I lack some of thy instinct.
>
> *1 Henry IV*, II iv 361–7

This is not (yet) Hal's revenge. Though satirically turning the tables even as the reality of his own world makes itself felt to him through this alien medium, the Prince is none the less still content to appear in translation, putting his own implicit inverted commas around that word 'instinct'. He still includes Falstaff, he still contains their differences within the shared language of the jest, preserving some sort of fellowship of reference. Later Warwick will explain it thus: 'The Prince but studies his companions/Like a strange tongue' (*2 Henry IV*, IV iv 68–9). But what temporarily the Prince does here, in bringing back 'some of thy instinct' and improvising a longer sequence, is with retrospective quickness to knit together the often uneasy counter-community which the cheerful anarchy of Eastcheap still constitutes in the play.

Such improvised exchanges and tie-ups help give form to a society, in a deep sense of that term; and Eastcheap is at least for the time being an alternative holiday-world for the Prince, albeit one borrowed from the prospect of its future subordination. A social body survives in so far as, essentially undamaged, it can find room to absorb into its very constitution those excrescences, licences, nascent changes, or divergences that may come to life at any moment. 'A state without the means of some change is without the means of its conservation.'[3] How far in lending himself to Eastcheap, Hal absorbs Falstaff, or Falstaff Hal, is always, on the knife-edge, an abidingly dark interest. But in either case how sequences get built up, how sustained, how turned round into shapes other than a linear one, is part of that law of social conservation from Hooker to Burke which works by means of grafting, assimilating and regenerating. 'I lack some of thy instinct.' It is no wonder that the scene before us leads on immediately to the parody of Falstaff standing for the King while the Prince plays himself, until the two change places and the Prince acts his father and Falstaff the Prince. For Eastcheap and civil society likewise change places with each other, at one moment versions of the same basic thing, at the very next threats to each other again. These shifts of shape and level were implicitly in mind from the very moment when the Prince said to Falstaff, 'These lies are like their father that begets them': in such a context there was always going to have to be a more serious pick-up of those words 'father' and 'begets' and 'lies'.

The way in which one moment invents the next brings the meaning of 'sequence' nearer to the gravitation of thought found in a series of sonnets than to the succession of sovereigns in Holinshed. A small but definitive instance of the very moment of kinetic rather than predictable sequence may be seen in what is thought to be one of Shakespeare's own revisions from Quarto to Folio in *King Lear*. Lear's embarrassing self-anatomy satirically directed at Goneril is printed as prose in the Quarto[4]:

> *Lear* Doth any here know mee? why this is not *Lear*, doth *Lear* walke thus? speake thus? where are his eyes, either his notion, weaknes, or his discernings are lethargie, sleeping or waking; ha! sure 'tis not so, who is it that can tell me who I am? *Lears* shadow? I would lerne that, for by the markes of soueraintie, knowledge, and reason, I should bee false perswaded I had daughters.
> *Fool* Which they, will make an obedient father.

But it becomes this in the Folio:

> *Lear* Do's any heere know me?
>   This is not *Lear*:
>   Do's *Lear* walke thus? Speake thus? Where are his eies?
>   Either his Notion weakens, his Discernings
>   Are Lethargied. Ha! Waking? 'Tis not so?
>   Who is it that can tell me who I am?
> *Fool* *Lears* shadow.

> I iv 223–8

As the Renaissance philosopher Telesio put it, in the work *On the Nature of Things According to their Own Proper Principles* which inspired Campanella: matter may be 'decompressed and dilated' or 'compressed in itself and reduced'. In Shakespeare too it may be stretched or contracted.[5] The Quarto goes on and on with terrifying fluency – as though Lear could not really stop to 'lerne' that he is no longer Lear inside as well as out, but must go on quickly past his own words, gradually losing his mind even in keeping its sarcastic purpose, externalizing most when most unable to take anything in. But the cruellest change in the Folio, pulling the man up short and making him hear something of himself, is that which takes 'Lear's shadow' out of Lear's mouth and puts it into the Fool's:

> *Lear* Who is it that can tell me who I am?
> *Fool* Lear's shadow.

'It opens a gap. . . . The poetic space can scarcely be played across. Within it, the Fool's words resonate.'[6] A hole opens beneath Lear's feet – deeper than that which threatened either Feste or Falstaff but of that same Shakespearian underlyingness. Indeed, the whole play does not merely go on and on successively, but down and down.

Thus Shakespeare here creates a force-field, where one character may speak for another's fears better than he can himself. Shakespeare moves matter to a new space where he can then let it, as of its own accord, take on a further magnetic resonance. For in the Folio, 'Lear's shadow' may be simultaneously the answer not only to 'Who I am?' but also to 'Who can tell me?' And if it is the answer to 'Who can tell me?', then it may mean that only Lear's shadow side, deep in the dark of his mind, can tell him who now he really is; or that Lear's shadow is now the Fool himself, cryptically shadowing Lear and telling him what his own deeper mind can hardly bear to register. 'Can *you* make no use of nothing, nuncle?' cries the Fool (I v 115), making the King remember Cordelia. The most frightening possibility is of course that all the alternatives belong together: that the Fool is both separate from and part of Lear's distracted mind, the Folio version at once separating Lear's speech from itself and then returning it to him; and that the shadow side of the brain, behind Lear's folly and inside his Fool, is the only place where the sense of being but a shadow of oneself can bear to be thought.

When a history becomes a tragedy, that dark area of meaning is where the deposed Richard II's *un*regal thoughts have to go on, like 'thoughts . . . in their dumb cradles' (*Troilus and Cressida*, III iii 199). That is to say, unregal thoughts are for Richard unshaped thoughts, mental content without form, shadowy thoughts that have not yet a shape in the reality of the external world to give them even internal identification. It is these thoughts, especially when they are on the very verge of shape, that most excite Shakespeare.

As we have seen in Chapter One, the opening of poetic space and of resonant fields is vital to Shakespeare's sequences. Coleridge, writing of *The Tempest*, said:

> One admirable secret of his art is that separate speeches do not appear to have been occasioned by those which preceded and which are consequent upon each other, but to have arisen out of the peculiar character of the speakers.[7]

But Shakespeare no sooner opens up these *gaps* between characters than he makes an *overlap* across them. Again a fool best knows how to orchestrate these sequences – first in the parallelisms of *Twelfth Night*:

> *Clown* Good madonna, give me leave to prove you a fool.
> *Olivia* Can you do it?
> *Clown* Dexteriously, good madonna.
> *Olivia* Make your proof.
> *Clown* I must catechise you for it, madonna. Good my mouse of virtue, answer me.
> *Olivia* Well sir, for want of other idleness, I'll bide your proof.
> *Clown* Good madonna, why mourn'st thou?
> *Olivia* Good fool, for my brother's death.
> *Clown* I think his soul is in hell, madonna.
> *Olivia* I know his soul is in heaven, fool.
> *Clown* The more fool, madonna, to mourn for your brother's soul, being in heaven. Take away the fool, gentlemen.
>
> *Twelfth Night* I v 55–70

Just as those parallelisms work like a version of rhyme itself, so the comedy works catechismally here like some looser descendant of religious wisdom-teaching. For the wisdom ensues not by 'separate speeches . . . [which appear] to have been occasioned by those which preceded'. Rather, it emerges more democratically, through the very use of differences in station, and also more surprisingly – by finding, it seems, the right time half by chance, half by wit. Thus the Fool himself stays in the one place, while his name goes across to the other. 'Take away the fool, gentlemen.' For the Fool, unbound by intentions and designs of his own, best knows how to use contingency.

Here is another fool, setting it up more slowly:

Lear A bitter foole.
Foole Doo'st know the difference my boy, betweene a bitter foole, and a sweete foole.
Lear No lad, teach mee.
Foole That Lord that counsail'd thee to give away thy land,
      Come place him heere by mee, doe thou for him stand,
      The sweet and bitter foole will presently appeare,
      The one in motley here, the other found out there.
Lear Do'st call mee foole, boy?
Foole All thy other Titles thou hast given away that thou wast borne with.
Kent This is not altogether foole my Lord.
Foole No faith, Lords and great men will not let me, if I had a monopolie out, they would have part on't, and Ladies too, they will not let me have all the foole to my selfe, they'l be snatching . . .

                                  King Lear, I iv 145–52[8]

Again 'teach me'. But Shakespeare's teaching is not merely one person mechanically following the instruction of another, his superior. Like Shakespeare, the Fool stands one person in one place, another in another, then without their moving begins to make them mentally change places. The fact that, structurally, rhyme is somewhere at the bottom of this process is made explicit here in the Fool's chant. As Lear stands in for the bad counsellor, so, bitter-sweet, the Fool also stands for a version of those external humiliations that now beset Lear. It is as though as Lear tries to whirl centrifugally away from madness, the Fool spins him centripetally back to his folly, trying to substitute the one for the other. 'Opposites act in this manner as a counterforce.'[9] The Fool does not try the impossible – to replace bad with good, or hate with love – but offers in lieu of the mere consolation of an Adrian or a Gonzalo the cruel truth lovingly embodied in a rueful friend. Shakespeare, that is to say, eschewing straightforward means often has to work back-to-front, by 'instance contradictory', like a fool.[10] If the Fool says he thinks Olivia's brother is in hell, she will then have to say she knows his soul is in heaven. If the Fool starts by saying everything he can against Lear, then if anything is left thereafter it is genuinely *for* Lear. The Fool cannot act like Prospero with that other great 'yet' of his in the play:

> Though with their high wrongs I am stung to th' quick,
> Yet with my nobler reason gainst their fury
> Do I take part.
>
> *The Tempest*, V i 25–7

No more than Lear himself, can the Fool be like Prospero before his enemies and haltingly *hold* within him some of the painful evil of the world:

> A hit B? B hit C? – we have not enough alphabet to cover the condition. A brave man will try to make the evil stop with him. He shall keep the blow. No man shall get it from him, and that is a sublime ambition. . . . What are the generations for, please explain to me? Only to repeat fear and desire without a change? That cannot be what the thing is for, over and over and over. Any good man will try to break the circle.[11]

The Fool cannot break the sequence; like so many other characters in the play, he can only allow it to pass through him in modified form.

If there is any possibility of a sequence other than this passive passing on of the human parcel, it arises in Shakespeare only from something connected with the holding power of language: the power to take from a visible thing its name, its word, to hold its very thought in mind rather than let its force automatically use you. Only thus may you then re-employ that power elsewhere instead, mentally – as does Kent coming into the space opened between the sweet fool and the bitter fool to say:

> This is not altogether foole my Lord.

He does not merely say: this is not altogether foolish. He takes the word 'foole' from the thing itself, as if it were a thing now in itself, and, finding room thereby even in the midst of trouble, makes free use of the word as active thought.

This is the opposite of all Henry IV can do when he finds himself telling his own dissolute son about the rebellion of Hotspur and his party. Henry cannot detach any meaning, he is locked into a sequence:

> For all the world
> As thou art to this hour was Richard then
> When I from France set foot at Ravenspurgh,
> And even as I was then is Percy now.
> Now by my sceptre, and my soul to boot,
> He hath more worldly interest to the state
> Than thou the shadow of succession. . . .
> And what say you to this? Percy, Northumberland,
> The Archbishop's Grace of York, Douglas, Mortimer,
> Capitulate against us and are up.
> But wherefore do I tell these news to thee?
> Why, Harry, do I tell thee of my foes,
> Which art my nearest and dearest enemy?
>   *1 Henry IV*, III ii 93–9, 118–23

The cry at the heart of these history plays is 'What are the generations for, please explain to me?' For that is virtually what Henry, Earl of Richmond cries when crowned King Henry VII at the end of *Richard III*, in a prayer full of horror at the generations corrupted:

> England hath long been mad, and scarred herself;
> The brother blindly shed the brother's blood;
> The father rashly slaughtered his own son;
> The son, compelled, been butcher to the sire;

All that divided York and Lancaster,
United in their dire division.
O now let Richmond and Elizabeth,
The true successors of each royal house,
By God's fair ordinance conjoin together.

Richard III, V iii 23–31

It is a massive point to be making: dynasts exist only to establish a succession, yet this greatest blessing of all has been felt in these years as a curse.

In place of the succession from father to son, Henry IV likewise sees a dismally ironic succession of things from himself to Hotspur, as from Richard to Hal. Not only has Henry IV, envying Northumberland his Hotspur, the wrong Harry to son:

O that it could be prov'd
That some night-tripping fairy had exchang'd
In cradle-clothes our children where they lay,
And call'd mine Percy, his Plantagenet!
Then would I have his Harry and he mine:
But let him from my thoughts.

1 Henry IV, I i 85–90

but Hal is also more like the Richard whom Henry deposed, that 'grew a companion to the common streets':

And in that very line, Harry, standest thou.

1 Henry IV, III ii 85

Thus, when the King speaks to the Prince of his 'foes', in terms of logical sequence this ought to be because the Prince is the King's most natural ally. As Ramus put it in chapter xiii of his *Logic* (1574):

The relatives are co[n]trarie affirmatives, of the which the one hathe his being of the mutuall societie & affection with the other, for the which cause they are called Relatives: as, he is a father which hathe a sonne, & he is a sonne which hathe a father for by this mutuall relation they are and cease to be bothe at once.

But that formal and logical relationship turns sourly psychological here. Henry and Hal need each other and yet, inside that, cannot bear each other, and thus exist in dangerous mutual dependence. As with any rebellious son, Hal's temporary sense of freedom is itself borrowed from the very relationship he resists. And at some level he himself knows this – and knows that all the time he wastes is only a form of desperately bored and unreal waiting upon the reality of succession. For very early in *1 Henry IV* he secretly says that all in good time he will 'this loose behaviour throw off'

> And pay the debt I never promised.
>
> I ii 203–4

Meanwhile apparently without a son who can substantiate 'the noble image of my youth', the father finds only the alternative succession – 'my grief/Stretches itself beyond the hour of death'

> when I do shape
> In forms imaginary th' unguided days
> And rotten times that you shall look upon
> When I am sleeping with my ancestors.
>
> *2 Henry IV*, IV iv 54–61

The very circuits of the king's brain are shaped by that sequence of events, now made thought, which he thus has to follow out. So, Henry IV finds the word 'ally' taken from his lips and catches there instead the thought of the prince himself being

> my nearest and dearest enemy.

'Enemy': the word strikes with violence. As with Kent and 'fool', a word has become transferred – but here only as a terrible continuance of the sequence. 'A hit B? B hit C? – we have not enough alphabet to cover the condition.' So C hits B back, and so on. The King is hurt by his son and gives pain back to him; he fights battles both inside and outside his court; it is all becoming so much the *same*. Yet there are still some differences taken to heart, albeit without room for a separate vocabulary for them.

In the Shakespearian dynamic, betrayal by a friend – let alone a son - is harder to bear, inside, than the most constant hatred of a more external foe. By the same kind of rule (since Henry IV mentions him), Richard II urged his queen to leave England:

> Weep thou for me in France, I for thee here;
> Better far off than, near, be ne'er the near.
>
> *Richard II*, V i 87–8

He cannot bear to think of her remaining only just outside the wall of his prison. Let the physical space truly reflect the emotional distance. Let the thought be bearably shaped in terms of the very miles between us. But let not my son be my *nearest* enemy. For in that last case the pain goes so far inside precisely because of the lack of external correspondence: my son, my enemy. It is simpler to be Hotspur whose inner thoughts, according to his wife, match his outer actions even in sleep:

> In thy faint slumbers I by thee have watch'd,
> And heard thee murmur tales of iron wars,
> Speak terms of manage to thy bounding steed,
> Cry 'Courage! To the field!' . . .
> Thy spirit within thee hath been so at war
> And thus hath so bestirr'd thee in thy sleep.
>
> *1 Henry IV*, II iii 48–51, 57–8

This supercharged spirit is not essentially at war *with itself*: the inner life here is only the exuberant outer life carried over into a different place.

There used to be a simpler world for Henry IV too. At the end of *Richard II* Exton entered with the coffin of his murdered predecessor:

> Great king, within this coffin I present
> Thy buried fear.
>
> *Richard II*, V vi 30–1

There is dead Richard; there is your inner fear laid out too to rest: as if by magic, the two are one.

But now with his own son felt as his 'enemy', all Henry IV

himself can do, in order to try to regain a balance, is hit back out again accordingly. 'But wherefore do I tell these news to thee?/Why, Harry?'

Shakespeare's too must have been strange times for the idea of succession. The only play to celebrate 'generation' at the close is *Henry VIII* – presumably in the person of Elizabeth who herself is not a source of succession, but as virgin queen deliberately denies succession and is instead the phoenix.

What is the point? 'What are the generations for? Only to repeat without a change?' The history plays are the apotheosis of Shakespeare's boredom with sequences that actually go hardly anywhere at all. These plays contain a deeply irritated weariness and frustration articulated most of all through Henry IV himself:

> Are these things then necessities?
> Then let us meet them like necessities.
>
> *2 Henry IV*, III i 92–3

But necessity in this world is such a merely *external* thing: people are not called into being by it as by a felt certainty within themselves meeting an event, but give themselves to it as though to the next thing that must happen once a sequence has been set going. In that sense these things are only 'like necessities', not the thing itself. Yet so overdetermined are these plays by the knock-on political sequence within them that any space outside the sequence can only become otiose in the end, like Hal's looseness or like Falstaff himself. As we have seen, there are marvellous improvised rhythms created in the meantime, as – to give a further instance - when a bored Prince, subtler than any Antonio or Sebastian, works a second contrapuntal sequence off poor Francis's monotonous reply of 'Anon' to Poins's peremptory calls for attendance:

> *Prince* Nay but hark you, Francis, for the sugar thou gavest me, 'twas a pennyworth, was't not?
> *Francis* O Lord, I would it had been two!
> *Prince* I will give thee for it a thousand pound – ask me when thou wilt, and thou shalt have it.
> *Poins [Within]* Francis!

Francis Anon, anon.
Prince Anon, Francis? No, Francis, but tomorrow, Francis; or, Francis, a-Thursday; or indeed, Francis, when thou wilt.

1 Henry IV, II iv 57–66

Suddenly verbal space becomes significant again in that misplaced pick-up of anon – Have the money *anon*, Francis? No Francis! So unlike your humble self . . . !

But the improvisation seems more gratuitous or negligible than it is, say, in *Twelfth Night* where what is transitory still has passing depth and where sequences have an opened-up space within them. In the histories there is not that heart-echo – 'It gives a very echo to the seat/Where love is thron'd' (II iv 21–2) – that there is when Malvolio, unknowingly overheard, rehearses his fantasy put-down to Sir Toby:

Malvolio 'You waste the treasure of your time with a foolish knight' –
Sir Andrew That's me, I warrant you.
Malvolio 'One Sir Andrew.'
Sir Andrew I knew 'twas I, for many do call me fool.

Twelfth Night, II v 77–81

– or, again, after Maria exits:

Sir Andrew Before me, she's a good wench.
Sir Toby She's a beagle, true-bred, and one that adores me: what o' that?
Sir Andrew I was adored once too.

Twelfth Night, II iii 178–81

Self-forgetfully delighted to recognize himself – even as a fool! or a fool adored – Sir Andrew finds that big word 'once' like something out of Bottom's dream: 'once' long ago, but only 'once' and very very briefly. These comic and sad parts of life find more welcome and more autonomy for them in *Twelfth Night*. For in this play's vision of life, offering as it does so much more congenial room to Shakespeare, it is less clear what should or should not be treated as merely incidental moments – indeed, perhaps everything should be allowed more than it is, when anything could all too easily be less:

What is love? 'Tis not hereafter . . .
    What's to come is still unsure. . . .
Then come kiss me, sweet and twenty:
    Youth's a stuff will not endure.
                                    Twelfth Night, II iii 48–54

It is more possible here for the little touches momentarily to seem as if their very littleness could be important – as if the quick disproportionate emotion they provoke could grow to something more in some other potential play that is hinted at but not fully developed here. What will come of anything is always 'unsure'.

Yet with these embryonic hints, it is not in the histories as it is in the other plays: in the family tree of the histories there is less tolerance of any nascent life-force that unsurely

            diverts his grain
Tortive and errant from his course of growth.
                                    Troilus and Cressida, I iii 8–9

Increasingly after the death of the large all-or-nothing figure of Hotspur, the 'seeds and weak beginnings' of things are held within a very limitedly political sense of 'the hatch and brood of time' (*2 Henry IV*, 84–6). In the *Henry IV* plays in particular, whatever temporarily finds extra room becomes indolently superfluous and finally forgettable. Francis is dismissed – 'Away, you rogue, dost thou not hear them call?' – as Maria is not. Sir Andrew Aguecheek is adored by the play in which he appears, as Justice Shallow is not when he recounts his past affairs:

> I do see the bottom of Justice Shallow. Lord, Lord, how subject
> we old men are to this vice of lying.
>   *2 Henry IV*, III ii 296–8

Falstaff's 'we' there is not sympathetic but predatory; he uses his own faults only to spy out the faults of others. Similarly in the configuration of these plays, as Hal mocks Francis, so Falstaff in an equivalent model of power later mocks his own conscripted recruits - and it is hard to say who is imitating whom, where everybody acts only the role that space allows them.

It is not in the histories as it is, for example, with Barnardine in *Measure for Measure,* whose stubborn refusal to fit in with the duke's plot –

> I have been drinking hard all night, and I will have more time to prepare me . . . I will not consent to die this day, that's certain.
>
> > *Measure for Measure,* IV iii 52–5

– is none the less allowed its due of life:

> Duke　A creature unprepar'd, unmeet for death;
> 　　　　And to transport him in the mind he is
> 　　　　Were damnable.
>
> > *Measure for Measure,* IV iii 66–8

To transport him would be to be as damnable as he is. The inconvenience of comedy is here allowed. Indeed, the Duke is content even for the religious terms, upon which reprieve is granted the creature, to seem very close to complicity in Barnardine's cunning engineering of his own let-off. If the object of the pedantic moralist is to find out the bad in everything, Shakespeare's object – says Hazlitt quoting from *Henry V* –

> was to show that 'there is some soul of goodness in things evil'. Even Master Barnardine . . . speaks for himself. . . . In one sense Shakespeare was no moralist at all: in another, he was the greatest of all moralists.[12] .

But he was not so generous in *2 Henry IV.* There is finally no such comic space affordable for a sinner such as Falstaff in the histories.

It is as though a history was always used to diminish possibility – diminishing it precisely, as Raleigh writes near the beginning of his *History of the World,* 'by the comparison and application of other men's forepassed miseries with our own like errors and deservings'. The very way that life diminishingly becomes history in the *Henry IV* plays is thus by a sort of dying – like the very death of Hotspur:

> 　　　　　how much art thou shrunk!
> When that this body did contain a spirit,
> A kingdom for it was too small a bound;
> But now two paces of the vilest earth
> Is room enough.
>
> > *1 Henry IV,* V iv 87–91

Delighted and stimulated by his own incapacity to stop himself, this was the big risk-loving man who knew that, if he lived, he lived 'to tread on kings' (V ii 85) and, since not, is now trodden on by them. Hotspur either made reality or was unmade by it: dignity, like history, was to him a thing conferred retrospectively. It was because his reinforcements were doubtful, and the king's certain, that doubt itself became the ground for action. 'O God that one might read the book of fate', says Henry IV. Then if all were seen, 'the happiest youth' – even youths as apparently different as Hotspur here or Henry himself years earlier – 'viewing his progress through'

> Would shut the book and sit him down and die.
>
> *2 Henry IV*, III i 56

Shut up Holinshed, with all the deadening power of the factual as the solely actual:

> where the Historian in his bare *Was* hath many times that which wee call fortune to over-rule the best wisdom.[13]

Shakespeare shared Sir Philip Sidney's objection to the futilities of historical action: the 'bare *Was*'. Hotspur really was; but historically he failed. Henry IV must live historically, think politically. 'A man who wanted to feel historically through and through would be like one forcibly deprived of sleep. . . . There is a degree of sleeplessness, of rumination, of the historical sense, which is harmful, and ultimately fatal to the living thing, whether this thing be a man or a people or a culture'[14]:

> O sleep, O gentle sleep
> Nature's soft nurse, how have I frighted thee,
> That thou no more wilt weigh my eyelids down,
> And steep my senses in forgetfulness?
>
> *2 Henry IV*, III i 5–8

The way that Henry IV's sleep is disturbed is so very different from Hotspur's. History lived consciously in terms of sequence – such that the future is conceived of as only what will become a subsequent form of memory – is fatal to the living thing in

Shakespeare which must move and develop in fractional advance of consciousness.

Where is the room for real thinking, rather than pragmatic calculation, in an historical sequence of events? For example, Octavius's claim 'The time for universal peace is near' (*Antony and Cleopatra*, IV vi 5) is essentially a battle speech – politically intended to create as much as foresee an imperial Pax Romana, itself a world apart from the 'new heaven, new earth' of the contemporaneous birth of Christianity (I i 17). Even if Shakespeare does find room for disinterested thinking, as he does in the time-out of *Troilus and Cressida*:

> *Paris* But I would have the soil of her fair rape
> Wip'd off in honourable keeping her. . . .

> *Hector*   Thus to persist
> In doing wrong extenuates not wrong,
> But makes it much more heavy.
>
> II ii 149–50, 187–9

still even this thought – the very thought that surrounds Henry IV – is the slave of history. Shakespeare could take only the bare bones of the history plays from Holinshed; none of his plays is so dependent upon his invention. But it is invention as filling-in as much as bringing to life. These plays are slaves – that is their political subject-matter - and never more so than when involved in the attempted invention of free life. They are like more theatrically successful variants of *Troilus and Cressida*.

In *1 Henry IV*, as we have seen, Falstaff acts the part of the Prince's alternative father. At one inventive moment, compounded out of a mixture of cruelty and guilt in Hal, Falstaff is actually made by the Prince to stand in place of his own father – to 'examine me upon the particulars of my life' (II iv 371–2). As King, Falstaff acts all too well the father's disappointment in his son: only the son a moment later can act it out better. There is a strange psychological magic in this acting out – a mixture of taunting and haunting by which the two of them both take the place of the father in bad faith and yet still call him into being. Not one of them is quite as in control as he wishes or seems. Even the King himself is at once the missing person here and yet the most consistently present one.

It looks like comedy, like play-acting, even like parodic exorcism, but it is as though a person can become all too easily what utterly opposes him, simply by a change of place:

> *Falstaff [half as Prince]* No, my good lord; banish Peto, banish Bardolph, banish Poins – but for sweet Jack Falstaff, kind Jack Falstaff, true Jack Falstaff, valiant Jack Falstaff, and therefore more valiant as he is old Jack Falstaff, banish not him thy Harry's company, banish not him thy Harry's company, banish plump Jack, and banish all the world.
> *Prince [half as King]* I do, I will.

II iv 468–75

It is impossible to know which is more disturbing – the extent to which the characters are overtaken by their roles, or the extent to which, for all the confused movement between them, they are more than ever before nakedly themselves. There is Falstaff, pleading in manipulating and manipulating in pleading till he does not know one from the other; there is Hal, playing and warning and despising – despising by play, despising in play, warning that it is play, and hardly knowing the difference between despising himself and despising others.

Both these people – the Prince as much as Falstaff – are counterfeits even when they play themselves. The word 'counterfeit' haunts the play:

> What art thou
> That counterfeit'st the person of a king?

V iv 26–7

What art thou? It is a question to ask of both Hal and Falstaff in act II scene iv. Falstaff later tries to say that his counterfeiting death on the battlefield was no counterfeit – Death itself is the counterfeit, argues Falstaff, whereas he claims to stand for sheer life, without so-called honour: 'I lie, I am no counterfeit' (V iv 114). But there is still so much trickery in such a life, still so many lies in Falstaff's version of honesty. And though that might be tolerable in a private area of the plays, the history plays themselves draw all private areas into the public arena. Falstaff would have influence, would even be Lord Chief Justice – and again it is hard to know which would be more sickening: that this is delusion or that it

could be a real possibility. There is no getting to the bottom of
Falstaff or of Hal, as there is with Shallow. They have none: for
as long as they can be, they are improvisers outside a sense of
life-time. The Prince does not exist until he is king: that is all the
Prince is, someone not really existing till king. For action does not
change the Prince; only the death of his father and the ceasing to
be prince at all do that. As soon as battle ceases, the Prince at the
opening of *2 Henry IV* is back at the same old odds with his father,
as though he had forgotten all that his actions by the end of *1 Henry
IV* had proved him to be:

> King Thou hast redeem'd thy lost opinion,
>   And show'd thou mak'st some tender of my life
>   In this fair rescue thou hast brought to me.
>
> *1 Henry IV*, V iv 47–9

Only when the tender is formal service in the heat of action can
some tenderness go with it. The old psychological difficulties of
the relation of father to son are what exist when occupation's
gone; in this play our modern psychological patterns are only
what happens when nothing else does. In a word, people who
belong to a sequence – the Prince to the future succession, Falstaff
to banishment and to death rather than to the office of Lord Chief
Justice – are never anything but false in temporarily denying it,
even if the sequence itself is so blackly tedious a necessity. Yet Hal
and Falstaff cannot accept the sequence.

But they cannot deny it either. Like a ventriloquist, Falstaff as
King commends Falstaff as Prince's guide, but the scene works
precisely because *everyone* there knows it is a lie, albeit at present
still a funny one:

> And yet there is a virtuous man whom I have often noted in thy
> company, but I know not his name. . . . and now I remember
> me, his name is Falstaff.
>
> II iv 413–14, 419–20

At the next moment the Prince turns it all round – not in
repentance but ostensibly to give the alternative view of Falstaff.
But deeper even than that, in replacing Falstaff as his father's
stand-in, Hal is now ambiguously turning on himself in the person
of Falstaff:

Swearest thou, ungracious boy? Henceforth ne'er look on me. Thou art violently carried away from grace, there is a devil haunts thee in the likeness of an old fat man.

II iv 439–42

The Prince as father identifiably drives out of himself 'that *father* ruffian' (448). The jealousy Hal feels for Hotspur fuels the jealousy used by his version of Henry IV to expose Falstaff.

Yet such configurations of substitution, such twists and turns, are not genuine alternatives to the dominant sequence – as counterfeits and blinds, they merely delay while still foreshadowing it: 'I do, I will.' A vacuum opens around those words, lying in wait for the ignoring present. The characters play with substitution as an idea, as an alternative: thus even while the king wishes it could be proved that

> some night-tripping fairy had exchang'd
> In cradle-clothes our children where they lay,
> And call'd mine Percy, his Plantagenet!

I i 86–8

the Prince himself parodies the preference by acting out the part of Hotspur in jealous jest:

> I am not yet of Percy's mind, the Hotspur of the north, he that kills me some six or seven dozen of Scots at a breakfast, washes his hands, and says to his wife, 'Fie upon this quiet life, I want work'.

II iv 99–103

But what is behind Hal's parodic imitation – both of Hotspur and of his father's admiration for Hotspur – is in fact the desire for sequential replacement, when:

> This gallant Hotspur, this all-praised knight,
> And your unthought-of Harry chance to meet.
> For every honour sitting on his helm,
> Would they were multitudes, and on my head
> My shames redoubled! For the time will come
> That I shall make this northern youth exchange
> His glorious deeds for my indignities.

III ii 140–6

No fairy exchanged the children. Instead, one Harry must take the place of, make an exchange with, another.

And increasingly, replacement is what substitution gives way to as *1 Henry IV* is succeeded by *2 Henry IV* – because linear replacement is what substitution in these plays has always really stood for:

> God knows, my son,
> By what by-paths and indirect crook'd ways
> I met this crown, and I myself know well
> How troublesome it sat upon my head.
> To thee it shall descend with better quiet,
> Better opinion, better confirmation,
> For all the soil of the achievement goes
> With me into the earth. . . .
> And now my death
> Changes the mood, for what in me was purchas'd
> Falls upon thee in a more fairer sort;
> So thou the garland wear'st successively.
>
> *2 Henry IV*, IV v 183–90, 198–201

In making the act of dying also an attempted act of killing what was wrong in the life and the reign, this is the father's bid 'to make the evil stop with him . . . [to] try to break the circle' - but not to form a new shape, only to ensure that the succession may go on and have a foreseeable future. The essential structure remains in place, only Henry IV and Falstaff become sacrificial scapegoats to it, saving Hal from any of the disorientating thoughts of a Hamlet inheriting an ill-shaped time:

> My father is gone wild into his grave,
> For in his tomb lie my affections;
> And with his spirits sadly I survive.
>
> *2 Henry IV*, V ii 123–5

> Presume not that I am the thing I was;
> For God doth know, so shall the world perceive,
> That I have turn'd away my former self;
> So will I those that kept me company.
>
> *2 Henry IV*, V v 56–9

In their stead, the Lord Chief Justice succeeds to Henry V 'as a father to my youth' (V ii 118), according to a sort of rhyming conveniency which is the equivalent of the act of marriage in the comedies but is here achieved according to the symbolic pattern rather than the inner feeling of a family relationship. If this artifice is not merely cynical or pragmatic but is a real achievement, it is because the secondary institution of succession still carries in *2 Henry IV* echoes of the more dynamically primitive states of sacrifice and purgation:

> By a constitutional policy, working after the pattern of nature, we receive, we hold, we transmit our government and priv-ileges, in the same manner in which we enjoy and transmit our property and our lives. The institutions of policy, the goods of fortune, the gifts of Providence, are handed down, to us and from us, in the same course and order. Our political system is placed in a just correspondence and symmetry with the order of the world, and to the mode of existence decreed to a permanent body compounded of transitory parts. . . . The whole, at one time, is never old, or middle-aged, or young, but in a condition of unchangeable constancy, moves on through the varied tenour of perpetual decay, fall, renovation, and progression. Thus, by preserving the method of nature in the conduct of the state, in what we improve we are never wholly new; in what we retain we are never wholly obsolete.[15]

The king is dead, long live the king. All other places are refilled accordingly. The power of assimilation in the conservative state of Hooker and of his descendant, Burke, allows the nation constantly to reshape itself as something always different, always the same.

This then, says Holinshed, is the story of how Henry V came 'to put on him the shape of a new man'.[16] And impressively, the mechanisms within the *Henry IV* plays do not differ from those spa-tial shapings and temporal dynamics discussed in Chapters One and Two – save in one tell-tale respect: their devitalizing imprisonment in the sequence of history. For the political art may be modelled on a version of natural survival, but it is still an art. And it is as though the forces in these plays were themselves parodies of the original forces that brought life into being – secondary duplicates that overtake the social world in de-enlivened memory of how

necessity calls life into being, according to the shapes available to
it. The process Campanella describes –

> All bodies abhor the existence of a vacuum, and they rush, with
> natural impetus, to fill such a void in order to conserve the
> community entire.[17]

– becomes in the histories the grim filling-in of the power
vacuum.

Henry IV himself embodies the weary cost behind the necessity
of stable succession. Otherwise, the nearest to an understanding of
what such an historical sense of things kills comes almost naturally
from Hotspur, that otherwise least reflective of men, as he lies
dying before Hal:

> O Harry, thou hast robb'd me of my youth!
> I better brook the loss of brittle life
> Than those proud titles thou hast won of me;
> They wound my thoughts worse than thy sword my flesh.
>
> 1 Henry IV, V iv 76–9

'Wound my *thoughts*' carries over the world of the play's action
into a different dimension *even though* those thoughts are still
'the slaves of life, and life, time's fool' (V iv 80). In death the
inner meaning of being a soldier goes further with Hotspur than
anything else, but it goes deeper only through the idea of mortal
wounding. Nonetheless, metaphor as fast and deep as this is the
sign in Shakespeare of a big original force which is usually tamed
or lost in the histories – the sign in this case of something unnamed
inside a character seizing upon the opportunity of terms to call
itself into being and express itself in life even at the very last. It
is that something which can speak of 'my youth' as though with
impersonal compassion. For 'my youth' is not simply something
Hotspur *has* – youth. 'My youth' is what he *is* to whatever dying
thing it is that now speaks so simply through him. After the death
of Hotspur, as we have seen, the way is clearer for the succession
of *2 Henry IV*.

How therefore recent modern critics have come to separate out
Shakespeare's political interests as predominant, when that interest
is clearly so reluctant and so bleak and seen as so damaging to all
implicated in its secondary version of necessities, is astonishing.

But perhaps this emphasis is bound to preponderate when critics associate role-playing in the theatre with role-playing in the world of kingship and power politics. 'Theatricality', says Greenblatt, 'is not set over against power but is one of power's essential modes. Henry IV tells Worcester, "I will from henceforth rather be myself,/Mighty and to be fear'd, than my condition" (*1 Henry IV*, I iii 5–6). "To be oneself" here means to perform one's part in the scheme of power rather than to manifest one's natural disposition.'[18] But if for Shakespeare playing a part is the only way in which power can manifest itself, then theatre and the life it represents have become a travesty of themselves. For Shakespeare, theatre is not wholly become, as Agnew argues in *Worlds Apart*, a representation of the fabricated processes of role-playing, hypocrisy and power-broking in a new market economy – apt though that may be for a play such as Ben Jonson's *Bartholomew Fair*. Shakespeare also still belongs to the old tradition of *theatrum mundi*, as I shall try to show in Chapter Four.[19] True drama – that is to say, the generation on stage of something equivalent to sheer life-forces – occurs when, to meet the pressure of circumstances, action and not merely acting is released, and an act of being is called forth, like a word of realization in the midst of inarticulate trouble. 'I don't have any sense of or interest in history as a reality', says Peter Brook speaking of his vision of Shakespearian creativeness:

> What I am much more interested in is the way that we live in our present . . . is a greater possibility of seeing what is actually happening than the duller vision with which we live through our everyday lives. . . . There are many complex, archaic things that I look at as coming not from history.[20]

The histories themselves banish the archaic. It is the backwards substitution of Henry IV for Hal by the father's death, reversing as it does the sequence of substitutions theretofore, that *makes* history far more than does the forward-looking accession of Henry V which it allows. History is a death-force. And for Shakespeare fully to release himself and his power of life, the history play needed to become a tragedy. In *Richard II* it already had.

2 PERSONAL HISTORIES

In the tragic history of *Macbeth* the irrevocable sequence of events
and consequences becomes 'tedious' to the protagonist:

> I am in blood
> Stepp'd in so far, that, should I wade no more,
> Returning were as tedious as go o'er.
>
> *Macbeth*, III iv 135–7

The witches show Macbeth Banquo's descendants, a show of eight
kings succeeding him, the 'line' stretching itself on and on, it seems,
to the crack of doom. 'If 't be so,/For Banquo's issue have I fil'd
my mind' (III i 63–4). The inexorably linear sequence he himself
started has now emphatically got Macbeth, even as it goes on past
him: all he can do now is increase its speed even if it means making
it get him more. 'This push/Will cheer me ever, or disseat me
now' (V iii 20–1). A sort of desperate stoicism, a laughing of the
world to scorn, a rejoicing in the superficiality of mere outcomes, a
boredom with being cabin'd, cribb'd and confin'd with fears about
security: all this makes Macbeth want to win for ever or lose once
and for all – as if either of those two would do, providing it is
all finally over. If the course turns out to be self-destructive, still
it will not be suicide: 'I'll fight, till from my bones my flesh be
hack'd' (V iii 32) - for only the outcome may show whether this was
defiance or the death-instinct, Macbeth himself no longer knowing
the difference. But at some level Macbeth does not care about
outcome any more. The most he will do is make that external
sequence, which robs him of himself, as much and as ruinously
him as possible, till all of himself and life itself is tedious to the
man: 'To-morrow, and to-morrow, and to-morrow . . .' (V v 19).
The Folio prints it thus:

> To morrow, and to morrow, and to morrow,
> Creepes in this petty pace from day to day,
> To the last Syllable of Recorded time:
> And all our yesterdayes . . .

Suddenly the word 'tomorrow' is opened up again in its original
formation. I have heard Ian McKellen seize on that dominant

'to' and then carry it over not only from 'day to day' but from 'day to day To . . . the last syllable' – when until the very last possible second, one had expected a third 'day', to match the three tomorrows.

> Despite the fact that few are aware of it, from the very moment that we began to speak some change has occurred; and during the very instants of syllabification some little life has passed away.[21]

'During the very instants of syllabification', just before pro-nouncing 'the last syllable', McKellen momentarily slurred over the line-ending 'from day to day/To . . .' before restoring it retrospectively. It was a small thing, but only small because it took place in an instant of time which almost immediately disappeared back into the sequence of verse and time. For in that instant the modulating syllables, coming together one way, turning another, are like tiny seeds of micro-meaning in time:

> If you can look into the seeds of time,
> And say which grain will grow, and which will not,
> Speak then to me.
>
> *Macbeth*, I iii 58–60

To be sure, Shakespeare needs grammar just as he depends on story, to give some sort of meaningful order and consequence. But given that necessary basic order – which like rhyme is at once both a support and a pressure of limitation – he wants within sequence a resonance of meaning that has room, even for a brief moment, to be free.

Actors are aware of such embryonic possibilities in those pauses which seem to lie amidst the very life of things before they quite settle into completed temporal sense. For there is, as we saw in the comparison between the Quarto and Folio versions of the dialogue from *King Lear*, a sheer fluidity in Shakespeare's lines which is rich in the possibility of one thing flowing in and out of another. Consider the reality of this micro-language as shown in a rehearsal of the following sequence of dialogue from *Twelfth Night*:

Orsino How dost thou like this tune?
Viola It gives a very echo to the seat
  Where love is thron'd.
      [*Quick cue*]
Orsino   Thou dost speak masterly.
      [*Pause*]
  My life upon't, young though thou art, thine eye
  Hath stayed upon some favour that it loves.
  Hath it not, boy?
      [*Quick cue*]
Viola   A little, by your favour.
Orsino What kind of woman is't?
      [*Quick cue*]
Viola   Of your complexion.
Orsino She is not worth thee, then. What years i'faith?
      [*Pause*]
Viola About your years, my lord.
Orsino Too old by heaven. Let still the woman take
  An elder than herself . . .

        Twelfth Night, II iv 20–9

The cast discuss the dynamics of Shakespearian rhythm. The director John Barton says to Judi Dench as Viola:

When Orsino says, 'She is not worth thee then. What years i'faith?' and you have a *short* verse line, 'About your years, my lord', Shakespeare has actually built a pause into the verse there, because it's a short line of six syllables. It's as if there's a pause of four missing beats. What we have to decide is whether that pause comes before or after the line.

Judi Dench decides it should come *after*, giving Orsino time to take in what she has said –

it's such a wonderful pay-off for him to say, 'Too old, by heaven'.

Moreover, pausing after 'About *your* years, my lord' also leaves Viola time to hear (and be a little scared of) herself *and* to wait upon Orsino. On the other hand Judi Dench also says, 'I feel I want to pause *before* "Of your complexion"':

> *Orsino* What kind of woman is't?
> *Viola*   Of your complexion.

'Because she's caught out there, isn't she?' To which Barton replies:

> There's always a third option about a pause. You can, as it were, pause *within* the words. When you say, 'Of your complexion', you could pick up the cue at once but then *feel for* the rest of the line: 'Of . . . (*pause*) . . . your complexion'.[22]

This is *feeling for* the meaning in every sense – as if words could be like a putting-out of feelers, looking for meaning; as if one could have a tacit feeling for one's own meaning, seeing it in the very midst of its formulation. And that is what is so moving about Viola: the way that she is at once prompting, and being overtaken by, the sheer rhythmic spell of what she is saying, as she both reveals and disguises her love for Orsino:

> *Viola*   Ay, but I know –
> *Orsino* What dost thou know?
> *Viola* Too well what love women to men may owe:
>   In faith, they are as true of heart as we.
>   My father had a daughter loved a man,
>   As it might be perhaps, were I a woman,
>   I should your lordship.
> *Orsino*   And what's her history?
> *Viola* A blank my lord: she never told her love.
>   *Twelfth Night*, II iv 105–11

Emphatically, that is what momentary micro-pauses in the very midst of things are about in Shakespeare: the *hidden* inner histories that get explosively left behind as the sequence moves on so quickly; the silently resonant meanings that lie on the other side of 'a blank'. Meaning and feeling rush in to fill the tiny vacuum between '*And* what's her history?' and 'A blank my

lord', or between 'A blank my lord:' and 'she never told her
love'. In Shakespeare, the speeches between people and, indeed,
the very parts of a sentence 'enjoy touching one another, and
maintain and conserve themselves by this mutual contact': for,
all things 'so hate being disjoined and separated' that if one part
is pulled away from another, even by a pause, it will be followed
somewhere, somehow.[23]

What a spectator or a reader finds himself or herself doing in
Shakespeare is still holding in mind those embryonic hints of story,
which are at once so powerfully sketched and then jettisoned by
the sudden verse. 'Every reader of Shakespeare feels at some time
that he is creating what he reads, and is participating in the actual
process of art.'[24] That is what John Bayley, following Morgann,
means when he speaks of finding the novel behind the play:
the novel is that sense of inner character and history which the
power of the poetry in moving ever onwards leaves behind it as
resonance.

Shakespeare's dynamic use of disproportion is one such form
of shorthand. Sometimes he may formally or grammatically
subordinate an idea which ought to be allowed its full moment.
As Bolingbroke wryly puts it, when Richard abruptly remits his
banishment from ten years to six: 'How long a time lies in one little
word' *(Richard II,* I iii 212). Four years in a second's speech. It is a
classic statement of that sudden moment of uncertain gear-change
in a Shakespeare play. For consider likewise Macduff's discomfiture
in the face of Malcolm's sudden disclosure that after all he is not bad
but good, that he will save and not betray his country:

Malcolm   Why are you silent?
Macduff Such welcome and unwelcome things at once,
             'Tis hard to reconcile.

                                             Macbeth, IV iii 137–9

It is harder to reconcile than Macbeth's '"Fear not, till Birnam
wood/Do come to Dunsinane"; – and now a wood/Comes toward
Dunsinane' (V v 44–6) – for that at least fitted, however terribly.

Richard II extends that brief subordinate moment of transition in
the midst of historical process. It becomes almost two plays, shifting
as it does, with the deposition of Richard himself, from public and

political in the first half to personal history in the second. But even in the first half of the play Gaunt, the very figure of honourable succession in England, still stands for something left out of account in the political world:

> Richard Why uncle, thou hast many years to live.
> Gaunt   But not a minute, king, that thou canst give.
>
> > *Richard II*, I iii 224–5

The King can take away life, and from a sentence of banishment can remit time, but at the limits of natural mortality he has no writ to give either life or time. In the context of a public council decision on the banishment of his own son Henry Bolingbroke, Gaunt feels personally obliged to forfeit that extra, human point of view. But he had still expected it to be taken up by others in his stead, to keep it alive and remembered:

> Richard Thy son is banished upon good advice.
> > Whereto thy tongue a party verdict gave.
> > Why at our justice seemst thou then to lour?
> Gaunt   Things sweet to taste prove in digestion sour.
> > You urged me as a judge, but I had rather
> > You would have bid me argue like a father.
> > Oh, had it been a stranger, not my child,
> > To smoothe his fault I would have been more mild.
> > A partial slander sought I to avoid
> > And in my sentence my own life destroyed.
> > Alas, I looked when some of you should say
> > I was too strict to make mine own away.
>
> > *Richard II*, I iii 233–44

There is an admirable Hooker-like belief here in the way that there should be room for movement in a civil society to provide cover for its members. If a father is made judge and cannot exercise for his own what he would for another, then another judge should take over and embody at another level the mitigation that the father-principle stands for.

But so often there is not room for such mutual reshaping in Shakespeare's world. So many of his tragedies – *Othello, Hamlet,*

King Lear, Antony and Cleopatra – clearly begin from the sudden
arising of an historical split between public function and what then
emerges bewildered as private character. With occupations gone,
places lost, kingships abdicated, and beliefs and trust in the world
disabused, character takes form in the otherwise empty space as
precisely what is left when a person is made redundant and
functionless. 'From the *place* of loyalty to his king, Gaunt is
patient. From the *place* of loyalty to his blood, he is in despair.'[25]
He cannot hold the different places together in one place. And
what happens to Gaunt in the first half of *Richard II* happens all
the more to Richard himself in the second; but in Richard's case,
after the public ending, the play *stays* with what is left behind in the
personal realm and lets the mere historical sequence go on past.

The points of hesitating transition between one structure and
another, those embarrassing moments of deep pause betokening
the loss of sequence and the difficulty of conservative assimilation,
constitute the very subject-matter of *Richard II*:

> *Bolingbroke* Are you contented to resign the crown?
> *Richard* Aye – no. No – aye, for I must nothing be,
>   Therefore no 'no', for I resign to thee.
>   Now, mark me how I will undo myself.
>
>   *Richard II*, IV i 199–202

It is not as though 'yes and no' come out together there. It is 'aye'
in one mind, then a split second later 'no' in another. He is torn
between the two, without a space to occupy between them. He
cannot get out of them – all he can do is put them together
again, turn them round: 'No – aye' – as if to say, who knows
which? what difference if I care? And the Folio spelling of 'I'
for both 'aye' and 'I' increases the aurally registered complexity:
there will be no I if I say aye. 'Therefore no, no' likewise flows
into 'no "no"' as the only way I can say aye, undoing my I by
a double negative to which I could not otherwise assent. But
in those micro-seconds between the first sounding of 'aye' and
'– no', or its somersaulting round into 'No – aye', the time
between thoughts, the person between opposites and all that is
involved in the changes of mind are held in the barest of all slow
motions:

A stress is born in time, and in sound, meaning and emotion; but it also stands outside time in a sort of minor, eternal present, a trembling instant which half stands still, partly resisting the flow of the line which creates it. It probably represents a little model of how our minds relate the instant of time to the flow of time.[26]

Little models are important in the histories – the garden in *Richard II*, the discussion of careful building in act I scene iii of *2 Henry IV*. But usually they are offered discursively as ways of getting thoughts accepted in the social world. The use of rhythmic stress, though more than a 'bare was', is only a scarce heard feeling for a thought which can get neither quite into nor out of the world's time. With a rhyme-structure which makes especially clear what can or cannot get into it, the first half of *Richard II* is full of people thinking thoughts that can barely *be* thought. Gaunt tries to get Bolingbroke to 'suppose' his banishment voluntary and so make a virtue of necessity, but he cannot (I iii 281 ff.); Green says of banished Bolingbroke, 'Well, he is gone, and with him go these thoughts' (I iv 37); Richard will not really allow thought of Gaunt's death, 'So much for that' (II i 155); York says to Richard, '[You] prick my tender patience to those thoughts/Which honour and allegiance cannot think', only to hear Richard respond with 'Think what you will, we seize . . .' (II i 207–9); Ross says to the would-be conspirator Northumberland, 'We three are but thy self . . . Thy words are but as thoughts' (II i 275–6). The little model of a stress, which finds some time for expression in the midst of things, has of itself hardly any status in bringing thoughts into reality to those who will not hear its unshaped thought. 'Thought in its dumb cradle.' And yet what the humiliatingly stranded and bewildered speech of the bereaved and unavenged Duchess of Gloucester does, with such bare awkwardness, is try to find time for itself in the world:

I take my leave before I have begun,
For sorrow ends not when it seemeth done.
Commend me to thy brother Edmund York.
Lo, this is all. Nay, yet depart not so;

Though this be all, do not so quickly go.
I shall remember more. Bid him, ah, what?

Richard II, I ii 60–5

'Nay . . . what?' As with Gaunt himself, to whom she thus speaks, there is no time for her here. For Gaunt himself is just as grotesquely pushed out, for all he thought 'the tongues of dying men/Enforce attention' (II i 5–6). His last words of warning are mocked to his face by a king who threatens to kill a dying man for taking advantage of the extra dimension provided by that final condition.

But in the play's second movement it is the deposed Richard who, as more and more is taken away from him, now must try to find some place for himself, or some self to take refuge in. For as Bolingbroke puts it, to Richard's request 'Then give me leave to go': 'Whither?' (IV i 313). The very word opens the vacuum around Richard. And if there is no place for a Richard outside, then like a cornered rat he has to run around looking for a way out from within:

> Oh that I were as great
> As is my grief, or lesser than my name,
> Or that I could forget what I have been,
> Or not remember what I must be now!

Richard II, III iii 136–9

In the game of tennis, players move from individual points, to games, to sets, to matches, all the time as the stakes increase, having none the less to come back to individual points in order to progress. So here if Richard is going to rebuild something which he can be, he likewise is going to have to find something to build up from – starting from the possibilities in the blanks, the pauses and stresses, the hints of nascent meaning. 'Who is it that can tell me who I am?' He tries one starting-point after another: to be as great as is my grief over my loss of greatness, or to be as diminished inside me as is my name without; to forget what I have been or not remember what I am now. But they are all higher versions of 'aye – no, no – aye'. If one repeated thought or one thought merely following obviously upon another is boring to Shakespeare, then two thoughts - two split and mutually weakening alternatives – may be worse when they serve only to create a continuous cycle between them. Yet Richard has to try to make the want of something into the thought of something; he has to make the thought of what he now is into something he can be. He seeks that crucial thing in Shakespeare's poetic thinking - a breathing-space arising out of the caesura, a nidus, a place of lodgement which is also a breeding-place.

'Every thought', said Keats, 'is the centre of an intellectual world'[27]: potentially, as 'a sort of minor eternal present', every thought may develop into what it represents in shorthand – namely, a way of being. Shakespeare is so supremely intelligent that he can think what seem to be a thousand thoughts or half-thoughts or fractions of thought in a few minutes. Most are let go or perish by the way; a few are pursued and may become persons or worlds; some will be found to have contributed later, as in a version of retrospective stress. But Shakespeare knows that there is all the difference in the world between having a thought and that thought coming into full being as a person. What Richard seeks to do is turn a point of thought into a centre of being:

> A generation of still breeding thoughts,
> And these same thoughts people this little world
> In humours like the people of this world,
> For no thought is contented . . .
> Thoughts tending to ambition, they do plot
> Unlikely wonders: how these vain weak nails
> May tear a passage through the flinty ribs
> Of this hard world my ragged prison walls,
> And, for they cannot, die in their own pride.
> Thoughts tending to content flatter themselves
> That they are not the first of Fortune's slaves,
> Nor shall not be the last, like silly beggars
> Who, sitting in the stocks, refuge their shame
> That many have and others must set there,
> And in this thought they find a kind of ease,
> Bearing their own misfortunes on the back
> Of such as have before endured the like.
> Thus play I in one person many people,
> And none contented. Sometimes am I king,

Then treasons make me wish myself a beggar,
And so I am. Then crushing penury
Persuades me I was better when a king,
Then am I kinged again, and by and by
Think that I am unkinged by Bolingbroke,
And straight am nothing. But whate'er I be
Nor I nor any man that but man is
With nothing shall be pleased till he be eased
With being nothing. . . .
For now hath time made me his numbering clock.
My thoughts are minutes . . .

Richard II, V v 8–11, 18–41, 50–1

'And, for they cannot' has a dying fall – the life is going out of the thought-tendency's momentum. Things try to live, try to establish alternative company and supportive traditions, but begin to die again as soon as they feel themselves to lack real contentment or be insufficiently full of themselves to last on their own. Richard's is a slow, extended speech because it is thought in lonely abstract, without the pressure of external necessity to call it into being, with only the felt sense of a lack of necessary function instead. It is like an experiment in abstract mind. For although the ideal state of a Gaunt, a Hooker, or a Burke might just have strength to accommodate many changes and many peoples, for certain the mind of a single prisoner such as Richard cannot find, microcosmically, sufficient hold for as many thoughts. Richard barely has a name here: he is a mind in prison, almost the forgotten abstract mind of the world itself. Before, the crown around his brows seemed to enclose the whole of England. Now, he feels like a thinking heart suspended within the flinty ribs of the whole world's body. His thoughts, unable to become real, instead become merely the beating counters of the minutes of imprisonment.

All things seek to conserve their own life, say Telesio and Campanella alike. Living things cannot bear the vacuum of being nothing: to be nothing and yet still to exist makes no liveable sense. If people cannot move one way, they will seek another; they will try to break out of the sequence of events which is destroying them and 'refuge their shame'. So the displaced king is in his cage – claustrophobically enclosed as though within his own mind, yet with so much gratuitous room in which to think.

Granted, it is important for the country that Richard II is deposed. But once achieved it is not a very interesting requirement. The tragic dimension that opens up in Richard may threaten to be impotently luxurious in the man's estranged self-pity – Shakespeare is alert to every overlapping nuance – and yet his situation is finally more metaphysically powerful than history can ever be. For when Richard seems to us so much *more* for seeming nothing to and in himself, then losing seems disturbingly more important at some level than winning is.

It is as if a hidden metaphysic is disclosed by loss and defeat in the world. And that is itself the subject of the late plays, as alternative metaphysical histories.

The Winter's Tale transmutes the very idea of continuous sequence. Act IV scene iv is the longest scene Shakespeare ever wrote - the pastoral scene of comic obliviousness and of love between Florizel and Perdita, the new generation. As a result, the audience is amazed to think it can have these new feelings so soon after the terible old feelings of the previous act with the trial, death and belated vindication of Hermione to the utter ruin of Leontes. It is startling that, emotionally at least, one has forgotten the previous act and sequence, until the older generation threatens to ruin things again, this time in the person of Polixenes.

We then come back to the old world in act V. And act V of *The Winter's Tale* retrospectively invokes two allied structures - two forms of sequence we have already looked at in the *Henry IV* plays – which it then goes on to deny, in the name of a deeper, more archaic and primary sense of life.

As we have seen, one of the history plays' favoured structures is that of linear replacement, rather than truly abiding memory. But in *The Winter's Tale* Paulina, who in every sense 'hast the memory of Hermione' (V i 50), stands guard against the King's taking a wife in place of his lost queen. The place must be held open, the vacuum filled only with feeling. There are to be no pragmatic short-cuts in this complex sequence. The order in which things are to be done is vital. Twice in the first scene she intervenes – once extendedly against those who would have Leontes wed again: 'here is none

worthy,/Respecting her that's gone' (34–5), 'Remember mine'
(67); and once again when both a servant and Leontes express
deep admiration for Perdita:

> Servant Ay, the most peerless piece of earth, I think,
>   That e'er the sun shone bright on.
> Paulina   O Hermione,
>   As ever present time doth boast itself
>   Above a better gone, so must thy grave
>   Give way to what's seen now!
>
> V i 94–8

> Paulina   Sir, my liege,
>   Your eye hath too much youth in't; not a month
>   'Fore your queen died, she was more worth such gazes
>   Than what you look on now.
> Leontes   I thought of her,
>   Even as these looks I made.
>
> V i 223–7

A person cannot be a substitute for a subtle process: when Paulina
has to try to be one such and hold the fort, she is always going
to make of subtlety something rough. Though she herself will not
'give way', because the past itself must not, still her very fidelity
is always a touch hard, a touch comic – like a sign of her being
only one person and thus flawed. 'What, sovereign sir,/I did not
well, I meant well' (III iii 2–3). But when Leontes says to Paulina,
'I thought of her', his remark is not simply personal and defensive:
there is in it, unbeknownst to him, an innocent process of nature's
impersonal memory that makes him think of Hermione even as he
looks on Perdita. This man has lived for sixteen years, stuck fast
in his past. The sequence of dear life must be unfrozen, must be
taken up again. But it is not a straightforward sequence. Leontes
must begin to go back and forth. And here at the sight of Perdita,
Leontes begins again to have almost youthful thoughts rather than
just old memories.

The other secondary structure that the end of *The Winter's
Tale* summons from the histories only to eschew is the allied
one of counterfeiting, copying, or substituting. In the histories,

character can be subsumed into function, but here Shakespeare is more deeply anxious for its irreplaceability. Thus the statue of Hermione is offered as no more than an 'ape' of Nature (V ii 99), a lively 'mock' of life (V iii 19). Leontes fears 'we are mock'd with art' and, feeling induced to kiss the statue as if it were alive, cries, 'Let no man mock me' (V iii 68, 79). Long-dead intuitions begin to lead Leontes to the real thing, despite all the fear and scepticism he has learnt thereafter. For Julio Romano cannot, like God, put breath into his work (V ii 97–8): 'What fine chisel/Could ever yet cut breath?' (V iii 78–9). Hermione is not to be replaced by another woman and cannot be replaced by a piece of art. This is to be real.

Efforts at substitution are well meant but misplaced. Seeing Leontes's distress at the sight of Hermione's statue, Polixenes wants to be the good man who can stop the sequence of pain by holding it in himself for others, rather than pass it on: 'To take off so much grief from you as he/Will piece up in himself' (V iii 55–6). Paulina, similarly, invokes the statue to life by sacrificially offering to take Hermione's place in death: 'Come!/I'll fill your grave up' (V iii 100–1). It is as if by calling these former dynamisms into minor roles, Shakespeare is forcing himself beyond them. The end of *The Winter's Tale* finally demands back again the primary not the secondary processes of life.

That is why memory in this act, not allowed to be a thing of the past, is of the *present*. Memories begin to form themselves in the shape of the young people such as Florizel, or in the return of the old ones such as Camillo. Thus when Paulina sees Florizel, she thinks again of Mamillius: 'he had paired/Well with this lord' (V i 116–17), just as their fathers long before them 'were as twinn'd lambs' (I ii 67). But then at the mention of 'our prince' Leontes adds:

> Prithee, no more; cease; thou know'st
> He dies to me again, when talk'd of . . .
>
> V i 118–19

This is the very thing that killed a Lear. She dies to me again. But in *The Winter's Tale* the present pain is but the very vehicle of past virtue:

Leontes   Whilst I remember
                Her, and her virtues, I cannot forget
                My blemishes in them.

                                            V i 6–8

He cannot remember the one and forget the other, and he will remember. This, however hard, is better than Richard's 'Oh that . . . I could forget what I have been,/Or not remember what I must be now' because it breaks the circle, by involving the two opposite thoughts simultaneously in one. Leontes is a better man now when he knows how bad he has been, though knowing how bad he has been makes him feel worse. And that paradoxically mutual involvement of good and bad is part of some *deeper* structure of life that the reunions in the second and third scenes have to deal with – that sudden mix of joy and sorrow which, when Edgar finally revealed himself to his father, killed Gloucester:

> the changes I perceived in the king and Camillo were very notes of admiration . . . the wisest beholder, that knew no more but seeing, could not say if th' importance were joy or sorrow . . .
>
> *The Winter's Tale* V ii 10–11, 16–18

Did you see the meeting of the two kings? . . . Then have you lost a sight which was to be seen, cannot be spoken of. There might you have beheld one joy crown another, so and in such manner that it seemed sorrow wept to take leave of them, for their joy waded in tears.

> *The Winter's Tale*, V ii 40–7

Paulina   I'll draw the curtain:
                My lord's almost so far transported that
                He'll think anon it lives.
Leontes   O sweet Paulina,
                Make me to think so twenty years together!
                No settled senses of the world can match
                The pleasure of that madness. Let 't alone.
Paulina I am sorry, sir, I have thus far stirr'd you: but
                I could afflict you farther.
Leontes   Do, Paulina;

For this affliction has a taste as sweet
As any cordial comfort.

The Winter's Tale, V iii 68–77

Shakespeare makes us so aware that he is not letting us *see* those first two reunions: 'the wisest beholder, that knew no more but seeing, could not say if th' importance were joy or sorrow', 'Then have you lost a sight which was to be seen, cannot be spoken of'. Again, material that could have been expanded into a story in itself is contracted so as to force, as all the more finally present, the last reunion of all. A resonant and charged presentness – always so much Shakespeare's immediate and quick concern – is what this scene is all about, for everything is gathered into this present till the King is almost 'ready to leap out of himself' (V ii 49–50) and sorrow itself seems to weep to take its leave. In Paulina's quick, deep words as she bids the statue awake and descend:

'Tis time.

(V iii 99)

It means, Now is a good time; but also, this is Time itself coming into being. This is the nidus – what Wordsworth called the hiding-place of his power and the recovered source of his memories, which for Shakespeare, in the midst of his swift flow, is that pre-conceptual source of being from which all later conceptualizations emerge. It is the magical place which brings to free verse something of the power of generative memory that rhyme itself gives in Sidney's account of its power to beget and to knit.[28] 'I like your silence', says Paulina, articulating just such a generative space between Leontes and the statue (V iii 21).

The memory of guilt is made a present pain again in these scenes. The pain is persevered with for the sake of what it bears witness to. And finally with the painful sight of the statue, memory is externalized, made present outside:

Chide me, dear stone, that I may say indeed
Thou art Hermione; or rather, thou art she
In thy not chiding; for she was as tender
As infancy and grace. . . .

> O, thus she stood
> Even with such life of majesty, warm life,
> As now it coldly stands, when first I woo'd her.
> I am asham'd: does not the stone rebuke me
> For being more stone than it?
>
> V iii 24–7, 34–8

As the pain of memory stands to the life held within it, so likewise
the cold to the warmth it gradually gives way to. For that is what
Paulina is now recovering to warm and dear life – not a statue, not
even just Hermione, but Leontes himself, inside, even as he looks
without him at the apparent past: 'when first I woo'd her'. In the
words of Bruno, we 'are always gathering something inside from
the outside, and sending outside something from the inside'.[29] As
Leontes begins to enter into a sense of relatedness again, it is that
shift of line from 'Chide me' to 'or rather, thou art she/In thy not
chiding', in the very midst of the formulation of thought, which is
a sign of Shakespeare's sense of *life*. 'For she was . . . tender.'

Superficial events create straightforward sequences. But deep
structures in Shakespeare create a force-field, a sensed rhythm,
an area of structural resonance in which one element of life is
not separable out from another but all are immersed together, as
joy and sorrow here, in a saturated solution of the thing itself.[30] A
force-field establishes itself thus:

> Paulina   It is requir'd
>   You do awake your faith. Then all stand still:
>   Or – those that think it is unlawful business
>   I am about, let them depart.
> Leontes   Proceed:
>   No foot shall stir.
> Paulina   Music, awake her; strike! [*Music*]
>   'Tis time; descend; be stone no more . . .
>
> V iii 94–9

This is like a secondary mode made primary again – the secondary
mode of remembering turned into an actual bringing back to life.
For it is as though there were now a primary tie felt suddenly
between 'awake your faith' and 'Music, awake her'. Likewise,

even while Paulina stops Perdita kissing the statue by telling her it is 'but newly fix'd, the colour's/Not dry', Camillo tells Leontes his sorrow is too sore laid on, sixteen winters cannot blow it away nor can sixteen summers dry it (V iii 47–51): there is some intuitive association between the sorrow inside Leontes and the statue before him, between taint and paint – the very language catches it.

But internal intuitions were what betrayed Leontes in the first place. He has already learnt one of those secondary lessons that so pained Hamlet – that passionate feelings and the objects of them may be quite separate. For his suspicious feelings about Hermione and Hermione herself, though overlapping in place, were in truth distinct. The result of such knowledge is cautious self-scepticism at best, distrustful paralysis at worst. A second nature must be learned. Yet the sequence of this play would then again unlearn it. Act V turns from memories to the people they stand for; it takes Leontes from that mental asylum into which he has retreated on the rebound from the grievous mistakes made in reality, back out into the real again.

For at some deep, original level many of Shakespeare's human beings are never quite made either political or jaded by experience, but still do go on functioning instinctively as though emotions were beliefs, were signs of union with the world outside, were secret messages given almost physically by the world itself in the language of human sensation. They sense 'a touch, a feeling' from the world (*The Tempest*, V i 21). As long as they are really alive, they cannot help it. Richard II says he knows that the earth he feels to greet him on his return to England is actually 'senseless' (III ii 23); the senseless firewood cannot really sympathize with the tale of the fall of a king told around the fireside (V i 46). The deathlike limbo, the increasingly lonely echo-chamber, in which Richard speaks makes these things already fallacies and fancies even as he talks all too slowly of them. But in the sudden heat of life, the very language of human expression seems to bespeak an underlying belief, impossible to surrender, in the union of man and world, name and thing, emotion and its object.[31] 'This is not altogether *fool*, my lord', says Kent. The loss of my proud titles, cries Hotspur, '*wound(s)* my thoughts worse than thy sword my flesh'. 'He *dies* to me again, when talk'd of.' In all these cases, a word is transferred – as though still bearing power from the place it was taken from, still

giving renewed power to the mind which apprehends it. When
Leontes looks at the stone and calls himself *more stone* than it, it is
still the same process of feeling, even in reverse by feeling the lack.
Campanella writes:

> Hope and fear are tendencies to flee evils or pursue goods which
> are not sensibly present. Trust is sense of something which we
> are convinced is good: its contrary is diffidence or mistrust. Faith
> is the mother of trust because it is the sense of good, although the
> object is not present. True imagination is when the spirit takes in
> something and thinks of it as it is, not confusing it with another;
> proof is when the spirit of something is so affected that it cannot
> be moved in any other way, but every motion reveals the things
> to be as it is.[32]

'It is requir'd/You do awake your faith' – not least the faith that
there can still be unity between the emotion and what, outside, it
stands for within.

Hermione now promises Perdita:

> thou shalt hear that I,
> Knowing by Paulina that the Oracle
> Gave hope thou wast in being, have preserv'd
> Myself to see the issue.

V iii 125–8

while Leontes says to Paulina:

> Lead us from hence, where we may leisurely
> Each one demand, and answer to his part
> Perform'd in this wide gap of time, since first
> We were dissever'd . . .

V iii 152–5

The story of how, like the statue 'Lonely, apart' (V iii 17),
Hermione managed to 'preserve' herself for sixteen years – if
only by knowing that her own existence held out some oracular
hope of the existence of her lost child. Of how Leontes, thinking
his wife and children lost through his own sin, lived out the time

as if it were a long final gap, a sense of 'nothing' experienced both as dead end and endless pain. Of how Perdita, like 'the spring to th' earth' (V i 151), has in all that time unconsciously grown to give the old that 'hope' and 'issue' which she herself, being young, embodies yet scarce feels the need or value of. All this, imagined together, in an instant retrospectively creates the novel behind the play – the story so different from the lives the characters thought they were living during all that interim. Sixteen years are imagined in the split-second of that word 'preserv'd' (what went into it!) – sixteen years when none knew this was only a gap and not an end. That sudden Shakespearian glimpse of a greater scale of time – the time by which these sixteen years turn out to have been only after all a 'wide gap', wounding but not fatal – that glimpse, I say, is the revelation of a deeper sense of sequence, a longer and a bigger view that sweeps past premature conclusions:

> The reason of motion is the renovation and rebirth of that body which cannot be perennial. . . . The things that cannot be perennial as individuals . . . perpetuate themselves as a species.[33]

In the twentieth century perhaps only Lawrence's *The Rainbow* is of equivalent scale – the rainbow renewed over all the generations. 'A world ransomed, or one destroyed' (V iii 15).

At the close of the subtle sequence of *The Winter's Tale* inner things – memory, emotion, thought – are drawn out again into the life and the people they too often and too sadly have stood in place of: pained memory too often in lieu of the hope that life could come back; emotion hardly daring to call itself belief; thought not risking itself as a form of sensing. In short, history itself is brought back to life.

Yet Paulina is not performing magic or miracle – and not just because Mamillius remains dead or Hermione is aged or so much time has been lost. Rather, she is trying to break to Leontes the real story without its breaking him. He somewhere knows, even before he dares secondarily to acknowledge it, that this is the real Hermione before him. But Paulina has to lead him gradually through it all, in ritual sequence, letting him release his intuitions into her definite shaped thought. 'I like your silence', she says, covering the initial gap of shock. But now, she hints to him, I am afraid that you will think 'anon it moves' (V iii 21, 61). She does not rush into it; rather, she backs into it, gently devious but also reverent: I could afflict you farther . . . Or shall I redraw the curtains? 'It appears she lives' (V iii 117): appears is on the very borderline between revelation and scepticism. Can you believe it? If you can, can you take it? Always in counterpoint there is fear – Paulina's fear that this reunion is dangerous and may be too much for Leontes; Leontes's fear that it may be too little, too good to be true, that he is only mocked with art, like Alonso in *The Tempest*: 'If this prove/A vision of the island, one dear son/Shall I twice lose' (V i 175–7). If so, she dies to me again. Yet, says Paulina, 'Do not shun her/Until you see her die again; for then/You kill her double (V iii 105–7). There has to be fear for anyone who intuitively believes that losing may somehow be a gain.

Paulina and Leontes have become allies in trouble. What she says outside him, upon her tongue, is only as bad as what he feels inside, 'in my thought' (V i 19). In this co-ordination, she knows from her own recent experience the dangerous mix of feelings through which she guides the king – it is as if Shakespeare writes out in prose the blueprint for her:

> the noble combat that 'twixt joy and sorrow was fought in Paulina! She had one eye declined for the loss of her husband, another elevated that the Oracle was fulfilled: she lifted the princess from the earth, and so locks her in embracing as if she would pin her to her heart, that she might no more be in danger of losing.
>
> V ii 72–8

So too with Leontes:

> Our king, being ready to leap out of himself for joy of his found daughter, as if that joy were now become a loss, cries 'O, thy mother, thy mother!'
>
> V ii 50–4

'Turn, good lady,' says Paulina, 'Our Perdita is found' (V iii 120–1). *Our* Perdita. 'Look upon your brother,' says Leontes to Hermione, pointing again to Polixenes at last (V iii 147). These turns are not simply from sorrow to joy but to a fourfold family amalgam of the two – joy in sorrow and sorrow in joy. For, as it all comes together at the end of *The Winter's Tale*, what is most impressive is still that mix of joy and sorrow even in the careful breaking of the joy on all sides. We normally think of joy and sorrow as two different, even two opposite things. But here the sudden thought is: what if joy and sorrow were not even separate, though we have no name, no concept by which to unite them. What makes *The Winter's Tale* so near perfect is what makes *Twelfth Night* so near perfect too: that joy and sorrow are somehow not separate but the span of the same life-stuff; that life is most full when the two are, incredibly and almost unbearably, part of each other - and thus part of something greater than can be described in terms that are either optimistic or pessimistic but can only be called, in Middleton Murry's phrase, 'the thing which is':

> The world which Shakespeare represents to us, or the Nature which represents itself to us through him, is not a world to which faith is the appropriate attitude of mind: it is a thing which simply is. If it satisfies us, it is because existence itself has come to satisfy us; if it terrifies us, it is because existence itself still terrifies us; if we seek in it a morality, it is because we seek a morality in existence; if we can only be reconciled to it by faith, it is because we still need faith to reconcile us to existence. Lear says to Edgar: 'Thou art the thing itself'; and so we to Shakespeare.[34]

When joy and sorrow are inseparable they are no longer like temporary moods or possible attitudes; they are more like the gamut or range of *everything* that could be felt, all at once, in 'dear life'. For in the mix of tragi-comedy we are at the limits that make a human being almost 'leap out of himself' or burst smilingly. 'The things that cannot be perennial as individuals perpetuate themselves as a species.' The person can hardly contain the process. Yet in *The Tempest*, as we shall finally see, he tries to.

3   'THERE, SIR, STOP'.

If transformation goes on in all the plays, it goes on least of all in the histories and most of all in the late plays, where it becomes their very subject. Before turning to *The Tempest*, I must briefly recall how the late plays, as alternatives to the histories, are born out of

the variations that, in Shakespeare, comedy performs upon tragedy
and tragedy upon comedy. For the difference between the greatest
late plays, *The Tempest* and *The Winter's Tale*, lies at the very end
of those variations.

In his shaping imagination, I have argued, Shakespeare is more
interested in levels than in lines. Or, more aptly, if he is going to
drive on in a strong linear sequence of story, he is interested in the
way that levels are compressed within the story-lines. The spatial
pressure of a sequence can create resistances that would prefer
incorporation in different dimensions but still are half included in
the onward drive of the action. To give an example: various sorts
of pressure, internal and external, force Coriolanus to work within
the forms of Rome, yet as he puts it:

> Know, good mother,
> I had rather be their servant in my way
> Than sway with them in theirs.
> > *Coriolanus*, II i 200–2

That is what it means to try to create a level of modification
('their servant in *my* way') within an ongoing structure, rather than
now 'crave the hire which first we do deserve' (II iii 112).

At least the tragedies try to find some place of freedom; the
histories can barely try. Like Coriolanus, the deposed Richard
desperately desires some force-field for identity to operate in,
albeit within the realm of necessity. But with Richard, it is too
often more a style than a place. All he can do is revenge himself
upon what is happening by showing and mocking its hidden reality
even when he is threatened by it:

> *Richard* Now, mark me how I will undo myself.
> I give this heavy weight from off my head
> And this unwieldy sceptre from my hand,
> The pride of kingly sway from out my heart.
> With mine own tears I wash away my balm;
> With mine own hands I give away my crown;
> With mine own tongue deny my sacred state;
> With mine own breath release all duteous oaths.
> All pomp and majesty I do forswear;
> My manors, rents, revenues I forgo;

My acts, decrees and statutes I deny.
God pardon all oaths that are broke to me;
God keep all vows unbroke are made to thee.
Make me that nothing have with nothing grieved,
And thou with all pleased that hast all achieved.

Richard II, IV i 199–213

A director describes this in performance:

He played with Bolingbroke as a cat with a mouse. The crown was dangled like a carrot, it was held high, gently offered, snatched away, the anguish of the virgin, refusing yet knowing ultimately the prize would have to be given away, determined to tease and frustrate, delaying the moment as long as possible.[35]

But performance is what it is – a ritualistic contradiction of Richard's own sense of power in this uncoronation. As the power passes from him, apparently by 'mine own' hand, it is a parody of freedom, mocking its own state in being forced while seeming forceful. Above all, it is an act of inversion: even here while Richard plays with Bolingbroke, in the wider context the silent Bolingbroke is still winning. 'Up, cousin, up. Your heart is up I know,/Thus high at least, although your knee be low' (III iii 194–5). Let us see the hidden political reality, let us shape ourselves accordingly. Yet Richard speaks as though a master in his own terms, not a servant in Bolingbroke's. When Richard cries, 'God save the king!', is it the old king he means or the new? Either satirically he now means Bolingbroke in succession or, within that, he still has faint hopes that he himself should be saved. But he is in a world of his own now: 'Will no man say, Amen?/Am I both priest and clerk? Well then, Amen' (IV i 172–3) – an unreal parodic world he cannot really inhabit even were Bolingbroke to let him try. It is strange to hear in Richard an inner voice and an outer voice at once. But so it is with Coriolanus, lonely in the midst of addressing others. The inner life is now only a *tone*, has just such a non-physical space for itself, if any space at all. If after all Shakespeare has a dominant political interest, in the wider sense of that term which Hooker allows, this is the ambiguous area it functions in – the simultaneous need for and resistance to social definition.

But it is in comedy that this need for different levels, even socially defined levels, finds its best and most convenient home. For what Shakespeare can do in act V scene ii of *The Winter's Tale* is take his major theme down to the level of the lower, minor characters:

> *Autolycus* I know you are now, sir, a gentleman born.
> *Clown* Ay, and have been so these four hours.
> *Shepherd* And so have I, boy.
> *Clown* So you have but I was a gentleman born before my father; for the king's son took me by the hand, and called me brother; and then the two kings called my father brother; and then the prince, my brother, and the princess, my sister, called my father father; and so we wept . . .
>
>

The Winter's Tale, V ii 136–44

Here is not only a repetition of the major theme of sadness in the midst of joy but, as with Mozart's Papageno, seriousness ('and so we wept') in the midst of comedy:

> and there was the first gentleman-like tears that ever we shed.

The sequence of the speech is complete with that comic return to the gentleman theme – the Clown still persisting with his point at his own level, still going on with his life according to his colours. Born again yet also a four-hour-old baby. Yet 'we must be gentle,' adds the shepherd-father, 'now we are gentlemen' (V ii 152–3). And to whom are they gentle? Autolycus!

Better such mixed-up divine idiots – like Dogberry with his 'God's a good man' (*Much Ado*, III v 35) – than more intelligent devils. Or, to transpose the same strain of thought into a quite different context:

> Better a witty fool than a foolish wit.
>
>

Twelfth Night, I v 34

For that is one of the secrets of Shakespeare's seemingly inexhaustible variety – his putting the same thing into a different place with a resulting mix of continuity and alteration. 'Better a witty fool than a foolish wit' is after all Coriolanus's 'rather be their servant in my way/Than sway with them in theirs' put into comedy. And Feste

puts the same thing again in a different context when he says he is
'the better for my foes, and the worse for my friends'. But how so,
asks the Duke, surely it should be the opposite?

> Marry, sir, [my friends] praise me, and make an ass of me. Now
> my foes tell me plainly I am an ass: so that by my foes, sir, I profit
> in the knowledge of myself, and by my friends I am abused.
>
> *Twelfth Night*, V i 11–12, 16–19

'Virtue that trangresses is but patched with sin, and sin that amends
is but patched with virtue' – anything that's mended is but patched
(*Twelfth Night*, I v 44–6). 'Our virtues would be proud, if our faults
whipped them not, and our crimes would despair, if they were
not cherished by our virtues' (*All's Well That Ends Well*, IV iii
61–3). As I argued in Chapter One, comedy - not history, not even
tragedy – is ever, as Dr Johnson claimed, Shakespeare's congenial
starting-point. The art of transposition that the Fool carries out
within comedy can also be employed at another level to turn
comedy itself suddenly to a higher seriousness. Tragi-comedy is
simply a development of that process, whereby suddenly one thing
is found in amidst another: sorrow in joy, friendship in foes, wit in
folly, virtue in sin, fault in virtue, seriousness in comedy.

Thus, out of the mouth of a fool who seems old can come songs
of young love, till the cynicism and disappointment that he half
disguises in jest become an underlyingly beautiful sadness in song:

> Not a flower, not a flower sweet,
> On my black coffin let there be strewn:
> Not a friend, not a friend greet
> My poor corpse, where my bones shall be thrown:
>   A thousand, thousand sighs to save,
>   Lay me, O where,
>   Sad true lover never find my grave,
>   To weep there.

> *Duke*   There's for thy pains. [*Giving him money*]
> *Clown* No pains, sir, I take pleasure in singing, sir.
> *Duke*   I'll pay thy pleasure then.
> *Clown* Truly sir, and pleasure will be paid, one time or
> another.
>
> *Twelfth Night*, II iv 59–70

Love and death, young and old, pleasure and pain – of all such mixtures and vicissitudes, Bruno, the philosopher of rich process, would say:

> we ourselves, and our things, go and come, pass and return; there is no thing [part] of ours which would not become alien [to us], and there is no alien thing which would not become ours. And there is not a thing we are made of that at times should not become other than ours, just as there is no thing which is ours, which at times we shall not be made of.[36]

Every thing will go into different levels, places, forms, shapes and sequences in order to preserve itself – inside us and outside us, in the individual or in the species, in joy and in sorrow. That is the Archimedean point outside the world by which Shakespeare may move the world and create his worlds, play after play. The song comes out of something inside the Fool, and yet continues its existence resonantly outside him. In chapter xxix of *De doctrina christiana* Augustine said that when a wicked man composes a discourse which contains goodness and truth, he draws from himself what does not belong to him. In Shakespeare things are more mixed: the Fool is not wicked, and his song is partly an expression of and partly a contrast with its own singer. We hold life-stuff for a moment and then pass it on as it passes on. 'Youth's a stuff will not endure.'

So the songs and great speeches in *Twelfth Night* belong half to the characters and half to the force of the situation which speaks through them:

> *Viola*   If I did love you in my master's flame,
>   With such a suff'ring, such a deadly life,
>   In your denial I would find no sense,
>   I would not understand it.
> *Olivia*   Why, what would you?
> *Viola*   Make me a willow cabin at your gate,
>   And call upon my soul within the house;
>   Write loyal cantons of contemned love,
>   And sing them loud even in the dead of night;
>   Halloo your name to the reverberate hills,
>   And make the babbling gossip of the air,

Cry out 'Olivia!' O, you should not rest
Between the elements of air and earth,
But you should pity me.

I v 268–80

Viola But if she cannot love you, sir?
Orsino I cannot be so answer'd.
Viola   Sooth, but you must.
Say that some lady, as perhaps there is,
Hath for your love as great a pang of heart
As you have for Olivia: you cannot love her:
You tell her so. Must she not then be answer'd? . . .
My father had a daughter lov'd a man . . .

II iv 88–93, 106

These wonderful speeches have a music of their own and a
resonance between each other, turning one way and then another
in complex relativism. The cadence at the end of the first line of
each of the following:

In your denial I would find no sense,
I would not understand it.

              you cannot love her:
You tell her so. Must she not then be answer'd?

even across the apparent differences of situation is none the less
fundamentally the same. In both there is a sort of reluctant and
helpless lamed halt in the face of a bar to possibility. For this is not
that active comic work of a Rosalind or a Benedick which has its
place elsewhere. And yet those pauses yield to the ear that listens
something almost magical. For the felt impossibilities – 'I would
not understand it', 'you cannot love her' – still seem to contain
something of the eternal and original possibility within them, more
sadly beautiful because unextortably lost:

Lamenting is altogether contrary to reioysing; every man saith
so, and yet it is a peece of ioy to be able to lament with ease,
and freely to poure forth a mans inward sorrowes and the greefs
wherewith his minde is surcharged. This was a very necessary
deuise of the Poet and a fine, besides his poetrie to play also the
Phisitian, and not onely by applying a medicine to the ordinary

sicknes of mankind, but by making the very greef it selfe (in part) also the cure of the disease. . . . Therefore of death and burials, of th'adversities by warres, and of true love lost or ill bestowed are th'onely sorrowes that the noble Poets sought by their arte to remoue or appease, not with any medicament of a contrary temper, as the *Galenistes* vse to cure *contraria contrariis*, but as the *Paracelsians*, who cure *similia similibus*, making one dolour to expell another, and, in this case, one short sorrowing the remedie of a long and grieuous sorrow.[37]

The bitter-sweetness of *Twelfth Night*, which is its own version of what is tragi-comedy in *The Winter's Tale*, is precisely the result of a sad but beautiful sense of pleasure – even in the pains and the losing, even in the recognition that such pleasure itself must be paid for in time itself. The sheer resonance of the language –

Halloo your name to the reverberate hills,
And make the babbling gossip of the air,
Cry out 'Olivia!'

– makes one dolour to expel another, *similia similibus*, as Viola makes the very air around echo and amplify the cry of love which she herself carries (so ambiguously) for Orsino. Language here is like what it makes of the very hills themselves – not an answer but a sympathetic echo of the disease raised to the point of crying beauty. 'We feel as we feel', says Campanella, meaning that we have emotions even as we have sensations:

Sense is passion; and memory is sense anticipated and renewed; and speech is sense of like for like; and just as many kinds of similitude as there are in the world – of essences, of qualities, of actions, of places, of times, of operations, of cause, of quantity, of sight, of figure, and of color – there are as many kinds of speech and syllogism.[38]

Viola's cry of poetry feels through words, as though words were themselves a medium for an emotional expansion of sensation. She makes and feels the senseless hills and air respond, 'like for like'. For every imaginative situation into which Shakespeare works himself has its own feel – and thence its own correspondent language or music:

like the sweet sound
That breathes upon a bank of violets,
Stealing and giving odour.

Twelfth Night, I i 5–7

Giving and stealing language, Viola makes 'the very greef it selfe (in part) also the cure of the disease' – until the language itself woos the story into going with it.

But *sympathy* in Shakespeare is a complex almost magical thing. There is indeed one side of him that is Paracelsian, that in *Twelfth Night* and *The Winter's Tale* goes with the pain *similia similibus*, for the sake of something other than pain in it. For it is not masochistic but paradoxical that 'this affliction has a taste as sweet/As any cordial comfort'.

Yet there is also another side, another language, that as with Galen brings catharsis only *contraria contrariis*:

why then the thing of courage,
As rous'd with rage, with rage doth sympathize,
And with an accent tun'd in self-same key,
Retires to chiding fortune.

Troilus and Cressida, I iii 51–4

This is the Shakespeare of King Lear raging against the storm, making the air echo him as he the air, in a way so very different in the end from Viola's. 'As fire drives out fire, so pity, pity' (*Julius Caesar*, III i 171), and the sympathy of *contraria contrariis* is the mode of the tragedies – which

do set the word itself
Against the word –
As thus: 'Come, little ones', and then again
'It is as hard to come as for a camel
To thread the postern of a small needle's eye.'

Richard II, V v 13–17

One 'come' drives out another. To that side I now turn – because it is from the way of the tragedies that *The Tempest* finally emerges. For all its masques and songs and shows, *The Tempest* is the most puritanical of all Shakespeare's plays, not going along with life and grief but countering them, against the grain. 'But this swift business/I must uneasy make lest too light winning/Make the prize light' (*The Tempest*, I ii 451–3).

There is still a music in *The Tempest* every bit as subtle and magical as that of *Twelfth Night*, but it is now framed by the second-order discipline of 'attend':

> *Prospero* Dost thou attend me? . . .
>   – thou attend'st not!
> *Miranda* O good sir, I do!
>
>   *The Tempest*, I ii 78, 87–8

There is a history to this. For it was in part through his own neglect that Prospero fell and was substituted. Far more than in *The Winter's Tale*, what follows is an art of *willed* memory: Prospero cannot now afford to forget 'The strongest oaths are straw' (IV i 52). A man who knows from his first life what mistakes he has made in the past through neglect of discipline, here has the power in a second life – if he now keeps discipline – single-handedly to stop the sequence and break the cycle, as never did happen in the histories.

The order in which things are done is now seen as a vital matter for care. When Ariel complains of more toil and demands liberty, he is chastened ('How now? Moody?') and forcibly reminded:

> *Prospero*   Dost thou forget
>   From what a torment I did free thee?
> *Ariel*   No.
> *Prospero* Thou dost . . .
>
>   I ii 250–2

– a nail drives out a nail, before ever the gentler dispensation can be allowed:

> *Ariel*   Pardon, master.
>   I will be correspondent to command
>   And do my spiriting gently.
> *Prospero*   Do so, and after two days
>   I will discharge thee.
> *Ariel*   That's my noble master.
>
>   I ii 298–302

Prospero is as puritanical as an Angelo: 'Mercy is not itself, that *oft* looks so' (*Measure for Measure*, II i 280). The noble master can only return and relent after the first principle is carried. Even though he knows in advance that he will eventually relent, if unpressurized and on his own terms, still he must go through the process step by step – always believing in it, at times genuinely flaring up at the memory of usurpation, yet at others subsiding into a somewhat weary adoption of the necessary routines of order. As in the histories, however tiring the repetition, right order depends upon correct sequence. Only in that sense is *The Tempest* 'Shakespeare's last history play'.[39] For Prospero's power is a duty, not a covert pleasure like Angelo's.

It is, moreover, a moral duty – not just a magical fantasy of control or an exercise in political or colonial repression. For Prospero must also exercise that power upon himself – even as he gives Miranda to Ferdinand:

> *Prospero* If I have too austerely punished you
> Your compensation makes amends, for I
> Have given you here a third of mine own life,
> Or that for which I live; who once again
> I tender to thy hand.
>
>   IV i 1–5

This is the Prospero of the austere 'yet': 'Why, that's my dainty Ariel! I shall miss thee,/But yet thou shalt have freedom. So, so, so'; 'Yet with my nobler reason 'gainst my fury/Do I take part' (V i 95–6, 26–7). For the very note of 'once again' is heard again minutes later when Prospero, his attention momentarily slipping for once, recalls himself from the masque back to the conspiracy of Caliban:

> *Ferdinand* This is strange. Your father's in some passion
> That works him strongly.
> *Miranda*   Never till this day
> Saw I him touched with anger, so distempered.
> *Prospero (To Ferdinand)*
> You do look, my son, in a moved sort,
> As if you were dismayed. Be cheerful, sir;
> Our revels now are ended. These our actors,

> As I foretold you, were all spirits, and
> Are melted into air, into thin air . . .
>
> IV i 143–50

The renewed resolve 'That for which I live; who once again/I tender to thy hand' is kin to that 'As I foretold you'. In the former case the remembered principle formally comes forward; in the latter it goes back again behind it all, declaring itself always there. But that Prospero can get so immediately to 'Be cheerful, sir' despite 'Our revels now are ended' is a transition he wishes the young to carry over – it is not really a thing he can any longer do for himself. Better to think of the young in a moved sort than his own disturbing passion; better to appease his own anger in comfort of the young's dismay. Be cheerful, but Prospero cannot be: 'Our revels now are ended.' He already knows his end, even while at another level he keeps on living and working his way. For him vulnerable emotions are held as private after-thoughts, as private to him and as superfluous to others as is an ageing man himself with thoughts of death. They are glossed over in his adjusting of his attire, 'So, so, so', or by his excusing himself, 'A turn or two I'll walk/To still my beating mind' (IV i 163–4). It is not 'my beating heart' but this is not because Prospero is heartless: rather, he will hold his heart's feelings nervily in an attentive mind and try to recompose the agitated beating there. It is the serious form of what Feste called patching – patching up the evil, patching over death.

It is by trying to *still* his beating mind that Prospero seeks to hold and absorb in himself the energy of his world's pain and evil, rather than reactively pass it on. 'A hit B? B hit C? . . . A brave man will try to make the evil stop with him. He shall keep the blow. . . . What are the generations for, please explain to me? Only to repeat?' All those knock-on forces, discussed in Chapter One, are what Prospero here at the end of affairs is trying to contain and transmute:

> Human mechanics. Whoever suffers tries to communicate his suffering (either by ill-treating someone or calling forth their pity).[40]

Prospero is mysterious because he does not finally 'communicate' in either of those ways; his silence is related to his death. He bears the play's problems and takes its irresolutions with him to the grave. When Alonso, Lear-like, says of the new daughter whose childhood banishment he sanctioned, 'how oddly will it sound that I/Must ask my child's forgiveness', Prospero immediately responds: 'There sir, stop' (V i 197–8). 'Do not infest your mind with beating on/The strangeness of this business' (V i 246–7). Stop the odd sounds; still the beating; yet hold on, in what must always seem Shakespeare's final play.

There is, as Eleanor Prosser has noted, a direct source for Prospero's austere moral 'yet' in Montaigne. The speech:

> Though with their high wrongs I am struck to th' quick,
> Yet with my nobler reason 'gainst my fury
> Do I take part. The rarer action is
> In virtue than in vengeance.
>
> V i 25–8

comes from the opening of Montaigne's essay 'Of Crueltie':

> Me thinkes vertue is another manner of thing, and much more noble than the inclinations unto goodnesse, which in us are ingendered. Mindes well borne, and directed by themselves, follow one same path, and in their actions, represent the same visage, that the vertuous doe. But vertue importeth, and soundeth somewhat I wot not what greater and more active, than by an happy complexion, gently and peaceably, to suffer it selfe to be led or drawne, to follow reason. He that through a naturall facilitie, and genuine mildnesse, should neglect or contemne injuries received should no doubt performe a rare action, and worthy commendation: But he who being toucht and stung to the quicke, with any wrong or offence received, should arme himselfe with reason against this furiously-blind desire of revenge, and in the end after a great conflict, yeeld himselfe master over-it, should doubtlesse doe much more. The first should doe well, the other vertuously; the one action might be termed goodnesse, the other vertue. For, it seemeth, that the verie name of vertue presupposeth difficultie, and inferreth resistance, and cannot well exercise it selfe without an enemie.[41]

A natural goodness is less creditable than the effort of self-overcoming. The one is the easygoingness of biological accident, the other a determined principle fought for against the natural grain. Virtue is like Galen's medicine: it fights against the body's unhealth. It is characteristic of Montaigne's tough-mindedness – and something that makes him kin to Shakespeare – to wish to make fine, inconvenient distinctions in the midst of overlapping similarities: 'Lo here the reason why when we judge of a particular action, we must first consider many circumstances, and throughly observe the man, that hath produced the same before we name and censure [or praise] it' (Montaigne, vol.II, p.114). If the Old naturally lose the sharp drives of lust it may indeed be good (Montaigne's unfussy shrug accepts peace wherever and however he can get it), but it is not virtue. Virtue is second thought, second nature.

Prospero is not a man of easy first-order goodness. He is manifestly still in a rage when he seeks formally to forgive the usurping Antonio:

> whom to call brother
> Would even infect my mouth, I do forgive
> Thy rankest fault – all of them – and require
> My dukedom of thee, which perforce I know
> Thou must restore.

The Tempest, V i 130–4

'The best we can do is to confront our inherited and hereditary nature with our knowledge of it, and through a new, stern discipline combat our inborn heritage and implant in ourselves a new habit, a new instinct, a second nature. . . . [But] second natures are usually weaker than the first.'[42] That extra clause 'which *perforce* I know/Thou must restore' is the mark of a man who sourly knows in advance that the forgiveness he can barely manage will be met by no free contrition in return.

Similar thoughts as to the sheer strain involved in implanting second nature must have struck Montaigne, moments later, in the midst of his improvised 'essai' of thought. For next thing, in a way that would surely have impressed Shakespeare as with the sight of a kindred free spirit, Montaigne turns round upon his own argument. He changes his mind not by an act of deliberation but by a sudden almost chance change of context and perspective – as though life in its multiplicity threw up in his mind the memory of a quite different thought:

> Hitherto I have come at good ease; but at the end of this discourse, one thing commeth into my minde, which is, that the soule of *Socrates*, which is (absolutely) the perfectest that ever came to my knowledge, would, according, to my accompt, prove a soule deserving but little commendation: For I can perceive no manner of violence or vicious concupisence in him: I can imagine no manner of difficultie or compulsion in the whole course of his vertue. . . . If vertue cannot shine but by resisting contrarie appetites, shall we then say, that it cannot passe without the assistance of vice, and oweth him this, by his meanes it attaineth to honour and credit?
>
> Montaigne, vol.II, p.110 (ch.xi, 'Of Crueltie')

In the soul of Socrates, and of Cato also, Montaigne saw 'so perfect an habitude unto vertue' that 'it was even converted into their complexion' – second nature seemed to have become first without the need for puritanical struggle *contraria contrariis*:

> It is no longer a painfull vertue, nor by the ordinances of reason, for the maintaining of which, their minde must be strengthned: It is the verie essence of their soule; it is her naturall and ordinarie habit.
>
> Montaigne, vol.II, p.113 (ch.xi, 'Of Crueltie')

This is the harmonious personality that Prospero, for all his power, cannot find in himself. Neither could Montaigne. But Montaigne shrugs, acknowledging that his own apparent virtues are really temperamental accidents, bits of natural good luck in the chance creation of his genetic character. Of the three types – the naturally easygoing, the strainers after second nature, and the harmoniously good – Montaigne belongs with the first as though it were closer in its sheer lack of strain to the third, which he admires most, than the second can ever be. But Prospero goes the opposite, more puritanical way. For here is the most powerful character

Shakespeare has ever created, aiming to make the whole shaping process of the plays the responsibility of his own person – a person who is not just a Paulina but analogous to Shakespeare himself. And yet for all his power he finds himself incomplete, in the second rank, unable to integrate virtue and nature, still in sad and pained effort.

He holds his enemies in his power. He addresses their spellbound bodies standing before him: 'Most cruelly/Didst thou, Alonso, use me and my daughter . . . You, brother mine' (V i 69 ff.). They stand like statues, yet statues so different from Hermione the innocent one. For, just before Prospero lets them come back to life, they cannot hear him who speaks to them as 'thou' and 'you'. It is as though he needs to get his thoughts about them *out* of himself and before them, as in a court of justice. These are no longer his thoughts and memories; they are people now, helplessly standing presently in front of him. He holds his very plan in a moment of suspended animation – as if to test himself between virtue and vengeance. Yet the dynamic memory of one little word from his subordinate spirit Ariel – the word 'human' – has struck Prospero from outside:

Ariel That if you now beheld them, your affections
     Would become tender.
Prospero   Dost thou think so, spirit?
Ariel Mine would, sir, were I human.

V i 18–20

There should be a slight but vital pause, like a dash, before 'were I' and again before 'human'. Just one word, but it is here the greatest and most powerful word in Shakespeare: it opens up the world and its whole history again; it makes a godlike figure again a man. The language itself turns back upon the man who gave Caliban words. For if it truly names him and names what he is, then it should be felt meaningfully within him, giving a very echo to the heart. The word 'human' brings something to life even as Hermione was revived. . . . And yet it still means sacrifice and pain to Prospero. He is not Montaigne's Socrates.

It is not that the idea of forgiveness is any big surprise of thought to Prospero. The idea that there are poor naked wretches in the world should not have been a surprise to Lear. But it is consonant

with the lucid austerity of *The Tempest* that what is not surprising
or original but obvious and already known should still be difficult,
painful and unheroically necessary to repeat. For *The Tempest* is
not a play of dramatic changes and sudden realizations so much
as subtly precise modulations and returns of what is or ought to
be *already* known. Prospero's plan to marry Ferdinand to Miranda
shows that forgiveness was always intended; yet both the marriage
and the forgiveness have to overcome sudden moments of renewed
reluctance. *The Tempest* is full of the subtlest post-dramatic changes,
a last play, with a mixture of the austere and the delicate. Thus,
as Prospero confronts his enemies in a ring, his words begin to
summon their thoughts back into them in place of his revenge:

> The charm dissolves apace,
> And as the morning steals upon the night,
> Melting the darkness, so their rising senses
> Begin to chase the ignorant fumes that mantle
> Their clearer reason. . . .
> Their understanding
> Begins to swell, and the approaching tide
> Will shortly fill the reasonable shore
> That now lies foul and muddy.
>
> V i 65–9, 79–82

The images are precisely descriptive of the way the play works its
modulated realizations: as dreamings and awakenings, hardenings
and meltings, darkenings and lightenings, the very ebbs and flows
of mind. Something is coming *back* into being in this play – not
in an excited rush but soberly, in the name of no more than
'reason' – rather as it did, more wondrously, for Miranda earlier:
something 'far off,/And rather like a dream than an assurance/That
my remembrance warrants' is coming to mental life now out of the
'dark backward and abysm of time' (I ii 44–5, 50). No sooner does
Miranda 'who art ignorant of what thou art', cry out on hearing the
piteous story of her and her father's past:

> Alack, what trouble
> Was I then to you!

than Prospero replies in a quite different tone from that of the
schoolmaster he is in the midst of being:

> O, a cherubin
> Thou wast that did preserve me.
>
> I ii 151–3

What she was *before* she can even remember being, is what he
gratefully recalls. But his private gratitude can barely find a proper
time or place for expression, when its object was then and is
now, by life's definition, so innocently unconscious of all that
her innocence gave and still gives to those who have outgrown
it. The best of Prospero – the bit of him that likewise admits to
loving 'my Ariel, chick' (V i 316) – has not quite got anywhere
to go. One of the saddest paradoxes of the play is that what the
young have and are, they themselves do not know – only the old
know it when they have it not. 'Tis new to thee' (V i 184).

Even here there is no way out of or above the Shakespearian
system of life. Even one such as Prospero no sooner seems to be
above it all than he feels excluded from it all; no sooner does
what is morally and publicly right than feels still privately bad in
himself about it. 'Dost thou love me master? No?' asks Ariel. The
note is not 'Yes?' as it would be to the young, but 'No?' And
Prospero replies with emotion as ever half hidden within the formal
relationship, 'Dearly, my delicate Ariel' (IV i 48–9) – not wanting
to hurt the delicate one, but even thus being hurt himself at some
private level where 'dearly' is also the fatherly cost. He must give
up his servant and his formal power. In this different version of
Henry IV and the death of the father, the rest is private.

Yet wherever the play ends up, even in the sad banality of death,
it got there by a series of subtle movements. *The Tempest* has its
players dispersed in troops about the isle (I ii 220), so that the
shifting dynamics both within and between the groupings make
up a sort of music:

Miranda   I might call him
          A thing divine, for nothing natural
          I ever saw so noble.
Prospero [aside]   It goes on, I see,
          As my soul prompts it. *[To Ariel]* Spirit, fine spirit, I'll
                    free thee
          Within two days for this.

Ferdinand   Most sure, the goddess
                On whom these airs attend . . .

                                                        I ii 418–23

No play of Shakespeare's is so full of multiply overlapping asides. There are here four different virtually operatic voices almost at the same time, two of them belonging to Prospero. As a man of experience, his very *voice* can do more than anyone else's, moving in and out of different dimensions of life and different depths of both tone and time – even though he can no longer reproduce youth's single note of innocent wonder. 'I do not know/One of my sex, no woman's face remember,/Save from my glass my own' (III i 48–50). Miranda only really has one tone of voice, virginally pure – but even that one Prospero, the man of many voices, himself 'prompts':

                Foolish wench,
        To th' most of men this is a Caliban,
        And they to him are angels.
    Miranda   My affections
        Are then most humble. I have no ambition
        To see a goodlier man.

                                                        I ii 480–4

It makes a most beautiful stop. That is one thing the generations are for.

The isle is full of noises. Temporarily, for as long as they can last, songs and sounds have a good influence upon others which disciplined morality itself, for all Prospero's efforts, can hardly match or sustain. One of the most beautiful of the play's modulations comes upon Caliban when he sees Stephano, his poor version of a Prospero-like god, suddenly startled by Ariel's invisibly mocking echo of the drunken party's tune:

Caliban Art thou afeard?
Stephano No monster, not I.
Caliban Be not afeard, the isle is full of noises,
        Sounds and sweet airs, that give delight and hurt not.
        Sometimes a thousand twangling instruments
        Will hum about mine ears; and sometimes voices,

That if I then had waked after long sleep,
Will make me sleep again, and then in dreaming
The clouds methought would open and show riches
Ready to drop upon me, that when I waked
I cried to dream again.

III ii 131–41

Immediately alongside the poetry of Caliban's address to Stephano, 'Thou wondrous man', comes Trinculo's prosaic aside: 'A most ridiculous monster, to make a wonder of a poor drunkard' (II ii 160). For when all the groups meet again at the end of the play, Caliban will learn what a thrice-double ass he has been to take a drunkard for a god. Yet suddenly here when Ariel's tune sounds, for all the surrounding folly, the positions change – and with them, in this auditory world, changes the very tone of Caliban himself: 'Be not afeard.' The beast is turned at once into an unconsciously superior and reassuringly compassionate creature trustingly at home in this world. He has betrayed this note before in attempting to rape Miranda. But for an instant here this gentler note of itself still releases the memory of that sleep of Caliban's – a sleep which the music interrupted from without, only to flow back inside it again at another level: 'voices,/That if I then had waked after long sleep,/Will make me sleep again, and then in dreaming . . .' Something has come over Caliban as by a turn of the sea – the 'awakening tide' of the play.

Yet for all that movement of the tide, there is nothing new under the sun, there is nothing new in the coming and the going of the very rhythms of the sea. There are (only? instead?) almost infinite shapings of the finite. The basic framework always comes back into place in this late play. Age surrounds the young. Awakening surrounds the dream, until the final sleep. Sometimes the voices that awakened Caliban did so only to make him sleep again and dream of what seemed to be on the very point of being 'ready'. Yet finally he had to wake up once more and cry to dream again. This is a version of what we might call Freud's stern reality-principle.

The fine tones and the beautiful notes, made in passing

> O, a cherubin
Thou wast that did preserve me.

Be not afeard

were I human

make a difference, yet something in them gets left behind by the very difference they have gone into practically making. There is no large structure of life which is as fulfilling as the tiny points that lead up to it: 'Yea, all which it inherit, shall dissolve' and 'leave not a rack behind' (IV i 154, 156). There is no utterly new way of being, only the austere return of a simple old one – forgive, die. The magic of *The Winter's Tale* and *The Tempest* is what Campanella called natural magic: translate Shakespeare's language into the language of a more mechanical understanding and what was magical seems commonplace.[43] There is no new discovery by Shakespearian philosophy that can quite live up to the promise of those powerful little moments and movements of utter complexity of meaning, like thoughts in their dumb cradles: there is only finally the spelling of them back out into the ordinary, finite, mortal world. And that, felt by Prospero as something very close to disappointing failure, is part of Shakespeare's truthful and creative agnosticism:

> It is a thing which simply is. If it satisfies us, it is because existence itself has come to satisfy us; if it terrifies us, it is because existence itself still terrifies us; if we seek in it a morality, it is because we seek a morality in existence; if we can only be reconciled to it by faith, it is because we still need faith to reconcile us to existence.[44]

Shakespeare's people cannot create a new world, cannot make new terms out of nothing; they can only remake and transpose the world's terms in their own ways. If Hamlet cannot live without belief, Coriolanus cannot live with it. Neither Prospero nor Shakespeare himself can finally get outside or above the world they create: like an island, it is 'rounded', 'our little life/Is rounded with a sleep' (V i 157–8). If there is some new world or some order of meaning beyond this one, such as might do justice to all that goes on so prolifically in the midst of the life of the plays, still with Shakespeare the limits are drawn tight, and filled almost to bursting-point, from the inside of this life. The beyond cannot be forced into being, and there is still so much 'ready' in the interim. 'Shakespeare's plays are so charged with matter that they can seem just as full of unrealised potential after a fine performance as before one.'[45] In my final chapter I shall turn to that sheer excess life of Shakespeare's within the theatre itself.

Chapter 4
The Living Thing:
Time, Place and Thought in Performance

1 'WHAT'S HECUBA TO HIM?'

It is the close identity of fastness to primal thinking that is my
subject in this final chapter. With Shakespeare there often seems
barely time for a word: the thought that finds a word by which to
be thought, in the almost physical pressure of time, seems even thus
to make us more conscious of the transience surrounding it. 'And
what seem'd corporal,/Melted as breath into the wind' (*Macbeth*, I
iii 81–2).

All the more is this so in the theatre. There it is no sooner one
thing than it is another:

> and faster than his tongue
> Did make offence, his eye did heal it up.
>> *As You Like It*, III v 116–17

Minds and bodies, thoughts and actions, words and thoughts: there
is barely time to register one before an audience is aware of the
other again, such is the movement all the time from one level to
another, within the basic physical setting of bodies on the stage.
Shakespeare is a dramatic creator *par excellence* precisely because
the point at which things *happen*, suddenly and dynamically – that
originating point at which either things come into being or one
thing becomes another – matters supremely to him: 'As the world
were now but to begin' (*Hamlet*, IV v 103).

In particular, it is the moment when a character suddenly seems
to have an *inside*, but an inside that must go on held within the
external world, that is so startling. So it is with disguise in *As
You Like It*:

Orlando Fair youth, I would I could make thee believe I love.

Rosalind Me believe it! You may as soon make her that you love
believe it . . .

As You Like It, III ii 375–8

Disguise becomes, beautifully, a way of our hearing what Rosalind
says to her unknowing lover even whilst we imagine what she is
thinking and feeling in her secret self at the very same time. In
Shakespeare, I have been saying, meaning has to go somewhere, has
to be picked up by someone. Here it is displaced upon an audience,
set outside the play, in a paradoxical and tender kind of sharing.

One way of talking about this Shakespearian close-packed speed
of emergence is thus through the idea of performance, a score given
voice and sound, a text brought to sudden, transient life on stage.
As Peter Brook puts it, Shakespeare is not a 'communicator' but
a 'creator' offering something deeper and more dynamic than can
the '"I communicate my message to you" level'.[1] In this chapter
I want to consider time and space within the theatre itself and to
look at Shakespeare's creation of sudden and new configurations at
once both in mind and on stage.

A recent novel by Graham Swift offers us the portrait of a
consciously ineffectual modern man, a failed but still enthusiastic
Renaissance scholar. Here he is thinking again – with more
simplicity than his academic practice had once allowed – about
Shakespeare on the stage. For his recently deceased young wife
had been a great Shakespearian actress:

> That moment when the performance begins! That magic
> moment when the lights go down and the curtain trembles;
> when the pretend thing, the made-up thing, becomes the real
> thing and the audience, in their dark rows, turn to ghosts. How
> can it be? Why should it be? What's Hecuba to him? That
> moment when things come alive.
>
> It doesn't always happen. There is good acting and bad acting
> (I know this). We sit in our seats and think of a thousand things.
> But she could do it, that simple, marvellous thing: she could
> bring things to life.

The writer ponders that last phrase, 'bring things to life', as if
he were a poet. His wife, that re-creator of life, is herself now

dead. Certainly no biographer could now bring things back to life - a biography, and perhaps even a realist novel, would be too flatly explanatory, too slowly considered, altogether too much after-the-event:

> They say I should write her biography. It has been put to me more than once – by friends, by a publisher or two. . . . The life of Ruth Vaughan, actress. Each time, it has come with the soft-toned hint that this might be, as it were, a cure for grief. But it seems to me it would be an impossibility, a falsehood, a sham. It's not the life, is it, but the *life*? The *life*.
>   How was it done?[2]

How can a Shakespearian play – so often more like a dramatic sketch than a totally finished oil-painting, so much a product of a visible set of artificial pretend-things such as disguise or overhearing – how can all this sometimes seem *more* real and immediate, more like sudden life, than writing that claims to be more realistic? It must have to do with Shakespeare's closeness to the very beginning of things – the bare stage, the play linguistically coming into being before our very eyes, the sudden emergence of mind. One of Shakespeare's last acts in the theatre was to make what was apparently a statue come back to life:

> No longer shall you gaze on't, lest your fancy
> May think anon it moves.
>   *The Winter's Tale*, V iii 60–1

And in a sense that was always what he had been doing. Even that space between the end of one line and the beginning of another can seem an invisible but magical stage-direction:

> I look'd toward Birnam, and anon, methought,
> The wood began to move.
>   *Macbeth*, V v 34–5

In both speeches it is: anon (pause) move. If this be magic, let it be an art.
    When Leonardo da Vinci wrote about painting in comparison

with poetry, and music, and carving, what he stressed was the miracle of re-creation, in making out of two dimensions something that seemingly has existence in three and visibly keeps that existence displayed for ever. In contrast Shakespearian drama, in its use of permanent written text made visible only in transient performance, might well seem less dignified a form - even to Shakespeare himself. Yet the actress's bereaved husband finds in Shakespearian acting sometimes a truer dynamic of art than in any other more retrospectively composed and steady form – precisely for its being, so to speak, for ever less permanent. 'The bright day is done,/And we are for the dark' (*Antony and Cleopatra*, V ii 192–3). No wonder the plays at the very heart of themselves depict transience so powerfully. The sheer once-and-for-allness of their dynamic transience offers an image of life *and* the death of life at once.

Every time, in performance, it takes just one unrepeatable second for an actor to get a line miraculously right or botch it. Orson Welles, playing Macbeth not so very well, suddenly reaches for the dagger of the mind, 'Come let me clutch thee: –' and at the felt word 'clutch' his reaching hand simultaneously, momentarily, closes itself upon thin air and falls, making him say, 'I have thee not' (and still the voice, physically thinking in the dark, goes on) 'and yet I see thee still.' How can it *be* that yet I see thee still? The unexplained is so immediately *there* in Shakespearian performance.

By 'performance', says Douglas Oliver:

> I do *not* just mean reading aloud but activating the reader's whole response to the work of art: intellectual, emotional and sonic. . . . [I mean] literature as an active performing art, sets of individual occasions renewed each time a poem or narrative is read.[3]

It is not new interpretations or new concepts that are necessary, but this sheer renewed coming-to-life, when we feel as though we are seeing Shakespeare as for the first time again. What I offer in this final chapter, as in my first one, is a way of thinking about Shakespeare which attempts to re-perform him on the page and in the mind, in a way dynamically analogous to performance to stage.

In *Characters of Shakespear's Plays* Hazlitt says in his essay on *Hamlet*: 'Other dramatic writers give us very fine versions and paraphrases of nature: but Shakespeare, together with his own comments, gives us the original text.' So often when we think about Shakespeare, we do indeed seem to have to go back to the imagined origins of affairs, to that primal dynamic behind creation which his art seems to uncover and depend upon. Shakespeare always begins each play afresh, always starts as if for the first time with the curtain rising upon the basic material of play-making.

Consider a Renaissance myth concerning the origins of theatre. Juan Luis Vives in his *Fabula de homine*, written about 1518, gives a fictional demonstration of the protean nature of human beings in a play called 'Life on Earth'. In *Fabula de homine* the gods, led by Jupiter, set up a theatre for their entertainment: the stalls and seats in the skies were to be occupied by the gods, the earth itself was made as a stage for the actors, comprising all the creatures upon it. But the greatest actor of all was found to be man. For man could change himself continually, putting on at will 'the shapes of a thousand wild beasts: namely, the angry and raging lion, the rapacious and devouring wolf, the fierce and wild boar, the cunning little fox, the lustful and filthy sow, the timid hare, the envious dog, the stupid donkey' – managing this extraordinary variety of earthly impersonations through the separated depiction of the many different passions he had within himself. 'After doing this, he was out of sight for a short time; then the curtain was drawn back and he returned a man, prudent, just, faithful, human, kindly, friendly . . . .' The gods burst into applause. It is marvellous, there seems no shape the creature cannot assume, he has played them all. But there is one more still:

> The gods were not expecting to see him in more shapes when, behold, he was remade into one of their own race, surpassing the nature of man and relying entirely upon a very wise mind. O great Jupiter, what a spectacle for them! At first they were astonished that they, too, should be brought to the stage and impersonated by such a convincing mime, whom they said to be that multiform Proteus, the son of the Ocean.

Almost literally, the gods hardly know where they are: 'the pretend thing, the made-up thing, becomes the real thing and the audience, in their dark rows, turn to ghosts. How can it be? Why should it be? . . . That moment when things come alive.' And then their astonishment at the magic gives way to their sudden applause. And the gods spontaneously decide to ask Juno to let this astonishing creature into the stalls with them, 'to make of him a spectator rather than an actor'.

They are too slow, it is too late for that, they can no longer continue merely to look down on this show. For before anything can be done, the man has changed again: 'he had transcended the characters of the lower gods and was piercing into that inaccessible light surrounded by darkness where Jupiter dwells, of kings and gods the king.' He takes the gods' breath away, he keeps on going, changing, (how far can he go?), pushing further and further up the scale of being:

> When the gods first saw him, they were roused and upset at the thought that their master and father had stooped to the stage. Soon, however, with composed minds, they glanced repeatedly at Jupiter's stall wondering whether he himself was sitting there or whether he had appeared masked in a play.

The audience looks for explanation, for distance, in order not to be taken over:

> Seeing him there, they gazed back again at man and then at Jupiter. With such skill and propriety did he play Jupiter's part that, up and down, from Jupiter's stall to the stage, they kept glancing . . .[4]

Samuel Johnson in his great *Preface* to Shakespeare famously remarked that 'The truth is that the spectators are always in their senses and know, from the first to the last, that the stage is only a stage, and that the players are only players.'[5] But even if we never forget that we are in the theatre, and indeed all the more strangely for our physical confinement there, the mind can find itself spinning in ways analogous to Vives's description. For, as I must now try to show, the most 'magical' moments in the theatre are mentally analogous to that point at which the eye doubles back and forth between Jupiter on stage and Jupiter in the stalls. Such

an audience as Vives describes finds even in itself what it is fearful
of considering in looking at the two Jupiters: *that minds and their
thoughts move*, do not simply stay put in their bodies – even though
they also do have to keep coming back to them.

In Shakespeare's geometry, invisible lines of relation go back
and forth across the stage and between stage and auditorium. The
boundaries of reality are not as solid as they literally appear to be.
For we see the characters: they are not just fictional, they exist.
But they do not see us. We are not in their presence, although they
are in ours. Yet although the characters and we do not occupy the
same *space*, we do all occupy the same *time*.[6] So from our distance
we bear witness to Hermione's helpless but self-aware innocence
and there is nothing we can do:

> Since what I am to say, must be but that
> Which contradicts my accusation, and
> The testimony on my part, no other
> But what comes from myself, it shall scarce boot me
> To say 'not guilty': mine integrity,
> Being accounted falsehood, shall, as I express it,
> Be so receiv'd. But thus, if powers divine
> Behold our human actions (as they do)
> I doubt not then but innocence shall make
> False accusation blush, and tyranny
> Tremble at patience. You, my lord, best know
> (Who least will seem to do so) my past life . . .
>
> *The Winter's Tale*, III ii 22–33

Hermione can distinguish her *self* from the false position in
which she is put, but 'mine integrity', she also knows, will still
be vulnerable to being misinterpreted. Meanwhile, surrogately
moved as her alternative audience, we are still not those people
on the stage who should 'best know', nor are we 'powers divine'
either. Although we are as it were in the gods, uncomfortingly we
are not them.

We watch King Lear holding his head in his hands and, says
Stanley Cavell, 'There is nothing we can do and we know there
is nothing we can do. Tragedy is meant to make sense of that
condition.'[7] But 'make sense of' in Shakespeare may mean only
'put into words':

Lear O! let me not be mad, not mad, sweet heaven;
       Keep me in temper; I would not be mad!

King Lear, v 43–4

Lear physically holds his head in his hands because *inside* that head –
in an invisible dimension only available to the audience through the
operation of words upon their imagination – he may well be going
out of his mind. Once again, we are not 'sweet heaven' to answer
that desperate prayer of a lonely mind implosively overtaken by
thought of its own increasingly insanity. But the rule is simply
this: the more Shakespeare opens the distance between stage
and audience, the more he then closes it again emotionally. In
Shakespeare's fixed and bursting medium, the audience feels for
the characters emotionally and imaginatively precisely because it
cannot get near them at the more direct, physical level and, in real
life, might not even want to.

Sympathy is always paradoxical in Shakespeare's theatre. Lear
and Hermione are human beings at the limits of what they can
know or do about themselves, in lieu of other people knowing or
helping them. But if we as audience stand emotionally in place of
those who cannot or will not help, the characters themselves are
experiencing their helplessness for us, reminding us of ours, like
ritual substitutes or scapegoats. No wonder in some secondary sense
we *feel for* Lear or Hermione, when at a deeper and more primary
level they are feeling for us, almost literally in the theatre in *place* of
us. With the whole space tense with such overlaps, sympathy here
is archaic, closer to magic than to liberalism.

People in the audience see part of themselves in some character
on the stage, even as within the play that character sees part of
himself in someone else, or part of someone else in him. The same
dynamic happens everywhere.

Thus Lady Macbeth feels something of herself has gone into her
husband, leaving her oddly small and even lonely in asking now
powerlessly, 'What's to be done?':

Macbeth Be innocent of the knowledge, dearest chuck,
         Till thou applaud the deed. Come, seeling Night,
         Scarf up the tender eye of pitiful Day.

Macbeth, III ii 44–7

It is in part her own former language that he now speaks: 'Come, you Spirits/That tend on mortal thoughts, unsex me here' (I v 40–1).

Conversely, even as Hamlet felt himself contaminated by the actions of his uncle, Claudius equally seems to feel something of Hamlet inside him when he cries: 'So like the hectic in my blood he rages' (*Hamlet*, IV iii 69). It is not just an external description, it really feels as though Hamlet has got lodged under his very skin, as Lear feels it with his daughters:

> But yet thou art my flesh, my blood, my daughter;
> Or rather a disease that's in my flesh,
> Which I must needs call mine.
>
> *King Lear*, II iv 219–21

The world seems made of life-stuff that keeps going in and out of the supposedly fixed boundaries of the individual self: it invades, it is expelled, it comes back to mind, it takes part of you even from yourself.

And so too at the same time between stage and audience. For let us take this thought of invisible associations back to Shakespeare even at his earliest stages.

In *The Comedy of Errors* the Syracuse side of the two sets of twins, Antipholus and Dromio, finds in Ephesus a strange world which seems unthinkingly to know them and claim them for its own. Why do they keep being recognized, given a ready-made wife or mistress, abused for they know not what?

> Luciana   Why prat'st thou to thy self and answer'st not?
>   Dromio, thou drone, thou snail, thou slug, thou sot.
> Syr. Dro.   I am transformed, master, am I not?
> Syr. Ant.   I think thou art in mind, and so am I.
> Syr. Dro.   Nay, master, both in mind and in my shape.
> Syr. Ant.   Thou hast thine own form.
> Syr. Dro.   No, I am an ape.
> Luciana   If thou art chang'd to aught, 'tis to an ass.
>   *The Comedy of Errors*, II ii 193–9

This is a beautifully comic version of Vives on the magical protean capacity of human beings – not least because these powerful changes (drone, snail, slug, sot, ape, ass) come helplessly upon the pair from *outside*. The two look at each other as if they were, inside themselves, their own baffled audience while at the same time, outside, the involuntary actors. What are all these others seeing in us? Meanwhile the unanxious real audience is thus released from part of its own role to begin to imagine, half seriously: what is it like to be inside those two bodies up there, with minds which seem to have no place save through speaking one to another? 'I am transformed, master, am I not?' Significantly it is only in aside that Antipholus of Syracuse can say at the scene's end:

Am I in earth, in heaven, or in hell?
Sleeping or waking, mad or well advis'd?
Known unto these, and to myself disguis'd.

III ii 212–14

'To myself disguis'd': that is poignantly paradoxical. It is about becoming a stranger to oneself within, when not recognized from without as what you think you are. Like the situation in which it is uttered, the language itself has a meaning too big for an Antipholus entirely to retain in himself. For Antipholus takes that *externally* referring word 'disguis'd' *into* himself, as if metaphor in Shakespeare were also itself a sign of how this world can be turned around, inside-out, outside-in. Meanwhile the very thought that the character's situation provokes, but which he himself cannot quite have or, having, cannot quite understand inside the play, is shifted on to the audience, witnessing tenderly in his place outside.

In Shakespeare, that is to say, we are more than usually aware that the way in which the audience is outside the play is not just determined by the sheerly physical nature of the setting. There is an invisible mental process involved – which is not simply that of sitting back and being detached. For there are complex rebounds that take place between stage and audience – as if in the room of the theatre there was one whole thing going on, albeit between two different places, on stage and in the auditorium. There is an *atmosphere* going in and out and around all the human shapes and forms in the place, like the magic atmosphere of Campanella's world where everything is full of sensation and feeling.

And what keeps the audience mentally off the stage is, I say, only part of the same dynamic as can happen within and between characters on it. In *Much Ado About Nothing* Benedick says:

> I do much wonder that one man, seeing how much another man is a fool when he dedicates his behaviours to love, will, after he hath laughed at such shallow follies in others, become the argument of his own scorn by falling in love; and such a man is Claudio.
>
> II iii 7–12

and this immediately before his own fall into love! But then immediately after it he remarks:

> Well, every one can master a grief but he that has it.
>
> III ii 26–7

It is clear that the two speeches are two different sides of the same coin. He first of all says: I cannot understand how people can put themselves into such a situation, knowing what they did beforehand outside it. And then he argues: Even though a person would be wiser outside, I cannot now see how one can possibly get out there again. Thus, things are said about the view from within and the view from outside that the audience, outside looking in, is itself kindredly privy to in the spatial dynamics.

The whole of *As You Like It* is based upon people feeling the same feeling and yet still feeling different from each other. Phebe replies to love-sick Silvius's cry of you-wait-till-it-happens-to-you:

> But till that time
> Come thou not near me; and when that time comes,
> Afflict me with thy mocks, pity me not,
> As till that time I shall not pity thee.
>
> III v 31–4

But (thirty lines later) she falls in love herself, with the disguised Rosalind, and softens. Silvius then comes back at her with:

If you do sorrow at my grief in love,
By giving love, your sorrow and my grief
Were both extermined.

III v 87–9

But if the Phebe who loves Rosalind unsuccessfully now feels like
the Silvius who is hopelessly in love with *her*, even so she still loves
Rosalind and not Silvius. She may feel the same, she may even thus
feel sympathetic; but though half of her is like Silvius in being the
victim of unrequited love, the other half is unlike him, and more
like Rosalind is to her, in being that unhappy love's unloving cause.
This might make a more complex character understand both Silvius
more and Rosalind more, whilst still having to remain herself – like
Viola caught in *Twelfth Night* between Orsino and Olivia. But
Shakespeare is not naturalistic: small characters may suddenly have
great language. And in such a case, with Phebe and with Silvius,
this language then seems to derive more from the situation than
the character, and the audience has more of the thought that Phebe
creates than she herself can or will. Shakespeare loves it when the
sheer predicament or being of a character far outweighs his or her
individual capacity for intelligence or selflessness: at some level the
deficiency does not matter to him – the thought still comes through
somewhere, for the sake of life itself and for the audience. For
suddenly, someone in the audience thinks: this is not just a Speech
but an *Idea* that emerges so quickly and insubstantially out of this
physical realm, out of the play itself, catching us. Thoughts are not
mere settled commentary, they are immediately embodied *as* (and
in and *from*) people on the stage. Shakespeare knows how thoughts
about a person are going on at the same time as the person himself
or herself who is their object; how the person may also get in the
way of those thoughts, almost physically preventing their separate
time and room; how to take the person away is then to see the
thoughts alone now taking the person's place – for Shakespeare can
use the trick of this thing inside his plays too:

She dying, as it must be so maintained,
Upon the instant that she was accused,
Shall be lamented, pitied, and excused
Of every hearer. . . . So will it fare with Claudio.

When he shall hear she died upon his words,
Th'idea of her life shall sweetly creep
Into his study of imagination.
>   *Much Ado About Nothing*, IV i 214–17, 222–5

The *idea* of her *life*. Sight, says Ficino, 'is midway between intellect and touch'[8]: when we look on as audience, it is as if, in the theatre, we are in on the very beginning of thinking. For there are moments when ideas rise beside or in place of persons, when seeing for one second gives way to thinking, or at another is close to reaching out emotionally in lieu of being able to touch or affect.

We are dealing here with how plays begin to make one think and think suddenly – with thought-in-performance erupting out of a physical situation. When Shakespeare creates thought it is not a casual and separate thing, to suit a detached spectator before a play or a viewer in front of a picture. It is thrown out of a play, like a displaced part of what it reflects upon, drawing the audience in to receive it.

It is as though the very place of thinking in relation to life on the stage is being almost literally worked out. Consider an example of *internal* overhearing – when characters become an audience to each other within the play, and when what an audience might have realized on behalf of a character is itself actually brought back on stage and re-embodied in that character there.

In *Much Ado About Nothing* it is not difficult to see the symmetry between Benedick thinking that he is secretly overhearing what Leonato makes up concerning Beatrice:

> O, she tore the letter into a thousand halfpence, railed at herself, that she should be so immodest to write to one that she knew would flout her. 'I measure him', says she, 'by my own spirit, for I should flout him, if he writ to me, yea, though I love him I should.'
>   *Much Ado About Nothing*, II iii 138–43

and Beatrice being tricked into overhearing Ursula and Hero's fictitious account of the love of Benedick:

Ursula And therefore certainly it were not good
			She knew his love, lest she'll make sport at it.
Hero Why, you speak truth. I never yet saw man,
			How wise, how noble, young, how rarely featur'd
			But she would spell him backward: if fair-fac'd,
			She would swear the gentleman should be her sister;
			If black, why, Nature, drawing of an antic,
			Made a foul blot; if tall, a lance ill-headed;
			If low, an agate very vilely cut;
			If speaking, why, a vane blown with all winds;
			If silent, why, a block moved with none.
			So turns she every man the wrong side out,
			And never gives to truth and virtue that
			Which simpleness and merit purchaseth. . . .
			But who dare tell her so?

											III i 57–74

In Chapter Two we saw how in *Love's Labour's Lost* Berowne was gloriously caught out, scoffing at hypocrisy most hypocritically. Here Benedick and Beatrice are courtiers who are one step on from Berowne. It is not that they first overhear and then are overheard; overhearing, each vulnerably sees a version of himself or herself as others see them, in one fell swoop. It is only when the friends externalize the habit of proud scorn which Beatrice and Benedick would characteristically each feel for the direct expression of the other's love, that Beatrice and Benedick can be free of that scorn within them. The disdain had become as much a pleasure as a defence: it is almost a shame to take it off and perhaps still not wise to walk naked. But just as with Claudio, soldier-turned-lover –

But now I am returned and that war-thoughts
Have left their places vacant, in their rooms
Come thronging soft and delicate desires

											I i 281–3

– so there is some intuitive law here: that something seen or overheard from without must take the very *place* of its equivalent within. And 'in their *rooms*/Come *thronging* soft and delicate desires': as I have tried to show in Chapters One and Two, it is the interaction of two such words as those that is the Shakespearian dynamic.

In both instances, with Beatrice as with Benedick, it is their friends who now, in their turn, are 'spelling backwards' these back-to-front protagonists, in order to make them more straightforward. For the lies are like truth: each cussed lover can confess a latent love only if the other already has – hence the double-bind. What we have here is Sidney's 'just exchange' done outside-in (that favourite mode of Shakespeare's): 'My true love hath my heart, and I have his,/By just exchange, one for the other given.' It only takes so simple a means to catch these two determinedly complicated characters!

Yet although such overhearing *is* a simple enough device, especially when done separately and successively, here the simplicity is doubled and redoubled upon itself. It is doubled of course in terms of the overhearing being done twice, once with Benedick and once again with Beatrice. For the two scenes must somehow fit together if the friends' plot is to work. But, to add to the emerging complexity – as if human complexity were only a series of multiplying variations played upon the model of simplicity itself – a redoubling also goes on within each scene separately. Thus Benedick, hearing how Beatrice measures her spirit by his, begins to measure his by what is now said to be hers. And Beatrice likewise is herself turned wrong (vulnerable) side out precisely by hearing how she does the same to men like Benedick. And both are wrong here, in falling for the friends' deception, unless in each being wrong they make the other right.

For all this, put together, is actually quite as hard to spell out and hold in one's head as any rhapsody on love by Ficino:

> He who loves another, but is not loved by the other, lives nowhere. . . . But where the beloved responds in love . . . a strange thing happens. Whenever two people embrace each other in mutual affection, this one lives in that; that one, in this. Such people exchange themselves with each other; and each gives himself to the other in order to receive the other. How they give themselves up while they forget themselves, I see. But how they receive each other I do not understand. . . . Certainly this one has himself, but *in* that one. That one also possesses

himself, but in this one. Certainly while I love you loving me, I find myself in you thinking about me, and I recover myself, lost by myself through my own negligence, in you, preserving me. You do the same in me. . . . And this again seems amazing. . . . I am closer to you than to myself, since I approach myself in no other way than through you as an intermediary.[9]

As Don Pedro says, 'The sport will be when they hold one an opinion of another's dotage. . . . That's the scene that I would see' (II iii 207–9): we too. But we have to wait for act V scene iv:

Benedick They swore that you were almost sick for me.
Beatrice They swore that you were well-nigh dead for me.

                                                               80–1

Is it symmetry or competition? Will it be their likeness or their mutual undoing? But before we can get to V iv, these two scenes, II iii and III i, are each a little invented world. If either were true, the world would go right. But neither is true separately and in themselves, and they can become true only if they can be matched together, married as it were. Otherwise, like rejected lovers, the scenes will 'live nowhere'. These two invented worlds are symmetrical, created out of the same principles. But they are also, as in a mirror, opposites. As so often in Shakespeare, the overlap that marks the relation of sameness and difference is crucial. According to Giordano Bruno,

we see such familiarity between one contrary and another that the one agrees more with the other than like with like. . . . Justice has no act except where there is error, harmony is not effectuated except where there is contrariety.

Conversely some things, 'physically, mathematically and morally', are simply too alike to produce harmony together:

The spherical does not repose on the spherical, because they touch each other at a point; but the concave rests on the convex. And, morally, the proud man cannot get together with the proud man.[10]

Here again is a situational geometry congenial to a mind like Shakespeare's.

But what has this to do with theatre? In fact, I want to say, actors do usefully recognize the underlying secret of such patterning dynamics of attraction and repulsion within performance-space. For example, Mark Rylance in an interview before a recent production of *Much Ado*:

> Since playing Hamlet I stumbled on some lecture courses on the hermetic and cabbalistic teachings of the Renaissance, and they proved really illuminating to my work, to the Shakespeare plays particularly. They opened doors to the basic structures that playwrights of that time may have been working with, in their attempts to mirror nature as closely as possible through those old observations of nature, and how the more invisible workings of nature seem to lie at the heart of it.

In Empedocles's twofold story, for instance, Love brings the elements of the world together, the many into one, while Strife keeps them apart, the one made into many – the universe itself constituted in the very sway between each other of these two primal forces. Hunger, says Bruno, is as like troublesome as is its opposite, satiety: we are only satisfied when in motion between the two, always on the move when what satisfies becomes what wearies. 'Love', says Ficino, quoting Dionysus the pseudo-Areopagite, 'we understand to be a certain grafted and mixing virtue.'[11] We need the mixtures. Thus with regard to *Much Ado* itself:

> There's always a plan, and it's always to do with uniting things, which is really the negative side of love, wanting to unite everything as quickly as possible. Whereas on the other [hand] . . . you have the more intellectual impulses: to separate, to take things apart in order to look at them. The extreme of that is to isolate things. Don John . . . is really to do with the intelligence, the side that limits the energy and makes it into form.[12]

Connect and separate, separate and connect. Beatrice and Benedick themselves use these forces at entirely practical levels to strive lovingly, as do actors in what the play calls 'working days', turning what seems solemnly abstract even into what is comic. Thus Beatrice as director, when Leonato elaborately offers his daughter Hero to Count Claudio:

> Speak, Count, 'tis your cue.
>
> II i 287

Go on, follow life's script while thinking yourself so very spontaneous! Then Beatrice (irritated, affectionate) to Hero, when Claudio, taking that cue, then goes on interminably about his love:

> Speak cousin, or, if you cannot, stop his mouth with a kiss, and let him not speak neither.
>
> II i 292–3

– for goodness' sake come on, and use young mouths properly: 'unite everything as quickly as possible'. But then says Beatrice, so used to herself, only half seriously sad, yet still separately and vulnerably so:

> *Beatrice* Thus goes everyone to the world but I, and I am sunburnt. I may sit in a corner and cry 'Heigh-ho for a husband!'
> *Don Pedro* Lady Beatrice, I will get you one.

Or, she replies to Don Pedro, will you yourself be the one? Don Pedro then follows suit, automatically or spontaneously, seriously in himself or matching her as one of a jesting pair – we do not know and nor perhaps does he or she yet:

> Will you have me, lady?

It is suddenly serious, dangerous, close: 'Will you have me, lady?' 'No, my lord . . .' She jokes him away whom she herself brought on: '– unless I might have another for working days: your Grace is too costly to wear every day'. These are 'the more intellectual impulses: to separate'. Then apologetically she asks him to accept something which is not a joke – she asks him to accept her for herself: you know me, it's all right isn't it for me to be this?

> But I beseech your Grace pardon me, I was *born* to speak all mirth and no matter.

At once Don Pedro again picks up, and can again work securely within, the comic language which is now her acknowledged characteristic, her safely beloved and implicitly familiar way:

> Your silence most offends me, and to be merry best becomes you, for out o'question, you were born in a merry hour.
>
> II i 299–314

It is all right, but not quite right. For all this is no more and no less than Beatrice's own now habitual pattern – not quite how she was born to be but what she has become. And only another who knew it and matched it, who was both similar enough to and sufficiently different from Beatrice, could take her and her way into the wider pattern of the pairing world. Indeed, Don Pedro immediately thinks of Benedick, and the plots of overhearing begin from there:

> *Don Pedro* By my troth, a pleasant-spirited lady.
> *Leonato* There's little of the melancholy element in her, my lord; she is never sad but when she sleeps, and not ever sad then . . .
> *Don Pedro* She cannot endure to hear tell of a husband.
> *Leonato* O, by no means, she mocks all her wooers out of suit.
> *Don Pedro* She were an excellent wife for Benedick.
>
> II i 320–9

When an audience, hearing Leonato and Don Pedro call Beatrice happy, knows that this is not entirely true, and yet that it would be no more true entirely to deny it, calling her wit simply a sorry defence, then indeed Shakespeare has succeeded in creating a character. Beatrice has become something more than the sum of the separate thoughts which people have of her.

And it is that defiantly *uninterpretable* quality, that excess called life, which remains so good in the final union of Benedick and Beatrice. For as II iii and III i must match, so the following, taken from the beginning and the end of the play, also come together in time:

> *Don Pedro* Well, as time shall try. 'In time the savage bull doth bear the yoke.'
> *Benedick* The savage bull may; but if ever the sensible Benedick

. . . let me be vilely painted, and in such great letters as they write, 'Here is good horse to hire,' let them signify under my sign, 'Here you may see Benedick, the married man.'

I i 241–8

Don Pedro How dost thou, 'Benedick, the married man'?
Benedick I'll tell thee what, Prince; a college of wit-crackers cannot flout me out of my humour. . . . In brief, since I do purpose to marry, I will think nothing to any purpose that the world can say against it; and therefore never flout at me for what I have said against it; for man is a giddy thing, and this is my conclusion. . . . Therefore play, music. Prince thou art sad; get thee a wife, get thee a wife! There is no staff more reverend than one tipped with horn.

V iv 98–107, 120–2

I am caught out, I know, but I am not going to be embarrassed (or not much), if what I am caught out by most of all is happiness. It's like Captain Wentworth at the end of Jane Austen's *Persuasion*, who ruefully 'must endeavour to subdue my mind to my fortune. I must learn to brook being happier than I deserve' – there are worse fates. Look at their change of heart, some may say of Beatrice and Benedick. Look at how they must really have loved each other all along, say others. Either way, retorts Benedick, I am not going to be reminded, or solemnly psychologized, or turned back in time when I am going forward with it. I am not going to be consistent, and I will think whatever suits my present happiness, even down to conclusions about general human inconsistency and its merits! Benedick mocks in himself, in Beatrice, and even more of course in everyone else, the illusion of living by 'no more than reason' (V iv 77). I will praise marriage not through objective reason but simply because I am going to be married – that is both utterly and straightforwardly fitting and wittily self-acknowledging of an impudent relativism. And if it comes to looking back then there is this to say to Don Pedro: 'Prince thou art sad; get thee a wife, get thee a wife!', recalling as it unknowingly does 'Will you have me, lady?'

In the end the problem of the reconciliation of Beatrice and Benedick in their two fooled-into-love scenes is simply overtaken

by events, by the beautiful interweaving of the Hero–Claudio plot.
As if through life's accidents, Hero's predicament subordinates the
tiresome luxury of detailed emotional negotiation to the quarrelling
couple's collaboration in a more immediate external necessity. Yet
when our two overhearing scenes are finally brought together in
the persons of Benedick and Beatrice meeting hereafter, the scenes
still have, in overlapping, to square with each other in the one big
outside world which they have sought to represent:

> *Benedick* And I pray thee now tell me, for which of my bad parts
> didst thou first fall in love with me?
> *Beatrice* For them all together. . . . But for which of my good
> parts did you first suffer love for me?
> *Benedick* 'Suffer love' – a good epithet, I do suffer love indeed,
> for I love thee against my will.
> *Beatrice* In spite of your heart, I think. Alas, poor heart! If you
> spite it for my sake, I will spite it for yours, for I will never love
> that which my friend hates.
> *Benedick* Thou and I are too wise to woo peaceably.
>
> V ii 56–67

It is still the old pattern of witty quarrel, for they need the old
form: with its familiar pleasures it even now protects the more
vulnerable content. But the most loving word there that saves the
day is no lovey-dovey word but simply, beautifully, and almost
involuntarily, 'my friend'. Beatrice makes sure that everyone
knows that she could still turn the neo-Platonic love-language
of Ficino inside-out into a new reason for spite: if you spite
your heart, I will too – out of pure loving sympathy! So too
with Benedick, protesting he will live in her heart, die in her lap
and be buried in her eyes – 'and moreover, I will go with thee to
thy uncle's' (V ii 95–6). It is the bathetic 'moreover' that is fine:
at once comic and practical, less important than the big stuff and
more so. Both Beatrice and Benedick are 'too wise' to admit to
themselves or to others the changes that have gone on beneath the
surface – 'for which of my good parts did you . . . ?' – there stop
and leave it: the changes weren't so very many, were more turns
than changes of the basic stuff, and anyway the thing works well
enough without further admission. For by the time they find out
how they were gulled into love, it is simply too late:

Leonato Come, cousin, I am *sure* you love the gentleman.

V iv 84

It is like 'and moreover': the secondary thing takes over from the apparently loftier flights of high passion, but with a tender message still left tacit and implicit in its apparently downright realism. 'And moreover, I will go with thee.' Beatrice and Benedick quarrel almost to the end and might still. The pair of them can still keep the old form of combative language going between them - but as something more like an old 'friend' than anything else. Successfully to make implicit changes whilst still remaining within the same basic structure as that pair do – this is one of the achievements of comedy, where minds in all their twists and turns are still at home and embedded in the play's accommodating pattern.

Thus, Benedick will bring to Beatrice a Benedick secondarily affected by Beatrice's alleged passion; Beatrice will bring to Benedick a second Beatrice moved by Benedick's supposed infatuation: as if (heaven forbid!) primary love, in both cases, never existed – or at least was never to be expressed by such as had resolutely once and for all passed over the stage of being Romeo and Juliet. Something went on between these two, years ago, before the play itself started, but we are never now to know quite what. In comedy, despite and because of old primal fractures in human nature, something consciously more *secondary* will do, serving as a sheer implicit language between two such as Beatrice and Benedick. The love poems they each wrote in private are used in evidence against them, for privately each of them wrote of their love even as they now half try to deny it. They are caught out again and they still escape. For it is their neo-denials and semi-reluctant admissions which actually contain the truer feeling of love precisely for half hiding it: 'A miracle! Here's our hands against our hearts!' 'A miracle' is both jest and earnest:

> Why do we think that Love is a *magician*? Because all the power of magic consists in love. An act of magic is the attraction of one thing by another in accordance with a certain natural kinship. The parts of this world, like the organs of one enormous living being, borrow and loan each other's natures. . . . Acts of magic, therefore, are acts of nature, and art is her handmaiden.[13]

'That magic moment when the lights go down and the curtain trembles.' So then, as the two borrow and loan each other's language in the grafting of love, Beatrice's earlier 'Speak cousin, or, if you cannot, stop his mouth with a kiss' is taken and given back in kind by Benedick:

> *Benedick* Come, I will have thee, but by this light I take thee for pity.
> *Beatrice* I would not deny you, but by this good day I yield upon great persuasion, and partly to save your life, for I was told you were in a consumption.
> *Benedick* Peace! I will stop your mouth. *[Kisses her]*
>
> V iv 92–7

The swift turn of defence of oneself into attack of the other is their form of sharing; for the risky insultingness of 'for pity', 'upon great persuasion', turns out actually to be both well appreciated and quite safe. And the cheeky bravado of these excuses is only equalled by their irrelevance. But it is the sheer excess of exuberant life-spiritedness over the minimalism of relevance and of underlying understanding that is the heartening triumph here.

I am saying therefore that the characters' implicit knowingness of their situation re-embodies the audience's underlying thoughts for us. And then the audience's thoughts and interpretations simply do not need to be spelt out: there is a reality in the relationship between Beatrice and Benedick which is greater than any interpretation of that relationship, and the relationship works well on its own. It is as if here, now, in invulnerable Beatrice and Benedick the thoughts are back *in* the life, in right proportion to it. And life in comedy is where there is always something bigger and more joyous, or something more alive, or something more likely to work – or simply just something more – than thoughts. At such a point it is as if in the experiment of theatre, human being itself is split into two attracted halves: one part of us goes with the play which in its continuous presentness is life itself; while the other part of us is ourselves as audience thinking about it – the audience, that is to say, as the repository for that thinking about life which has barely time or space for itself while life is being lived. In comedy it feels good that this is so, it frees life to be life; in tragedy for much the same reason and through much the same dynamic, it feels bad to be a mere helpless witness of pain and waste. It is not just 'I had rather have a fool to make me merry than experience to make me sad' (*As You Like It*, IV i 25–6); in *Much Ado* Beatrice and Benedick are too experienced to be sad.

2 THE WORD AND THE ACTION

Words without thoughts never to heaven go.

Hamlet, III iii 98

Comparing the arts, Leonardo put painting ahead of music, and seeing before hearing. Of hearing music, he said, 'As it is born so it dies'. Painting, in contrast, lasts independently and solidly and 'does not need to be reborn in numerous performances, like music'. Poetry too, thought Leonardo, can never be grasped as a simultaneous whole as, spatially, a painting can:

> The poet may wish to rival the painter, but he does not allow for the fact that the words with which he delineates the elements of beauty are separated from one another by time, which leaves voids between them. . . . A poem . . . does not achieve any more grace than music would produce if each note were to be heard on its own at various intervals, failing to produce any harmony – just as if you wished to show a face part by part, always covering the section previously shown. In such a demonstration . . . the eye cannot embrace all of it within its faculty of vision simultaneously.[14]

Is the greatest human art that which most seems to transcend time?

Perhaps the finest single thing in Shakespeare and certainly the greatest point in Hamlet's own life is:

> If it be now, 'tis not to come; if it be not to come, it will be now; if it be not now, yet it will come. The readiness is all.

Hamlet, V ii 216–18

But it is an achievement of poise and belief which although it is *about* time, and although it is attained as the end of the play's whole process of time, is also itself still *in* time:

Had I but time – as this fell sergeant, Death,
Is strict in his arrest – O, I could tell you –
But let it be.

V ii 341–3

Let it be, for 'it' does not stay still; there is no one else in the play who, recognizing the attitude, can take it out of the context that has created it and entirely save it, not even Horatio; its value is precisely that it goes back inside Hamlet's life, it goes into Hamlet's death. For this is Hamlet abandoning the idea that we can save our lives by *knowing* them. Knowledge of life cannot substitutively anticipate, compensate for, or replace what is its own subject: life as experienced in time. It is life in time, and a corresponding human attitude to life in time, that Hamlet finds again in place of his previous commitment to conscious knowledge. It forfeits any eternal grasp of the whole of life.

That the moment which the whole of a life has led up to, that the moment which gives that life its greatest possible view *of* life as a whole, should itself be not permanent and separate and final, but should be absorbed into acquiescence in whatever happens next – that is the sort of equivocal value that is consonant with performance as described by Leonardo on hearing music: 'as it is born so it dies'. To one such as Leonardo, Hamlet's all too hard-won wisdom is there only before it is gone.

But that is precisely the equivocal achievement of Shakespearian drama. There and then gone, Shakespearian drama is closer to life itself than to that substantial preservation of it against time which Leonardo believed great art should make for. But that is also the point of the thing for Hamlet: that the only real acceptance is acceptance where there is absolutely no saving consideration – the after-life in some shape or form – no, nothing at all held on to as part of some deal.

We have been witnessing how in Shakespearian drama poetry is made into the sort of performance-in-time that Leonardo took music to be: seeing made as transient as hearing; mortal thinking itself passing away through time. Actors learn to accept and even trust the process:

You play each scene or each beat, however contradictory, or however incompatible it seems with what has gone before or comes after. You play the moment for its integrity, for what it is. Then by the end of the play, the character is an accumulation of all those separate moments.[15]

But by the end of the play, the play is over, as in death. And the audience is often left in after-shock saying, all too late, as with Coriolanus to his mother (V iii 184):

> What have you done?

What *does* Shakespeare do – so quickly, yet so transiently? As I suggested at the end of my discussion of *The Tempest* in Chapter Three, he seems to have no permanent philosophy: so with what then does he leave us?

Shakespeare's art is the quintessential theatre, where the power of language meets most dramatically the force of time. Let us therefore take these questions about his drama to a practical rehearsal of some of Shakespeare's words, and follow the actors.

In a televised master-class some years ago Janet Suzman directed a drama student in a fast-moving soliloquy from *Much Ado*. It was Benedick's speech immediately after overhearing his friends' talk of Beatrice's secret love for him. I here print it, for reasons that will be clear in a moment, in the Folio punctuation, so flowingly if confusingly full of commas and colons where modern editors put full stops, dashes, or semi-colons:

> This can be no trick, the conference was sadly borne, they have the truth of this from Hero, they seem to pity the lady: it seems her affections have their full bent: love me? why, it must be requited: I hear how I am censured, they say I will bear myself proudly, if I perceive the love come from her: they say too that she will rather die than give any sign of affection: I did never think to marry, I must not seem proud, happy are they that hear their detractions and can put them to mending: they say the lady is fair, 'tis a truth, I can bear them witness: and virtuous, 'tis so, I cannot reprove it, and wise, but for loving me, by my troth, it is no addition to her wit, nor no great argument of her folly; for I will be horribly in love with her, I may chance have some odd quirks and remnants of wit broken on me, because I have railed so long against marriage: but doth not the appetite alter? a

man loves the meat in his youth that he cannot endure in his age.
Shall quips and sentences, and these paper bullets of the brain
awe a man from the career of his humour? No, the world must
be peopled. When I said I would die a bachelor, I did not think I
should live till I were married, here comes Beatrice: by this day,
she's a fair lady, I do spy some marks of love in her.

II iii 212–37

No pause, but suddenly and at once: 'I do spy some marks of love
in her.' Well, do you now, Benedick? You didn't want much per-
suading. . . . It's marvellous that Shakespeare tacitly communicates
these crude paraphrases within the tone and between the lines of
his elegance.

At any rate, the drama student in the master-class read the
speech through, on and on, hurriedly skidding off the surface
of it. He didn't know where to stop. When he did pause
or intonate, it was for too long. The words, as Leonardo put
it, became separated from one another by time, leaving voids
between them, 'just as if you showed a face part by part,
always covering the section previously shown'. The face which
the student wished to portray disintegrated in the very showing
part by part, without overlap. And indeed the Folio punctuation
makes the poor student's difficulty most understandable. Yet here
is the challenge of being Benedick – quickly preparing a change
of mind which has virtually happened already; having to change
gear here in the very racing of his mind and almost at the same
time having to try to hide that rather self-delighted moment of
transition that will (he already anticipates) cost him jibes. Half the
dupe of his own desires, half the exploiter of them, he brazenly
improvises morality out of desire: 'Happy are they that hear their
detractions and can put them to mending.' How do you show it
all – these transparent disguises that none the less must be seen
by the audience and not pointed to by the actor – and make it
come alive? In all its shifts and gear-changes Benedick's is so fast
a mind.

In a letter to Mrs Thrale in May 1780 Samuel Johnson writes of
just such speed of movement in referring to 'the noble disdain of
regularity . . . the graceful negligence of transition' which he finds
in Shakespeare's works:

Such were the transitions of the ancients, which now seem abrupt because the intermediate idea is lost to modern understandings.

It was precisely the tacit intermediate idea that Janet Suzman put back into Benedick's lightning-quick monologue for her modern student, turning it bit by bit into interior dialogue. I recall, doubtless roughly, those quick, half sly, knowing interruptions of hers, which tried to get the unspoken missing links of thought back into the student's speech:

> *Student This can be no trick*
> *Suzman [sotto voce]* Why not?
> *Student the conference was sadly borne*
> *Suzman* Ye-es. But what else?
> *Student they have the truth of this from Hero*
> *Suzman* And is Hero trustworthy?
> *Student [Nods]*
> *Suzman* What else?
> *Student they seem to pity the lady*
> *Suzman* Pity her? Why?
> *Student it seems her affections have their full bent*
> *Suzman* Oh! interesting . . . She then . . . Who? . . .
> *Student love me?*
> *Suzman* . . . loves you! What are you going to do, tell her to shove off?
> *Student why, it must be requited*
> *Suzman* Must! By you?

And so on. 'Other dramatic writers give us very fine paraphrases of nature but Shakespeare gives us the original text.' Janet Suzman's interjections were not like the paraphrases that literary criticism too often makes of Shakespeare. In their consciously shorthand simplicity, they *uncovered* some of the layers of that 'original' text – by getting the student to hear and speak the lines (rather than try to 'act' them at second hand), and to do so in monologue as a form of unconsummated mental dialogue. Her interrupting echoings were the externally physical equivalents in tone to what the mind feels and hears from itself in filling 'the voids' between the words. Shakespeare, I repeat, abhors those voids, as Leonardo

called them. It is as if in such rehearsals of Shakespeare we are
in at a version of the original act of rebounding interchange
between words and mind, mind and words. For Shakespeare
takes us as close to the fresh minting of thinking in relation
to the formation of language, and as close to the formation
of character by such an act, as we can ever get. Hamlet's
self-overtaking sentence

> I do not know
> Why yet I live to say this thing's to do
> Sith I have cause, and will, and strength, and means
> To do't

Hamlet, IV iv 43-6

is here, comically, Benedick's:

> When I said I would die a bachelor, I did not think I should live
> till I were married.

There is no use paraphrasing Shakespeare *except* in the quick instant
of hearing him. Turning him afterwards into a writer of steady
themes - 'appearance and reality' or 'the means of enpowerment'
or 'social ritual' - is precisely to use words in a way he does not, by
employing that safe paraphrase outside the experience of time itself
which concepts provide. For Shakespeare uses words dynamically
en passant - Hamlet's 'Why *yet* I live to say' - with thoughts
momentarily in time with the sudden present in which they are
spoken, and then left behind. 'Yet it will come.' Shakespeare, says
Peter Brook, does not offer us 'a series of messages' but a vibrating
'series of impulses that can produce many understandings'.[16]
   Thus Edgar, speaking of the accumulating sorrows of *King Lear*
in the Quarto, chorically receives and transmits the vibrating pulses
of the play:

> This would have seem'd a period
> To such as love not sorrow; but another,
> To amplify too much, would make much more
> And top extremity.

V iii 203-6

Grammatical periods do not govern or contain a play whose force pushes on over the line-endings and beyond any full stop to pain. There is here no steady build-up of character or story as in a nineteenth-century novel. Rather, through the succession of sudden words 'character and story are constructed from moment to moment, in an unexpected way: in the form of a *broken line*'.[17] Look at the energized words vibrating together in the knock-on white-heat of that broken line: 'too much' is 'much' become 'more' and almost immediately 'much more', till much more than 'much' and much more than 'too much' blows the circuit, tops extremity across the line-break, finds worse than worst beyond all normal bounds or periods of sense. It is like reading mental braille in the play's very darkness: for that is how Shakespeare is a linguistic discoverer of thought. His speed seems almost proportionate to the sheer amount of cumulative complexity forced into any one moment of expression – topping extremity. There is nothing else in the final short line, for 'And top extremity' means it is already too much. In turn the audience's apprehending gasp of emotion seems proportionate, in its shorthand register, to the weight and power and sheer recombination of thought that goes by too fast to be fully comprehended.[18]

Shakespeare simply gets his work into areas of dense energy, force-fields. The resultant thinking that is energized then feels like the immediate future of life, making 'much' 'more', rather than a conceptual consolidation or retrospective paraphrase of what has already been happening. 'The flighty purpose never is o'ertook,/Unless the deed go with it' (*Macbeth*, IV i 145–6). Shakespeare *goes after* his intimations, looks to give sudden conceptions life, before they have time to die on him.

In Shakespeare some of these thoughts of life themselves live and come into being as people or events; but some die, even as Isabella explained:

> His act did not o'ertake his bad intent,
> And must be buried but as an intent
> That perish'd by the way. Thoughts are no subjects;
> Intents but merely thoughts.
>
> *Measure for Measure*, V i 449–52

There is here a breath-taking vision of mental processes. The way in which action does not simply follow from intention but seems to come out from behind intention and overtakes it, the way in which intents and thoughts may or may not find embodiment in life, suggests something quite different from an idea of the mind as a mere calculating thing. 'O'ertake', 'buried', 'perish'd by the way': these are words embedded within the horizontal forward movement of the line in time, yet embedded as half-subdued metaphors slipped in from other levels of meaning, ready to explode even as the lines go past you. That tiny micro-pause between the end of one line and the beginning of the next

> And must be buried but as an intent
> That perish'd by the way

leaves 'intent' for a moment as bare potential like an embryonic thought seeking its realization or else doomed to fade. Which it is will be decided in a second: it is an image of thought's split-second decision as to what will or will not *come to anything* at the macro-level in Shakespeare's plays. For what Shakespeare has crowding upon his mind at such moments are nascent possibilities each suggesting itself linguistically, each calling for a chance to be and to have a future. Some live, some are dropped, some revive in other forms or as other plays. 'I had else been perfect', says Macbeth, hearing of the flight of Fleance (III iv 20): 'else', that safe future he had counted on, is already gone as he speaks it. Through a version of faith, Shakespeare trusts thoughts to come when they will in the working out of his processes – thoughts pagan and Christian, thoughts of good and of evil, thoughts operative or inoperable, as part of one's fate or despite it. Montaigne believed he was made up of thousands of these thoughts. Shakespeare set going a process by which anything can be thought but each, even wrong thing, in its own right time. If it be not now, yet it will come.

Therefore Mark Rylance is right to intuit a relation between Renaissance thought about the original patterns of natural Creation and Shakespeare's own parallel creation of verbal worlds of life, as a poetic maker. For Shakespeare belongs well with an age where an underlying technical language, like that of Pythagoras's mystic numbers, seemed to have innate access to more than technical concerns or concerns registered in a none the less technical way – in

sound and in vision, in the harmonies of music and the symmetries
of architecture. Equivalently, Shakespeare created a model through
which he could reproduce the underlying life-matrix and key into
the forces of creation itself. With his eye kept on the shape of
the situation, the situation created words for Shakespeare, and
those words before him themselves created human meanings as
it were behind his back, even as he wrote on. Shakespeare's is
thus what one philosopher, Michael Polanyi, calls mystic rather
than systematic thinking. Systematic thinking works mechanically,
according to models of scientific inquiry that, says Polanyi, have
come increasingly to dominate human thinking from the later
seventeenth century onwards, even to our own times:

> A problem may admit of a systematic solution. By ransacking
> my flat inch by inch, I may make sure of eventually finding my
> fountain pen which I know to be somewhere in it. I might solve
> a chess problem by trying out mechanically all combinations of
> possible moves and countermoves. . . . It is clear that any such
> systematic operation would reach a solution without crossing a
> logical gap and would not constitute a heuristic act.[19]

But Shakespeare does leap gaps and leave them behind him in
the wake of the mind's forward movements, eschewing the normal
time of logic, grammar and causal sequence for the sake of quicker
mental transitions. It is as though Shakespeare magically seizes a
word in the dramatic midst of things, a word like 'o'ertake' which
makes him think a thought – but a thought which (in the race for
meaning) he does not spell out explicitly so much as use tacitly in
his mind to let himself be taken to another word, the landing-stage
for another development 'by the way'. Shakespeare seems to hear
instantaneous pre-echoes from words and of more words, sounding
in his mind, setting up future lives in his imagination. He then
follows and overtakes those echoes or clues, like Macbeth in his
imagining the murder of Duncan, on the trail of what he has
already momentarily foreseen:

> Thou marshall'st me the way that I was going.
>
> *Macbeth*, II i 42

Or consider Laertes coming back to find his father dead
and his sister mad as a result – suddenly the whole situation

compresses itself together for Shakespeare and implodes in a single word:

> O rose of May!
> Dear maid – kind sister – sweet Ophelia –
> O heavens, is't possible a young maid's wits
> Should be as mortal as an old man's life?
>
> *Hamlet*, IV v 157–60

The discovered and discovering word is 'mortal': for *pace* Leonardo, it is not itself a 'separate' word but the expression of mind suddenly rushing in to see connection in the space between young maid's wits and old man's life. It is a more terrible and sudden version of what the player-king says in the simplified blueprint of the play-within-a-play. Much more slowly there, he warns of a queen's remarriage overtaking her previous vows: ''tis not strange/Even our loves should with our fortunes change' –

> Our thoughts are ours, their ends none of our own.
> So think thou wilt no second husband wed,
> But die thy thoughts when thy first lord is dead.
>
> *Hamlet*, III ii 195–6, 208–10

The explosively vibrating word there is 'die' – a word caught as metaphor in the midst of a situation suddenly throwing up terms by which to make itself thought. Even thus the play seems to discover its own meaning from within. For it is words such as this which in Shakespeare release the whole electric current of the play as they rebound between two speakers in dialogue or without dialogue go shuddering into the theatre's outer space. Without such explosions of meaning, we are only passive creatures pulled into the ongoing relativism of time: our thoughts going with whatever overtakes them, our loves with their fortunes, a young maid's wits going with an old man's life. But Shakespeare does not go along with things. Thought startles him, as a reminder of original things: the *mind* is mortal too, not just the body, and can die even before the body itself does. The force and position of that word 'mortal' in the question

> is't possible a young maid's wits
> Should be as mortal as an old man's life?

thus makes it not merely that Polonius's death causes Ophelia to go mad, as in some linear explanation, but rather as though Polonius's death now goes on as something lodged killingly inside Ophelia's brain. Hamlet is full of these Chinese boxes: thoughts contained amidst what they think about, while simultaneously what they think about is also still contained within them. Which way do we turn? 'A man may fish with the worm that hath eat of a king' (IV iii 27–8).

Shakespeare uses words as a discoverer in an age of discovery, not as an explainer. Trying to prevent discovery Lady Macbeth herself says that thoughts should 'die' with those they think on. Vainly she tries to will the two – thought and the reality it thinks on – into one:

> How now, my Lord? why do you keep alone
> Of sorriest fancies your companions making,
> Using those thoughts, which should indeed have died
> With them they think on? Things without all remedy
> Should be without regard: what's done is done.
>
> III ii 8–12

'Indeed' there is almost literal: in deed what's done is (I hope) over and done with. But this is not how thought can work either in Shakespeare or in Macbeth himself. For Shakespeare gets himself into the source of all shapes, what we might call some linguistic equivalent of the original gene-pool. A whole situation produces a word, a word which then compressedly contains that situation, like a mind a thought. Macbeth has murdered Duncan in his sleep – that is the situation spelt out in prose; now see, as if with Janet Suzman again, what Shakespeare does in poetry:

> *Macbeth* Methought, I heard a voice cry, 'Sleep no more!
>   Macbeth does murther
> *[Inner voice*   *Duncan?]*
>   Sleep, –
> *[Inner voice*   *What of it?]*
>   – the *innocent* Sleep.
>
> II ii 34–5

And I am *guilty*; the guilty lie awake at night. To die, to sleep – but then in Hamlet the sudden realization 'For in that sleep of death what dreams . . .' (and the subsequent words 'may come' are *already* out: the sense, as Dr Johnson says, connected more in the speaker's mind than on his tongue). Macbeth murders sleep. That is what sudden metaphor is: the higher meaning tied to the lower act, a creature's immediate mental realization of its own physical act and situation:

> Like those who live in a basement, with only one little window to the outside, do not see except through that window, thus we see nothing except through our senses. Nevertheless, we peep into the outside and with our mind we infer the existence of something beyond our senses, but only as much as our senses permit us to do. Our mind rises upon the senses, but is based upon the senses.[20]

Metaphor is a word suddenly making sense of sense itself, giving a mind to body as in that deep old metaphor of the mind's eye[21] which Macbeth tries to mask up. No wonder the making of metaphors is so characteristic of Shakespeare: they doubly *densen* the world; they help to realize that inextricable mixture of mental and physical that makes for the evolution of human meaning. Macbeth (as Hamlet himself might put it) is a man who has used daggers on another and now speaks daggers to himself. The mind, given by a word the very thought of what it has done, has then to live in the midst of the meaning of itself – if it can. In such a process, poor Ophelia

> *Divided* from *herself* and her fair judgment
>
> *Hamlet*, IV v 85

'as one incapable of her *own* distress' (IV vii 147), stands as a terrible demonstration of what can happen. Even while it is asked of Hamlet what 'hath put him/So much from the understanding of *himself*' (II ii 8–9), even while the ghost urges Hamlet in converse with his mother to 'step *between* her and her fighting soul' (III iv 113), Ophelia pays for them all. So often, by a mere word or two, the language of a play thus confusedly crosses minds, particularly minds divided or in need of division from themselves, and is lodged blurredly in the audience's memory, to give the audience an almost immediately retrospective sense of some mental whole getting unmade and made here – if there were time quite to gather it all.

Shakespeare's is not systematic but heuristic thinking. And heuristic thinking, says Polanyi, takes place when the mind *anticipates* reality, ahead of checking all the possibilities, in such a way as to open a path which seems to predict and indeed almost magically create the future. This, he argues, is the Pythagorean tradition of creative mind revived in the Renaissance by Copernicus and Kepler when, by their imaginative mathematics, they brought into being thoughts which were only later confirmed by experiment to correspond to reality. It was as if sheerly of themselves those thoughts were a dynamic replica of the prototypes by which reality itself was first created. Thus Kepler:

> What I prophesied two-and-twenty years ago, as soon as I discovered the five solids among the heavenly orbits – what I firmly believed long before I had seen Ptolemy's Harmonics – what I had promised my friends in the title of this fifth book, which I named before I was sure of my discovery – what sixteen years ago I urged to be sought - that for which I have devoted the best part of my life to astronomical contemplations . . . at last I have brought it to light, and recognized its truth beyond my hopes. . . . The die is cast, the book is written, whether to be read now or by posterity I care not; it may wait a hundred years for its reader, if God himself has waited six thousand years for a man to contemplate His work.[22]

Shakespeare's work has long since passed Johnson's test for greatness – length of duration and continuance of esteem, in far outliving his own century. For what seems so fast, so immediately present and so transient in him is, *pace* Leonardo, at the root of his permanent and lasting appeal. There is nothing more deep, more expressive of the source of human meaning and development, than Shakespeare's language – everything humans can *ever* think seems potential in it. In that sense Shakespeare's works continually make a future for themselves – not as monuments but as a dynamic life-force. In the midst of the plays' processes, we never feel we are ahead of Shakespeare, as moderns, but that we are always catching up with him and, equally, that he is in his language at

the very root of us. 'We that are young/Shall never see so much,
nor live so long.' Going back to Shakespeare, said Peter Brook in
The Empty Stage, is still the way forwards.

But without an example that may seem like mere hyperbole.
Here is a great example. Old Lear, shell-shocked, says before
Cordelia:

> Pray, do not mock me:
> I am a very foolish fond old man,
> Fourscore and upward, not an hour more or less;
> And, to deal plainly,
> I fear I am not in my perfect mind.
>
> *King Lear*, IV vii 59–63

Editors torn between the Quarto and the Folio can no longer be
quite certain how to print the lines, so tempted was Shakespeare
in the very life and death of his thoughts to refind in between the
lines invisible mental matter which could be spelt out further or left
as more implicit. But whether 'to deal plainly' is (as I prefer it) a
short line as in the Folio or printed at the end of a full line as in the
Quarto, emphatically the pause after it means that this speech never
feels like a past and settled thing, never feels as if we know what
is going to happen in it. It always requires and takes *its own time*,
however transiently. It is not permanent in the sense that Leonardo
meant, but it is always potentially new again in performance – for
if not renewed, if merely 'acted' in the sense that Janet Suzman
objected to, then it does not really, livingly exist. Shakespeare is
like a test of dynamic life: if Shakespeare becomes over-familiar
to you, then he and you are dead. Yet, in what Douglas Oliver
calls a sort of minor *eternal* present, unrepeatable but reperformable,
those words of Lear's can always come back to sudden life as an
'original text'. Lear struggles to bring himself to the threshold of
primal speech, of plain realization - a barely made-out admission of
thought painfully just ahead of him:

> And, to deal plainly,
> I fear I am not in my perfect mind.

In that innerly repressed sob of pain between the lines, there is this
silent recognition: Look what I have come to. One can feel the

future momentarily – the future thought coming to mind, where mind itself is so damaged – in between those two lines. This is why Peter Brook speaks of Shakespeare as offering a greater sense of the living present than modern thinking normally allows:

> we are constantly betraying reality, which we don't succeed in perceiving, grasping, and living, and we're continually diminishing and reducing it. It's always a highly diminished view of the present moment as it might be. The artist's vision . . . is a greater possibility of seeing what is actually happening than the duller vision with which we live through our everyday lives. The human faculty of apprehension is not static, but is a second-for-second redefinition of what it sees. Now to me the total works of Shakespeare are like a very, very complete set of codes and these codes, cipher for cipher, set off in us, stir in us, vibrations and impulses.

Shakespeare offers us 'a school for living', says Brook, because if we enter into relationship with those codes and vibrations, then in 'reincarnating' his vision through performance we are making a world 'in the present tense' again.[23] It is, I should add, a sense of the present shot through with the apprehended future of its own thought; a future that is never quite past, if we lock into it again. Shakespeare does not spell out all that lies in his transitions: he leaves things behind him, like that eternal momentary pause 'And, to deal plainly', to be performed again and again in the future. For those pauses are the deep, recurring places of life in which none the less humans do not seem allowed to rest or stay.

3   THE SCHOOL OF LIVING

Shakespeare is so fast, swallowing the immediate future into the fullest living present of thought and being, that even Hamlet can barely slow down the Shakespearian process. In his greatest soliloquy, the very syntactical workings of Hamlet's mind show that something in him already knows the way it must be: 'Who would bear . . . when he might his quietus make . . . But that the thought of something after death . . . makes us rather bear . . . Than fly'. But the list of injustices, customarily let go by in the world, is here held up for a moment after 'Who would bear':

Th'oppressor's wrong, the proud man's contumely,
The pangs of dispriz'd love, the law's delay,
The insolence of office, and the spurns . . .

For the sake of verbal revenge, Hamlet can find the freedom of a
second or two in which to hold on to those words separately, one
by one. It is as if the names were become the very things they speak
of so bitterly, in the very spittle of 'the insolence of office':

> and the spurns
> That patient merit of th'unworthy takes.
>
> *Hamlet*, III i 71–4

Yet very soon we have to see thought going back again into life and
into time, the words brought back together again into an ongoing
syntax within the sense of the world. Whatever the pain of those
'spurns', we have still to 'take' it: 'merit' has to take spurns from
the 'unworthy', which is the injustice; *and* merit has to bear it
'patiently', which, though even more unjust, is also part of its very
merit. Yet no sooner do these words go together, as in finished
sentences, than we – readers or actors but reperformers all – need
to keep them for a micro-second apart again. Why do we need to
do that? In order to prevent the thought that originally made those
lines being merely unthinkingly absorbed into them and made past.
In order that those brief moments of mental freedom should not
be completely absorbed into a set text or an old saw. That is
why theatre is so powerful, in its still momentary remaking or
recoining of what passes. If only, thinks Hamlet, he could hold
on to that principle of his being which invisibly makes thoughts
but is only incarnate in them, is found in their making and yet is not
transcendently separable from them. But Montaigne would reply to
Hamlet in his Leonardo-like desire for permanent transcendence,
even as he responds to Seneca:

> *Oh what a vile and abject thing is man* (saith Seneca) *unlesse he
> raise himselfe above humanity!* Observe here a notable speech,
> and a profitable desire; but likewise absurd. For to make the
> handfull greater then the hand, and the embraced greater then
> the arme; and to hope to straddle more then our legs length;

is impossible and monstrous: nor that man should mount over and above himselfe or humanity; for, he cannot see but with his owne eyes, nor take hold but with his owne armes.

> Montaigne, vol.II pp.325–6
> (ch.xii, 'An Apologie of Raymond Sebond')

Such a riposte, against the very idea of transcending time, is itself part of Montaigne's own story in time – a story which, again, is so close to Shakespeare as to make Shakespeare's ultimate difference from it all the more telling. For the last time I turn back to the contrast of Montaigne.

The longer he lived, the *less* consciously 'serious' Montaigne became – or better perhaps, the more he redefined his view of what mature seriousness should be. The crucial shift for Montaigne is from the early essay 'That to Philosophize, Is to Lerne How to Dye':

Cicero saith, that to *Philosophie is no other thing, than for a man to prepare himselfe to death*. . . . Accidents are not of such a necessitie, for most men passe their whole life without feeling any want or povertie, and other-some without feeling any griefe or sicknes. . . . But as for death, it is inevitable. . . .

They come, they goe, they trot, they daunce: but no speech of death. All that is good sport. But if she be once come, and on a sudden and openly surprise, either them, their wives, their children, or their friends, what torments, what out-cries, what rage and what despair doth then over-whelme them? . . . A man must looke to it, and in better times fore-see it. . . .

It is uncertaine where death looks for us; let us expect her everie where: the premeditation of death, is a fore-thinking of libertie. He who hath learned to die, hath unlearned to serve.

> vol.I, pp.73, 75, 79–80 (ch.xix)

– to this reversal of it in 'Of Phisiognomy', near the end of the *Essais*:

We trouble death with the care of life, and life with the care of death. The one annoyeth, the other affrights us. It is not against death, we prepare our selves, it is a thing too momentary. A quarter of an houre of passion without consequence and without annoyance, deserves not particular precepts. To say truth, we prepare our selves against the preparations of death. Philosophy teacheth us, ever to have death before our eyes, to fore-see and consider it before it come: Then giveth us rules and precautions so to provide, that such foresight and thought hurt us not. So doe Phisitions, who cast us into diseases, that they may employ their drugges and skill about them. If we have not known how to live, it is injustice to teach us how to die, and deforme the end from all the rest. Have wee knowne how to live constantly and quietly, wee shall know how to die resolutely and reposedly. . . . Me thinkes, [Death] is indeede the end, yet not the scope of life. It is her last, it is her extremity, yet not her object.

vol.III, p.307 (ch.xii)

'That to Philosophize, Is to Lerne How to Dye' is about vigilant consciousness in one who most knows himself to be an individual because he will die: 'In the confused mass of being, death cuts out that particular zone which is ourselves.'[24] The purpose of frequent thinking on death beforehand is that people might not be taken unawares by the 'sudden' end of what they supposed was still the very middle of an unfinished life with its hopes and plans. Instead of a life drifting in time, time is turned into thought and thus into that freedom from being slavishly at the mercy of mere contingency which at least lies in knowledge's permanence. For we always know it will happen some time: death is essential, is not in itself an accident, however abruptly it takes place. And what is always a physical possibility of our condition as mortals should, it is argued, become an established thought in that body's mind, a level above the vicissitudes of time and flesh. Hamlet could not have put it better.

But, arguably, there is a deeper 'unlearning to serve' in 'Of Phisiognomy', when Montaigne turns round on himself to cast off unnecessary and unprofitable anxiety in the past, and trust to a life's own contours, leaving the end till the end, without that being an undue irresponsibility. In his writing Montaigne follows only his own life forward. For in between the two essays Montaigne had actually had an accidental foretaste of death in a collision on horseback with a servant riding forth to greet him. It could have been the end then, suddenly, like nothing much at all, after all. 'Of Phisiognomy' is thus Montaigne's resultant shrug: death will happen anyway, like the universe it will go on daily without your thought – nor does it take long in itself. If it is 'sudden', it is also 'momentary'. It is the fear of death, the sense it can give a life of its limitation and its ungroundedness, which causes the trouble. So learn to live instead, since that is what the thought of death is really about. And let a life take whatever form it has, let it be a natural or a characteristic life, proudly – good and bad, in life and in death together. If we have known how to live, we may trust that we shall know how to die, fulfilled. If we have not known how to live, then we should not learn how to die well instead, giving the end a different shape from the whole. Montaigne would substitute *form* for *ending*. Let a life be what it is, or what it should be, or what you want it to be in future, but *now*.

This later attitude suits better with, and itself confirms, Montaigne's implicit form of writing. For there is no time when in the *Essais* he thinks he is outside or above time, ready to make a final conclusion. 'The extempore moment is always, by definition, "ahead",' says Terence Cave, as Montaigne's language continually 'pursues and displaces its own moment of presence'.[25] The work itself is experienced moment by moment, even by its own writer, as 'a shapelesse subject' since the subject comes into being not through 'external rule or method' but sheerly from improvisation emergent amidst the open spaces of Montaigne's mind:

> but gropingly. As in this: I pronounce my sentençe by articles, loose and disjoynted: it is a thing cannot be spoken of at once and at full. Relation and conformity are not easily found in such base and common minds as ours.
>
> vol.III, p.336 (ch.xiii, 'Of Experience')

Out of the impossibility of certain knowledge or constant being, Montaigne, as I argued in Chapter Two, found a sanction for making limited and relative attempts, present-tense essays, experiments in following up apparently chance remarks and thoughts rather than plans and schemes and categories. At times, as in the essay 'Upon some Verses of Virgil', he plays with his prose, relishing its turns and delays of climax as if it were a sexual thing. For sentences are not internally linked by the impersonal mechanisms of strict logic, but are felt physically, spoken 'in the ayrie body of the voice', 'without enterlacings in words, joyning ligaments and binding seames wrested in for the service of weake and unattentive eares' (vol.III, p.245, ch.ix, 'Of Vanitie'). Sentences thus fall from the pen in a livingly unconnected way, such that Montaigne feels what is in between them only as part of himself, of his implicit experience and of the leaping life of his mind, in motion. 'Thus improvisation, which might have seemed the antithesis of memory, is in fact dependent on its hidden activity' (Cave, p.131). Montaigne *finds himself* most when he hits upon that extra leap of experience into thought which suddenly discloses to him where he is going and what he is all about:

> If we have not known how to live, it is injustice to teach us how to die.

This is a landing-place. So it is, again, in the essay 'Of Repentance', when in the midst of saying so levelly that it is easy for an old man morally to repent of sensuality simply because biologically he is so much less susceptible to it, he breaks out in the very rhythm of conversation itself:

> Therein I see no conscience.

That sentence is personally definite, detachedly short in one dimension but full and large in another, an absolute 'no' coming not out of the structure on the page but of the mind and the experience of the person above it. '*Wherefore*', he says, gathering and launching himself again by that word, 'if there be any amendment, 'tis but diseased.' And that word 'diseased', which he writes and then at once hears again, triggers thought as surely as if thought were a form of proud and defiant anger:

> O miserable kinde of remedie, to bee beholden unto sicknesse for our health!
>
> vol.III, p.35 (ch.ii, 'Of Repentance')

The powerful, sudden sentence again characteristically results from a sense of paradox – 'O miserable kinde of remedie, to bee beholden unto *sicknesse* for our *health*'; 'If we have not known how to *live*, it is injustice to teach us how to *die*' – words rebounding off each other to bring together in Montaigne's mind a sane outrage at the sheer, usually unspoken, absurdity of merely normal human ways. 'Thus we ever hinder our selves' (vol.III, p.108, ch.xii, 'Of Phisiognomy'). Man is a giddy thing, said Benedick.

In what Peter Brook calls the school of living, both Montaigne and Shakespeare are improvisers in the present, letting thoughts happen in the space available, bringing a subject into being from out of the open spaces of the mind, following the movement of a life or a thought part by part and moment by moment, without that aspiration to the systematic in writers even so different from each other as Hooker and Ficino.

Indeed, Montaigne believed that he owed the way he wrote to the example of spontaneous freedom in thinking which originates most characteristically in poetry:

> I love a Poeticall kinde of march, by friskes, skips, and jumps. . . .
> Oh God, what grace hath the variation, and what beautie these
> startings and nimble escapes; and then most when they seem to
> employ carelessnesse and casualtie. . . . The best antient prose . . .
> shineth every where, with a poeticall vigour and boldnesse, and
> representeth some aire or touch of it's fury.
>
> vol.III, p.244 (ch.ix, 'Of Vanitie')

It must be said that nobody's poetry leaps faster across the spaces of thought than does Shakespeare's. So to put it another way round: Montaigne is almost what Shakespeare might have been like if Shakespeare had believed in writing essays not plays – and believed, moreover (as we saw in Chapter Two), in all that went with such a deep instinctive preference. But in making poetic plays, Shakespeare converts time into pressure, creating something which is not only as fast-thinking as the beliefs which an essay discloses *en passant*, but closer than is thought in an essay to a simultaneous embeddedness in sheer external life as well as the life within. Montaigne could explain it:

> we, and our judgement, *and* all mortall things else do uncessantly
> rowle, turne and passe away . . . both the judgeing and the
> judged being in continuall alteration and motion'
>
> vol.II, p.323 (ch.xii, 'An Apologie of Raymond Sebond')

but Shakespeare makes it happen:

> By the world,
> I think my wife be honest, and think she is not;
> I think that thou art just, and think thou art not.
>
> *Othello*, III iii 385–6

Not only does Othello seem to himself to move backwards and forwards but so to his mind do both Desdemona and Iago – the one right, the other wrong, the one false, the other true, in ironic tandem – until Iago has managed to embody what Othello will think of Desdemona even in what Othello will think of him. Emilia can manage a darkened version of Montaigne's witty pragmatic shrug from a more apparently normalized sense of life – when Desdemona asks her whether she would sexually betray her husband for the whole world:

> *Emilia* I would not do such a thing for a joint-ring, nor for measures of lawn, nor for gowns, petticoats, nor caps, nor any petty exhibition. But for all the whole world! Ud's pity, who would not make her husband a cuckold, to make him a monarch? I should venture purgatory for't.
> *Desdemona* Beshrew me, I would not do such a wrong for the whole world.
> *Emilia* Why, the wrong is but a wrong i'th'world; and having the world for your labour, 'tis a wrong in your own world, and you might quickly make it right.
>
> IV iii 68–78

This mental leap-and-turn not only takes its thinker from inside the system to outside, but, from outside it, then reforms what the thinker will be able to make of the system when back inside it again. It is that part of Shakespeare's linguistic and hence mental equipment which he usually gives to licensed fools. But Othello cannot use it, cannot really live in a world of his own – least of all by destroying her who is the world to him. He is still relative and still within an objective world which he cannot entirely subjectivize: by thinking of it he cannot get out of the world or stop being in it, indeed he cannot stop at all – as thus kissing Desdemona when asleep:

Be thus when thou art dead, and I will kill thee
And love thee after.

V ii 18–19

He already knows what will happen, he already imagines what he will feel afterwards, and he cannot stop himself.

Shakespeare too, I believe, could never stop himself. The very impulse not to stop drove him involuntarily the opposite way to that of Montaigne - from comedy to tragedy. Increasingly Shakespeare's people, if they cannot get out or up or above, do not, like Montaigne, pull back: 'The greatnesse of the minde is not so much, to drawe up and hale forward, as to know how to range, direct and circumscribe it selfe' (vol.III, p.379, ch.xiii, 'Of Experience'). Shakespeare's people, up until Prospero's 'There sir, stop', increasingly do seek to hale forwards if not upwards, do not go in if they cannot get above, but instead go on – dynamically, even desperately, but not just stoically.

Shakespeare had the sort of mind that, casting amidst the possibilities of life, might ask this: What sort of human being would it be who, seeing the point of 'Of Phisiognomy' succeeding 'That to Philosophize, Is to Lerne How to Dye', none the less still could not get beyond the *earlier* essay? It is that thought which makes for the writing of the tragedies: the reluctant thought of death as, still, above all. For if Comedy was most congenial to Shakespeare and, as we saw in Chapter One, most reveals his underlying code or template, none the less Tragedy is where he has to go and what he has to go through.

What counts in Montaigne is survival. But for better and for worse, the Shakespeare of the tragic vision of drama is concerned with something prior even to self-preservation – something more original and more primary, which the very dynamics of his method of thinking inevitably drove him to.

The survivor is a moderate man. But after *Hamlet* in particular, Shakespeare is not naturally moderate. The moderate man, says Montaigne, 'marcheth alwaies with the reines in his hand'; he knows 'as in too much speede, festinatio tarda est, Hastinesse is slow. Haste makes waste, and hinders and stayes it selfe: Ipsa se velocitas implicat; Swiftnesse entangles it selfe' (vol.III, p.259, ch.x, 'How One Ought to Governe His Will'). But Shakespeare is more in touch with the dangerous, ancient pre-mental world where, said D.H. Lawrence, 'connection was not logical but emotional. The word "therefore" did not exist.'[26] When sudden Shakespeare writes in *King Lear*, 'This would have seem'd a period/To such as love not sorrow', it is not as if he *loves* sorrow, it is not as though *that* is what makes him go beyond moderation. It is more as if Hamlet's

> Who would fardels bear,
> To grunt and sweat under a weary life,
> But that the dread of something after death,
> The undiscovered country from whose bourn
> No traveller returns, puzzles the will,
> And makes us rather bear those ills we have
> Than fly to others that we know not of?
>
> *Hamlet*, III i 76–82

has become this of Edgar's:

> O! our lives' sweetness,
> That we the pain of death would hourly die
> Rather than die at once!
>
> *King Lear*, V iii 183–5

where 'sweetness', like love, is no longer the word it used to be before the great catastrophe but is turned back upon itself, bitterly. It is of a language turned against itself, self-entangled and thus fighting itself, just as this almost suicidal play of *Lear* fights with its own life – and almost wants to resist that continuing life-spirit and life-caringness in its protagonists which is effectively killing them and destroying it. This is not the language that life speaks even in Montaigne's 'That to Philosophize, Is to Lerne How to Dye':

> To continue in this moderation, that is, neither to flie from life, nor to run to death (which I require of you) I have tempred both the one and other betweene sweetnes and sowrenes.
>
> vol.I, p.91 (ch.xix)

There is no such feeling of tempering in *Hamlet* or *Lear*. 'O! *our* lives' sweetness/That we the pain of death would *hourly* die': the very sounds run into each other and linger in place of that

monosyllabic 'rather than die at once': for we are forced to choose
not one death, but many. 'We must moderate ourselves', insists
Montaigne, 'betwixt the hate of paine, and the love of pleasure'
(vol.III, p.253, ch.x, 'How One Ought to Governe His Will').
But 'sweetness' is a bitter word for Edgar: only the more awful
taste of death could make us swallow such a description of life as
still, relatively, sweet.

Shakespeare's power in *King Lear* or in *Macbeth* is like the power
of force that Leonardo himself describes as going on and on and on
– 'Force', he says,

> is an invisible power which is created and imparted, through
> violence from without, by animated bodies to inanimate bodies,
> giving to these the similarity of life, and this life works in a
> marvellous way, constraining and transforming in place and
> shape all created things. It speeds in fury to its undoing. . . .
> Retardation strengthens, and speed weakens it.[27]

Thus Macbeth increasingly works upon himself as if upon an
inanimate object of his own will, wearing himself out to naught
with ever increasing speed of subtraction and ever decreasing light
of consciousness.

Shakespeare's tragic men 'hale forward'. They do so not least
because for Shakespeare himself thought is quintessentially not of
the past, as in the aftermath of consciousness, nor even of the
present, but of the future in the instant. That is to say, whatever
the content of a thought, whether it be about past or present, its
essential form of movement is forward. Even when the mind is
thinking about its own past, the future is almost always what the
mind is looking for in Shakespeare, as if it were life itself. Thus,
when Hermione cries to Leontes of his lost love for her:

> The crown and comfort of my life, your favour,
> I do give lost, for I do feel it gone,
> But know not how it went
>
> *The Winter's Tale*, III ii 94–6

that last line is no polite or curious inquiry about the recent past
but comes to mind (how, where, why?) as something already too
late almost for utterance, let alone amends, and left in her only to
be registered as bewildered pain.

The living mind seeks to overtake what it can only figure forth as ahead of itself until the evanescent shadowy thing is caught verbally. When Macbeth speaks of himself as left surrounded by

> Curses, not loud, but deep, mouth-honour, breath,
> Which the poor heart would fain deny, and dare not.
>
> *Macbeth*, V iii 28–9

there is hardly time now, so settled is his character and his fate, for Macbeth to separate 'would fain deny' from its sentence 'and dare not'. The space left between words, the sheer life of a mental leap, the very future itself, all are running out now. Life-thought – the very dynamic in Shakespeare – is nearly dead.

Where a mind can find no future for itself, we see the very syntax of a thwarted forward movement. As with Macbeth, so here with Claudius self-baffled and self-defeated:

> Pray can I not,
> Though inclination be as sharp as will,
> My stronger guilt defeats my strong intent,
> And, like a man to double business bound,
> I stand in pause where I shall first begin,
> And both neglect.
>
> *Hamlet*, III iii 38–43

The hanging middle line, '*Though inclination be as sharp as will*', goes first with '*Pray can I not*' which precedes it: 'Pray can I not, [even] though inclination be as sharp as will.' But then it immediately goes with '*My stronger guilt defeats my strong intent*' that follows, in the struggle for a word and for a future: '[Al]though inclination be as sharp as will, my stronger guilt defeats my strong intent.' 'Though inclination be as sharp as will' hangs trapped on either side, before and after, in a retributive travesty of Shakespearian instantaneousness:

> If a man were double fronted (as the poets have feigned Janus) . . . the same faculty of sight would address itself to see both before and behind at one instant, which now it doth by turning. . . . So the mind varieth . . . as the same faculty applied to . . . things past remembreth: to things future foreseeth: of present things determineth: and that which the eye doth by turning of

the head, beholding before, behind, and on each side, that doth the mind freely at once.[28]

Thus a line bespeaking an inclination and a will to goodness in Claudius cannot hold firm its resolve in time but is constantly absorbed into despair on every side, leaving the mind nowhere to look or go. No sooner present as a future possibility than it is past, the one better contrite part of Claudius goes back into the damned whole of him even as he speaks:

> but O, what form of prayer
> Can serve my turn? 'Forgive me my foul murder?'
> That cannot be, since I am still possess'd
> Of those effects for which I did the murder -
> My crown, mine own ambition, and my queen.
> May one be pardon'd and retain th'offence?
>
> III iii 51–6

No, 'tis not so above. '*Still* possess'd' (which cannot get rid of itself and re-emerges as 'retain') is Claudius's equivalent of Hamlet's 'Why *yet* I live': it comes as a reminding time-word in the very midst of utterance, to say, with Augustine, 'In these things there is no place to rest, because they do not last.' Such a speech can only rebound upon that mind which utters it, to see itself as trapped within the utterance as is 'my deed to my most painted word' (III i 53). In the drama of creation and evolution, thought in Shakespeare is literally thus a coming-to-mind – thought creating and conceiving the mind to bear and think it.

There is a terrifying mental innocence, as well as a pre-empted penitence, trapped within the guilt of a Claudius. And this is related to the fact that 'character' as such does not exist in Shakespeare, in the sense of fixed and ready-made people. Shakespeare's people are not at their own command: 'What is yours to bestow is not yours to receive' (*Twelfth Night*, I v 200). Only by dangerously giving themselves – and not merely lending themselves as Montaigne would have it – do they discover how much they indeed have in them. 'In his fullest living,' says D.H. Lawrence of Man, 'he does not know what he does. Altogether devoid of knowledge and conscious motive is he when he is heaving into uncreated space, when he is actually living, becoming himself.'[29]

And that is what life-thinking in Shakespeare's writing is like - a verbal heaving into that yet uncreated space ahead, thus trying to create it. 'Heaven does with us as we with torches do,/Not light them for themselves' (*Measure for Measure*, I i 32–3). Life goes outwards even as it forms itself. Thus as audience and readers we are, as Hazlitt indicates, in at the instant moment of 'the original text' when the characters and their future are being first realized, made, unmade – at the very boundary-point when thoughts become acts or acts are seen to have become everlasting consequences.

For Shakespeare's people do not make carefully weighed decisions in the extended present, in the light of their own clearly perceived self-interests. The people in *Lear*, do they *love* sorrow that they still cling to life as if it were *sweet*? Does Coriolanus think it is great to be hated when he says to the populace, 'Who deserves greatness,/Deserves your hate' (I i 175–6)? Does Hamlet really think that the less the substance of one's cause, the more intrinsically heroic is the undertaking of it, when he observes of Fortinbras: 'Rightly to be great/Is not to stir without great argument,/But greatly to find quarrel in a straw/When honour's at the stake' (IV iv 53–6)? When we hear such formulations we know that something has got itself put the wrong way round – even by just 'halfe a pegs turne' (Montaigne, vol.II, p.282, ch.xii, 'An Apologie of Raymond Sebond').

These utterances are not extrapolatable philosophies: there are none in Shakespeare. For truly *creative* thinking – in the deep sense that Shakespeare recalls for us, beyond cliché – is not like that, but offers something bigger. Utterances here are no more and no less than life-forces. And what Shakespeare offers is not thoughts so much as the very form of original thinking, primal life-thinking, too often forgotten in times dominated by the models of slow consciousness. It is *not* that Shakespeare isn't a conceptual writer; but that in so little time he has so many concepts, arising with absolute verbal force out of a situation only to be pulled back again relativistically inside it. Crowded Shakespeare has too many thoughts for just one ponderous concept.

Shakespeare does not give us something, like a solution; he seems to give us everything. Shakespeare sets going a process through scene after scene which of itself seems a model or a site for all those questions about life as it comes into being that one could ever ask – without himself being initially committed to anything other than the technical creation of the process.

Thus in the theatre, so many of the plays make us feel like this in the end: 'It is not a dispute or a story, but history happening, and we are living through it; later we may discover what it means, when we discover what a life means.'[30] But there is no time for 'later' in sudden Shakespeare. What seems as if it should be eternal or transcendent or conclusive is constantly returned to life-time.

Notes

ONE   DRAMATIC SPACE AND PERSONAL PLACE IN SHAKESPEARE

1 Russell Fraser, *Young Shakespeare* (Columbia, 1988), p.132.
2 Richard Hooker, *Of the Laws of Ecclesiastical Polity*, 1593, edited by A.S. McGrade (Cambridge, 1989), p.57 (book I, ch. 2.5).
3 William Empson, *Seven Types of Ambiguity*, 1930 (Harmondsworth, Middlesex, 1973), p.71. The line is an example of antimetabole, though perhaps even closer is that example of exchange of Sir Walter Raleigh's which is cited as one of Puttenham's figures of repetition – ploche or the doubler:

> Yet when I sawe my selfe to you was true,
> I loved my selfe, bycause my selfe loved you.

George Puttenham, *The Arte of English Poesie*, 1589, edited by G.D. Willcock and A. Walker (Cambridge, 1936), p.201.
4 Samuel Daniel, *A Defence of Rhyme*, 1603, in *Elizabethan Critical Essays*, edited by G. Gregory Smith, 2 vols (Oxford, 1967), vol.II, p.366. I am deeply indebted to T.R. Langley for his thoughts and teaching on rhyme.
5 ibid., p.362.
6 ibid., p.366.
7 Puttenham, *The Arte of English Poesie*, p.206.
8 Marion Trousdale, *Shakespeare and the Rhetoricians* (London, 1982), pp.65, 70.
9 Lucretius, *De Rerum Natura*, II, 688–98, translated by Thomas Creech: Titus Lucretius Carus, *His Six Books of Epicurean Philosophy*, 3rd edn (London, 1683), p.54. See also I, 823–7, which Creech translates:

> So in my Verse are Letters common found
> To many words unlike in sense and sound;
> Such great variety bare Change affords
> Of order i'th' few elements of Words.
>
> p.26

On a finite system of language having to stand for an infinity of thoughts and things, see Richard Mulcaster:

> The number of things, whereof we write and speake is infinite,
> the words wherewith we write and speake, be definite and within
> number. Whereupon we are driven to use one, and the same word
> in verie manie, naie, somtime in verie contrarie senses.
>
> *The First Part of the Elementarie* (1582)

and thus on the consequent necessity for 'compounded' terms,
Ralph Lever:

> *Plura rerum, quam verborum genera* (that is, more things, than there
> are words to express things by)
>
> *The Arte of Reason* (1573)

— quoted in Jane Donawerth, *Shakespeare and the Sixteenth-Century Study of Language* (Urbana, Il and Chicago, Il, 1984), p.109.

10 Ruskin, *Modern Painters*, vol.IV, part v, chap.xx, para.28.

11 Daniel, *Defence of Rhyme*, pp.365–6.

12 Quoted in Edward Grant, *Much Ado About Nothing: Theories of Space and Vacuum from the Middle Ages to the Scientific Revolution* (Cambridge, 1981), p.198. See also Thomas Fuller's witty application in *The Profane State*, 1642: 'Queen Joan . . . (hating widowhood as much as nature doth *vacuum*) married James King of Majorca', book V, ch.ii.

13 Nicholas Bonetetus, *Physica*, quoted in Pierre Duhem, *Medieval Cosmology*, edited by Roger Ariew (Chicago, 1987), p.234.

14 John Barton, *Playing Shakespeare* (London, 1986), pp.61, 141.

15 Iamblichus quoted in Robert Sorabji, *Matter, Space and Motion: Theories in Antiquity and their Sequel* (London, 1988), p.208; Carol Rutter (ed.), *Clamorous Voices* (London, 1988), p.43.

16 Grant, *Much Ado*, p.364.

17 ibid., p.197.

18 On the density of the medium for life and the rival claims of resistance, empty spaces and interpenetrability, compare Lucretius against certain peripatetic theorists who

> maintain that water yields and opens a penetrable path to the scaly
> bodies of fish that push against it, because they leave spaces behind
> them into which the yielding water can flow together. In the same
> way, they suppose, other things can move by mutually changing
> places, though every place remains filled.

Lucretius asks:

[But] how can the fish advance till the water has given way? And how can the water retire when the fish cannot move?

Or again:

if two bodies suddenly spring apart from contact on a broad surface, all the intervening space must be void until it is occupied by air. However quickly the air rushes in all round, the entire space cannot be filled instantaneously.
De Rerum Natura, translated by R.E. Latham, pp.38–9 (Harmondsworth, Middlesex, 1951), book I, 372–89.

19 Grant, *Much Ado*, p.197.
20 Agnes Heller uses this famous passage from Machiavelli's *The Prince* in order to show a change in basic life-rhythm that comes with the hurrying of history, outrunning the human capacity for flexibility – 'historical moments have become shorter than the span of human life. . . . Character, ways of thinking are scarcely formed, when they are obliged to accommodate themselves to changed demands and to take account of new human characteristics': *Renaissance Man* (London, 1978), pp.179–80.
21 On a world-view of knock-on effects where every action involves a counter-action, see John L. Russell, 'Action and Reaction before Newton' *British Journal for the History of Science*, vol.IX (1976), pp.25–38. I am suggesting that Shakespeare sets up, almost mechanically, reactions between different parts of both himself and his plays.
22 Ernst Cassirer, *The Individual and the Cosmos in Renaissance Philosophy*, translated by M. Domandi (Oxford, 1963), p.84.
23 Montaigne, *Essais*, 1603, translated by John Florio, Everyman's Library, 3 vols (London, 1980), vol.III, pp.375–6.
24 Philoponus, quoted in Sorabji, *Matter, Space and Motion*, p.25.
25 Telesio, Campanella's mentor, quoted in *Renaissance Philosophy*, vol.I, *The Italian Philosophers*, edited by Arturo B. Fallico and Herman Shapiro (New York, 1967), p.317.
26 John Berger, *Once in Europa* (London, 1991), p.136.
27 Compare with 'music, music', 'my loove, my loove' crying in the midst of the lines discussed in the following:

Ye have another sort of repetition when in one verse or clause of a verse, ye iterate one word without any intermission . . . And that of Sir Walter Raleighs very sweet

With wisdomes eyes had but blind fortune seene,

Than had my loove, my loove for ever beene.

The Greekes call him *Epizeuxis*, the Latines *Subiunctio*, we may call him the *underlay*, & methinks if we regard his manner of iteration would depart from the originall, we might very properly, in our vulgar and for pleasure call him the *cuckowspell*.

> Puttenham, *The Arte of English Poesie*, p.201

See also my essay 'On Repetition', *Swansea Review*, no.1 (April 1986), pp.1–13.

28 On place logic and the rhetorical use of loci, see Trousdale, *Shakespeare and the Rhetoricians*, especially pp.12–13 on how the character of Othello is brought into being through the fusing of different categories, such as 'form, figure, place, stock, name, country, time':

> If we borrow Lomazzo's categories, Othello represents in terms of stock, a Moor; in terms of place, the commander of an army for the Venetian state; in terms of figure, one who loved not wisely but too well. These all define him. They define him in terms of verbal categories that are places of invention as well as places of definition.

This bringing together of different rhetorical *places* is thus a process common to the creation of both metaphor and character. Verbally Shakespeare lays one sense over another: if a blind man may be said to see, it is because he sees *feelingly* (*King Lear*, IV vi 147). See also section 3 of Chapter Two below. With regard to rhetoric, I am also indebted, like everyone else, to the work of Brian Vickers.

29 Søren Kierkegaard, *The Sickness Unto Death*, translated by H.V. Hong and E.H. Hong (Princeton, NJ, 1980), p.94.

30 Giordano Bruno, *On the Infinite Universe and Worlds*, 1584, in D.W. Singer, *Giordano Bruno* (New York, 1950), pp.364–5.

31 Barton, *Playing Shakespeare*, p.57; compare Peter Brook, *The Empty Space* (Harmondsworth, Middlesex, 1972), p.18: 'Theatre is always a self-destructive art, and it is always written on the wind.'

32 On the analogical relation of place, human feeling and the orientation of meaning, see Pierre Duhem's provocative summary of the philosophy of John Buridan: 'The term *place* is to the term *surface* as a passion is to the subject it affects. Place is defined, as any passion should be, by the definition of the subject and by the terms that explain the particular *connotation* of this subject affected by the passion': *Medieval Cosmology*, p.239.

33 Montaigne, *Essais*, vol.I, ch.xxv, 'On Schoolmaster's Learning', in M.A. Screech's translation (London, 1991), p.154.

34 Kenelm Digby, *Two Treatises* (1644) quoted in Russell, 'Action and Reaction before Newton', p.32.

35 Philoponus in Sorabji, *Matter, Space and Motion*, p.25, where it is argued that matter alone is the first subject, but its three dimensions come further into realization when a layer of spatial extension is superimposed, forming a second subject from which qualities derive.

36 Compare Cassirer on Cusanus's '*docta ignorantia*': 'For far from excluding each other, separation and participation . . . can only be thought of *through* and *in relation to* each other': *The Individual and the Cosmos*, p.22. See also Thomas Nagel: 'How can it be the case that one of the people in the world is *me*?' – me who then suffers the double vision of 'conceiving the world as a place that includes the person I am within it, as just another of its contents': *The View from Nowhere* (New York and Oxford, 1986), pp.13, 63.

37 John Middleton Murry, *Shakespeare* (London, 1948), p.19.

38 See Jay L. Halio's New Cambridge edition of *King Lear* (1992), p.238, quoting P.W.K. Stone.

39 So Ruskin: 'Shakespeare is distinguished from Dante eminently by his always dwelling on last causes instead of first causes' (*Modern Painters*, vol.IV, part v, ch.xx, para.38, footnote). Dante, says Ruskin, 'invariably points to the moment of the soul's choice'; but Shakespeare, in the midst of an inescapable and entangling medium, dwells on 'the infinitude of result dependent seemingly on little things'.

TWO   SHAKESPEARE'S COMPOSITIONS

1 E.H. Gombrich, *Art and Illusion* (London, 1983), pp. 119, 176–7 (my emphasis). The quotation from *Lucrece* comes from stanza 204, lines 1422–8.

2 Maurice Morgann, 'An Essay on the Dramatic Character of Sir John Falstaff', 1777, in his *Shakespearian Criticism*, edited by D.A. Fineman (Oxford, 1972), pp.167–8.

3 Russell Hoban's characters speak of the pattern of mosaics thus:

Once the mode of repetition is established the thing goes on for ever. . . . However one looked at the pattern there could be no doubt that the stillness had become motion but I hadn't noticed at what point it had happened. . . . The motion in a tile pattern is intransitive, it does not pass; it moves but it stays in our field of vision. It arises from stillness, and I should like to think about the point at which stillness becomes motion. Another thing I should like to think about is the point at which pattern becomes consciousness.

Pilgermann (London, 1983), pp.113, 123, 118

Renaissance poetics are mosaic-like, particularly in the configurations of Shakespearian comedy. Of overlap in modern poetics, Les Murray writes: 'Humans are not rational, but poetic. For this reason, the world we have inherited is a vast texture of overlaid and overlapping poetries, often competing inside individual human heads' (*The Paperbark Tree* [London, 1993], p.356, 'Poemes and the Mystery of Embodiment').

4 Montaigne, *Essais*, 1603, translated by John Florio, Everyman's Library, 3 vols (London, 1980), vol.III, p.166 (ch.viii, 'Of the Art of Conference'). Hereafter cited as 'Montaigne'.

5 *Elizabethan Critical Essays*, edited by G. Gregory Smith, 2 vols (Oxford, 1967), vol.I, p.199.

6 Baldassare Castiglione, *The Book of the Courtier*, 1561, translated by Sir Thomas Hoby (London, 1966), p.49.

7 In *Love's Labour's Lost*, of course, that temporariness runs out before the end of the play: the death of a father in France, whom the audience has never seen, is given all the more power precisely in so far as it intrusively breaks the pattern. Something which should come later – after the marriage of the royals, or in another play, or at another stage of Shakespeare's career – characteristically is brought in earlier. Almost from the first, as with the left-over problem of Jaques in *As You Like It*, the stuff of inconvenience, if not tragedy, is present to Shakespeare but present as a breaking of the pattern only in so far as it is also a variation and transformation of it.

8 Richard Hooker, *Of the Laws of Ecclesiastical Polity*, 1593, edited by A.S. McGrade (Cambridge, 1989), p.92 (book I, ch.10.7). Hereafter cited as 'Hooker'.

9 See Philip Edwards, 'Person and Office in Shakespeare's Plays', *Proceedings of the British Academy* vol.56 (1972), pp.93–109.

10 Robert Sorabji, *Matter, Space and Motion: Theories in Antiquity and their Sequel* (London, 1988), p.209.

11 See James Black, 'The Unfolding of "Measure for Measure"', *Shakespeare Survey*, vol.26 (1973), p.124.

12 Giordano Bruno, *The Expulsion of the Triumphant Beast*, 1584, translated by A.D. Imerti (Lincoln, NB, 1992), p.187.

13 Compare Quintilian's 'there is always some difference which enables us to distinguish even the things which seem most like and most

equal to one another', quoted in Terence Cave, *The Cornucopian Text* (Oxford, 1979), p.38.

14 Cave, *The Cornucopian Text*, speaks of the *Essais* as self-sceptically superfluous, being both richly full and vainly empty: 'a discourse which, as it pours itself out, celebrates its own inanity' (p.321). For example, 'a discourse on death is necessary in order to remind the reader that death can be ignored' (p.304). Hereafter cited as 'Cave'.

15 John Bayley, *The Uses of Division* (London, 1976), pp.222, 228 (my emphasis).

16 Nicholas of Cusa, *On Learned Ignorance*, 1440, translated by Jasper Hopkins (Minneapolis, MN, 1981), p.89 (book II, ch.i).

17 Marion Trousdale, *Shakespeare and the Rhetoricians* (London, 1982), pp.35–6.

18 Compare the sort of technical rather than moral or political language that Marion Trousdale argues to be appropriate to a discussion of *Richard II*:

> The kinds of questions Shakespeare might have asked in pursuing such patterns are: not why Richard was deposed, but why might he have been deposed . . . not ought he to have been deposed, but what is there in his deposition that would make it possible to present a case on both sides.
>
> *Shakespeare and the Rhetoricians*, p.66

See also Chapter One above, note 28.

19 St Augustine, *Confessions*, translated by R.S. Pine-Coffin (Harmondsworth, Middlesex, 1974), p.80 (book 4.10). See Inga-Stina Ewbank's use of Augustine in her essay in Kenneth Muir's *Casebook on The Winter's Tale* (London, 1968), p.114.

20 Jacob Bronowski, *The Ascent of Man* (London, 1973), p.180.

21 Francis Bacon, *The Advancement of Learning*, 1605, edited by G.W. Kitchin (London, 1962), p.189 (second book, XXIII.14).

22 Agnes Heller, *Renaissance Man*, translated by R.E. Allen (London, 1967), p.118, quoting Machiavelli's *Discourses* (book III, discourse 22).

23 'The scene is the primary dramatic unit': Emrys Jones, *Scenic Form in Shakespeare* (Oxford, 1971), p.3. Cf. C. Hallett and E. Hallett, *Analysing Shakespeare's Action* (Cambridge, 1991). There is evidence to suggest that Shakespeare himself moved around scenes and parts of scenes that finally came to rest in act III, as if always testing whether there was any essential internal order involved in the sequence, and as though asking at another level Hamlet's own questions about the rightful place of things in Elsinore.

24 *Testimony: The Memoirs of Dmitri Shostakovich*, edited by Solomon
    Volkov, translated by A.W. Bouis (London, 1979), p.63.
25 Giambattista Guarini, *The Compendium of Tragicomic Poetry*, 1599, in
    Literary Criticism: Plato to Dryden, edited by A.H. Gilbert (Detroit,
    MI, 1962), pp.509–10.
26 Compare Cave on Montaigne's silent revisions of the *Essais* in an
    attempt to 'represent his life as uninterrupted *copia*. . . . In such ways,
    the search for coherence and continuity asserts itself momentarily
    over the vision of the endless fragmentation of experience' (Cave,
    pp.282–3).
27 D.H. Lawrence, *Aaron's Rod*, 1922 (Harmondsworth, Middlesex,
    1975), pp.200, 112.
28 In *Coriolanus: BBC TV Shakespeare* (London, 1984), p.27 (Henry
    Fenwick, 'The Production').
29 Erich Auerbach, *Mimesis*, translated by W.R. Trask (Princeton, NJ,
    1971), p.300.
30 Bernardino M. Bonansea, *Tommaso Campanella: Renaissance Pioneer of
    Modern Thought* (Washington, DC, 1969), p.155. Hereafter cited as
    'Campanella'.
31 See in particular G.C. Taylor, *Shakespeare's Debt to Montaigne*
    (Cambridge, MA, 1925).
32 Edward Dowden, *Shakspeare: His Mind and Art* (London, 1876),
    p.133.
33 Augustine, *Confessions*, pp.33–4 (book I.13).
34 John Masefield, *William Shakespeare* (London, 1956), pp.107–8.
35 ibid., p.110.
36 Marsilio Ficino, *Commentary on Plato's Symposium*, translated by Sears
    Jayne (Dallas, Tex., 1985), p.68.
37 Isaiah Berlin, *Vico and Herder* (London, 1976), p.14.
38 Such a world does not, like comedy, replace fallen primacies in an
    implicitly secondary mode, but makes a chaotic replica of the old
    order, where the best can be the very cause of the worst:

    Vives' original contribution to the study of human emotions
    began with his frequent observations about their complicated
    interrelations. . . . Love provokes fear; 'friends fear for their friends,
    fathers for their sons, wives for their husbands, and husbands for
    their wives'; envy is aroused by the love of concupiscence, and
    favor is occasionally stimulated by hatred 'which makes us lean
    towards the enemies of our enemies'. . . . On occasion passions
    change direction and intensity on account of external events or
    other causes. Sometimes 'envy can turn into compassion when
    misery succeeds happiness.' For this reason envious people are

compassionate and compassionate people are inclined to envy; jealousy can turn into hatred and favor.

Carlos G. Norena, *Juan Luis Vives* (The Hague, 1970), p.272

THREE SHAKESPEARE'S HISTORIES AND LATE PLAYS

1 *Renaissance Philosophy*, vol.I, *The Italian Philosophers*, edited by Arturo B. Fallico and Herman Shapiro (New York, 1967), pp.367–8.

2 Baldassare Castiglione, *The Book of the Courtier*, 1561, translated by Sir Thomas Hoby (London, 1966), p.150.

3 Edmund Burke, *Reflections on the Revolution in France*, 1790 (Harmondsworth, Middlesex, 1978), p.106.

4 The editors of the Complete Oxford Shakespeare reprint the quarto amended as verse:

> Doth any here know me? Why, this is not Lear.
> Doth Lear walk thus, speak thus? Where are his eyes?
> Either his notion weakens, or his discernings
> Are lethargied. Sleeping or waking, ha?
> Sure 'tis not so.
> Who is it that can tell me who I am?
> Lear's shadow? I would learn that, for by the marks
> Of sovereignty, knowledge, and reason
> I should be false persuaded I had daughters.
> *Fool* Which they will make an obedient father.
>
> *The History of King Lear*, scene 4 220–9

5 Telesio, *De rerum natura iuxta propria principia*, 1565, expanded 1570, 1586, quoted in *Renaissance Philosophy*, p.313. See also George Herbert, 'The Temper (I)' ('Stretch or contract me, thy poor debtor').

6 John Kerrigan quoted in The New Cambridge Shakespeare edition of *The Tragedy of King Lear*, edited by Jay L. Halio, p.267.

7 *Coleridge on Shakespeare*, edited by T. Hawkes (Harmondsworth, Middlesex, 1969), p.229.

8 See The New Cambridge Shakespeare edition of *The Tragedy of King Lear*, ed. Halio, pp.78–9.

9 Telesio quoted in *Renaissance Philosophy*, p.316.

10 See Harriet Hawkins, *The Devil's Party* (Oxford, 1985), p.11, on Bacon's 'instance contradictory' and Shakespeare 'forever citing the one black swan, even as he characteristically tends to confront the best possible case in favour of someone or something with the strongest (not the weakest) arguments that could possibly be levelled against it – and vice versa'.

11 Saul Bellow, *Henderson the Rain King* (Harmondsworth, Middlesex, 1966), pp.214, 297.

12 William Hazlitt, *Characters of Shakspeare's Plays*, 1817 (London, 1970), pp.252–3.

13 Sir Philip Sidney's *An Apology for Poetry* (1583) in *Elizabethan Critical Essays*, edited by G. Gregory Smith, 2 vols (Oxford, 1967), vol.I, p.168.

14 Friedrich Nietzsche, *Untimely Meditations*, translated by R.J. Hollingdale (Cambridge, 1983), p.106 ('On the Uses and Disadvantages of History for Life', 1874).

15 Burke, *Reflections on the Revolution*, p.120.

16 See Appendix I to the New Arden edition of *2 Henry IV*, edited by A.R. Humphreys, p.203.

17 Quoted in *Renaissance Philosophy*, p.362.

18 Stephen Greenblatt, *Shakespearian Negotiations* (Oxford, 1988), p.46.

19 In *Worlds Apart* (Cambridge, 1986), Jean-Christophe Agnew argues that in Shakespeare, theatre is now to do with the depiction of *mis*representations and self-fabrication in the new economic climate of power relations based not on faith but credit:

> The new drama showed, as no other genre could, how precarious social identity was, how vulnerable to unexpected disruptions and disclosure it was, and therefore how deeply theatrical it was. Everyone, dramatists seemed to say, was a player-king embroiled in a ceaseless struggle to preserve his legitimacy.
>
> p.112

Agnew quotes John Bulwer's mid-seventeenth-century writings, describing how a new Hobbesian economic man was now 'shoared upon the Continent of Change and confusion, where the inconstancy of his actions, and the various shapes he entertained, by the new modelling of his person, justly brought upon him the judgement of dereliction':

> All other creatures keep their ranks, their places and natures in the world; only man himselfe disorders all, and that by displacing himself, by losing his place.
>
> quoted p.96

I do not doubt the applicability of all this to the Iagos and Edmunds of Shakespeare's disrupted world. But I have tried to show that the dynamic changes of shape and place in Shakespeare's plays also belong to a wider and earlier view in which theatre is still a representation of a whole cosmology in little – a cosmology containing the sort of forces, apart from economic forces, which Campanella describes in terms of sympathetic magic. In Chapter Two I showed that acting as dissimulation was precisely what, in their different ways, and in comparison with Montaigne, both Coriolanus and Hamlet despised. See also Chapter Four on Vives and the ancient motif of the world as a theatre.

20 In Ralph Berry, *On Directing Shakespeare* (London, 1989), pp.149, 151. In Dollimore and Sinfield's *Political Shakespeare*, 2nd edition (Manchester, 1994), it is argued that Shakespeare's art is 'always political' (p.125); but Shakespeare's art is never 'always' any one thing, however pervasive. For example: Jonathan Dollimore, arguing that Antony wants to prove himself still the great warrior he once was, says 'That precipitates him into homosexual competition with Caesar, whose youthfulness makes him anxious . . . "There's sap in it yet"' (p.145). But 'precipitates' is indeed the word: the characters, the audience, or the readers, each at different times, find themselves unpremeditatedly thinking, 'Oh, *that* is what is happening now is it? It's now suddenly *become* political, or sexual, or criminal.' Thus it is not a matter of being ready with explanations, ideologies, or concepts, but of being overtaken by the pressure of events seemingly happening to take the experiential form of a recognizable category of sudden retrospective thought.

21 Petrarch, 'On the Remedies of Good and Bad Fortune', quoted in *Renaissance Philosophy*, p.6.

22 John Barton, *Playing Shakespeare* (London, 1989), pp.154–5.

23 Telesio quoted in *Renaissance Philosophy*, p.304.

24 John Bayley, *The Uses of Division* (London, 1976), p.185.

25 Marion Trousdale, *Shakespeare and the Rhetoricians* (London, 1982), p.73.

26 Douglas Oliver, *Poetry and Narrative in Performance* (London, 1989), p.19. In his analysis of some lines from Wyatt, Oliver refers to 'retrospective stress' in the midst of a line:

> So unwarely was never no man caught
> With stedfast look upon a goodly face
> As I of late; for suddenly me thought
> My heart was torn out of his place.

He writes of the dynamics of the third line:

> 'Of late' means 'recently', but, semantically considered, the pause makes 'late' almost literally late in that allied meaning because the word takes its time before the sound resumes quickly with 'for

suddenly'. . . . The pause after 'late' seems to increase my sense of how much 'late' was stressed, although I have *already* pronounced the word. This gives us a new concept, which I call 'retrospective stress'. . . . Part of our sense of a syllable's stress is cast back on to it afterwards, not from anticipation but from the real future (the pause). It is a minute puzzle of space-time that we think we heard, back in the past, a certain stress, but are able to add to our sense of what happened *then* by later events in the line. That is, the mind mistimes, if you like, a present experience, the pause, by posting its influence back to the notional instant when the voice stressed the syllable 'late' and by thinking that the influence took place then.

pp.34–5

It is as if the reader, looking forward, could hold on to the note of 'late', and hence the force-field created by it, a fraction of a second longer, and then find it jolted and altered almost before he realizes it.

27 Keats, letter of 13 March 1818.

28 See Sidney's *An Apology for Poetry*:

Verse farre exceedeth Prose in the knitting vp of the memory . . . the wordes (beside theyr delight, which hath a great affinitie to memory) beeing so set as one word cannot be lost but the whole worke failes . . . one word so, as it were, begetting another, as, be it in ryme or measured verse, by the former a man shall haue a neere gesse to the follower: lastly, euen they that haue taught the Art of memory haue shewed nothing so apt for it as a certaine roome deuided into many places well and throughly knowne.

Elizabethan Critical Essays, vol.I, pp.182–3

29 Giordano Bruno, *The Ash Wednesday Supper* (*La Cena de la Cenari*), 1584, translated by S.L. Jaki (The Hague, 1975), p.116.

30 'Campanella proposed notions of structural resonance . . . "per qualitatem sympathiae, sicut magnetis in ferrum"': Brian P. Copenhaver, 'Astrology and Magic' in *The Cambridge History of Renaissance Philosophy*, ed. C.B. Schmitt and Q. Skinner (Cambridge, 1988), pp.295–6. See also for a modern cosmological account of resonance in the living world, Rupert Sheldrake, *The Presence of the Past* (London, 1988): 'At the moment of insight a potential pattern of organized behaviour comes into being. This can be regarded as a new morphic field': p.173.

31 This is where I find Trousdale's continual re-enforcement of the

Renaissance distinction between *verba* and *res*, words and things, finally unhelpful. It leads her to see Shakespeare's rhetorical use of language as analogous to Iago's power of manipulation, in making Othello, like an equivalent audience, fall for the illusion of taking words for reality. But it is *also* true that Shakespeare's power of language is itself analogous to the untaught Othello's belief – 'to believe language real', or to believe at the very least that language naturally seems to be so (see Trousdale, pp.168, 171). Even Hamlet cannot bear it if he cannot trust 'words, words, words', as indeed he suspects he cannot. That alienating pain is one measure of his horror of the Fall. But near the end of Chapter One I argued that the gap between words and things was not inevitably a place of scepticism for Shakespeare but a space that Shakespeare used for quick, tacit thinking in the midst of his formulations.

32 *Renaissance Philosophy*, pp.375–6.
33 Bruno, *The Ash Wednesday Supper*, p.155.
34 John Middleton Murry, *Shakespeare* (London, 1948), p.20.
35 Michael Bogdanov on Michael Pennington in their *The English Shakespeare Company: 'The War of the Roses' 1986–1989* (London, 1992), pp.106–7.
36 Bruno, *The Ash Wednesday Supper*, p.156.
37 George Puttenham, *The Arte of English Poesie*, 1589, book I, ch.xxiv, in *Elizabethan Critical Essays*, vol.II, pp.49–50.
38 *Renaissance Philosophy*, pp.348–9.
39 Berry, *On Directing Shakespeare*, p.127.
40 Simone Weil, *Gravity and Grace* (London, 1952), p.5.
41 Montaigne, *Essais*, 1603, translated by John Florio, Everyman's Library, 3 vols (London, 1980), vol.II, p.108. See also Eleanor Prosser, 'Shakespeare, Montaigne and the "Rarer Action"', *Shakespeare Studies*, vol.I (1961), pp.261–6.
42 Nietzsche, *Untimely Meditations*, p.76.
43 *Renaissance Philosophy*, pp.374–5:

> All that scientists do in imitating nature and in working with her to bring about the ends of their arts is known as magic. . . . Now all arts, so long as they are not understood, are called magic; but after a while they acquire the status of common sciences. The invention of gunpowder and of printing was once regarded as magic; similarly, the use of lodestone – but now that everyone knows the art, it has become commonly accepted. So also with the art of clock-making; and all other mechanical arts just as easily lose their extraordinary status directly they become familiar to the ordinary man.

44 Middleton Murry, *Shakespeare*, p.20. Compare George Steiner's W.P. Ker Lecture, *A Reading Against Shakespeare*.

45 Brian Gibbons, *Shakespeare and Multiplicity* (Cambridge, 1993), p.211.

FOUR TIME, PLACE AND THOUGHT IN PERFORMANCE

1 Ralph Berry, *On Directing Shakespeare* (London, 1989), pp.141–2.

2 Graham Swift, *Ever After* (London, 1992), pp.252–3.

3 Douglas Oliver, *Poetry and Narrative in Performance* (London, 1989), pp.vii–viii.

4 Juan Luis Vives, 'A Fable About Man', in *The Renaissance Philosophy of Man*, edited by E. Cassirer, P.O. Kristeller and J.H. Randall Jr (Chicago, 1948), pp.389–90. This is an example of the sacred *cosmological* motif of *theatrum mundi* which Jean-Christophe Agnew argues in *Worlds Apart* (Cambridge, 1986) is superseded in Shakespeare's time by theatre as a reflection of the fabrications of a market *economy* in which people increasingly became actors – artificial performers, representatives and impersonators. In what he calls 'the gradual separation of . . . a market *process* from the particularity of a market-*place*', Agnew pays witness to the forces of sheer movement which indeed make place unstable in Shakespeare (*Worlds Apart*, p.41). Clearly the two views of theatre overlap in Shakespeare: I simply stress here the continuance of the older image, together with the sheer physical and spatial reality of the stage.

5 *Dr Johnson on Shakespeare*, edited by W.K. Wimsatt (Harmondsworth, Middlesex, 1969), p.70.

6 Adapted from Stanley Cavell, 'The Avoidance of Love' in *Must We Mean What We Say?* (Cambridge, 1976), pp.332–4.

7 ibid., p.330. Much of what I say about the way that theatre physically literalizes a vision of our condition is indebted to Cavell's argument that the catharsis of theatrical representation lies in its giving us a place as audience from which to witness and not intercede.

8 Marsilio Ficino, *Commentary on Plato's Symposium*, translated by Sears Jayne (Dallas, Tex., 1985), p.125.

9 ibid., pp.55–6.

10 Giordano Bruno, *The Expulsion of the Triumphant Beast*, 1584, translated by A.D. Imerti (Lincoln, NB, 1992), p.90.

11 Ficino, *Commentary on Plato's Symposium*, p.64. On Empedocles, see *Early Greek Philosophy*, translated by J. Barnes, Penguin Classics (Harmondsworth, Middlesex, 1987), pp.165–71. See also Bruno, *The Expulsion of the Triumphant Beast*, pp.89–90.

12 Quoted in *The Times*, 3 July 1993, p.14.

13 Ficino, *Commentary on Plato's Symposium* (VI.10), adapted quotation from Brian P. Copenhaver, 'Astrology and Magic' in *The Cambridge History of Renaissance Philosophy*, edited by C.B. Schmitt and Q. Skinner (Cambridge, 1988), p.275.

14 *Leonardo on Painting*, edited and translated by M. Kemp and M. Walker (New Haven, CT, 1989), pp.23–4.

15 Harriet Walter in Carol Rutter (ed.), *Clamorous Voices* (London, 1988), p.76.

16 Berry, *On Directing Shakespeare*, p.133.

17 Peter Brook's assistant director Jean-Pierre Vincent in *Peter Brook: A Theatrical Casebook*, edited by David Williams (London, 1992), p.254. As T.R. Langley has said, 'This would have seemed a period' is the disordered tragic development of Samuel Daniel's broadly comic principle of form happily constrained by rhyme: 'the certain close of delight with the full body of a just period well carried'. The body is tortured and racked in *King Lear*; the period is not just; there is no delightful close as the action goes on and on to its promised end.

18 For the characteristics of Shakespeare's mature style see Dowden, *Shakspeare: His Mind and Art* (pp.125–6), quoting Spedding:

> The opening of [*Henry VIII*] . . . seemed to have the full stamp of Shakspere, in his latest manner; the same close-packed expression; the same life, and reality, and freshness; the same rapid and abrupt turnings of thought, so quick that language can hardly follow fast enough; the same impatient activity of intellect and fancy, which having disclosed an idea, cannot wait to work it orderly out; the same daring confidence in the resources of language, which plunges headlong into a sentence without knowing how it is to come forth; the same careless metre which disdains to produce its harmonious effects by the ordinary devices, yet is evidently subject to a master of harmony; the same entire freedom from book-language and commonplace.

19 Michael Polanyi, *Personal Knowledge* (London, 1973), p.126.

20 Carlos G. Norena, *Juan Luis Vives* (quoting Vives) (The Hague, 1970), p.244.

21 See, in particular, *Hamlet*, I ii 185, and Sonnet 27; also Plato, *The Republic*, translated by H.D.P. Lee (Harmondsworth, Middlesex, 1965), pp.274–8 (part Seven, book Six, section 6, 'The Divided Line'): 'the real subjects of investigation being invisible except to the eye of the mind'.

22 Kepler, *Harmonices Mundi*, proemium to book V, quoted in Polanyi,

Personal Knowledge, p.7:

> What Kepler claimed here about the Platonic bodies was nonsense, and his exclamation about God's having waited for him for thousands of years was a literary fancy; yet his outburst conveys a true idea of the scientific method and of the nature of science; an idea which has since been disfigured by the sustained attempt to remodel it in the likeness of a mistaken ideal of objectivity.

23 Berry, *On Directing Shakespeare*, pp.149–50, 137 (modified).

24 Maurice Merleau-Ponty, 'Reading Montaigne' in his *Phenomenology, Language and Sociology*, edited by J. O'Neill (London, 1974), p.126.

25 Terence Cave, *The Cornucopian Text* (Oxford, 1979), pp.128, 130. Hereafter cited as 'Cave'.

26 D.H. Lawrence, *Apocalypse*, 1930 (London, 1981), p.42 (ch.vii).

27 *The Notebooks of Leonardo da Vinci*, selected by I.A. Richter (Oxford, 1977), p.62.

28 Timothy Bright, *A Treatise of Melancholy*, 1586 – another version of the mind's eye – quoted in Harold Jenkins's New Arden *Hamlet*, p.528.

29 D.H. Lawrence, *Phoenix*, edited by E.D. MacDonald (London, 1970), p.431 ('Study of Thomas Hardy'). See also Gabriel Josipovici, *Text and Voice* (Manchester, 1992), p.202 on Shakespeare's endless fullness. In contemplating the way that Shakespeare represents an original mode of being and thinking and acting, perhaps nothing is more suggestive than Hazlitt's youthful essay 'On the Principles of Human Action' (1805). For it is significant in relation to his later Shakespearian studies that Hazlitt himself as a young man wrote this essay in defence of something fundamentally more dynamic and more innocent in human thought and action than the prudential considerations of the Hobbesian man measuring his own present self-interests. Identity, says Hazlitt, is made up in retrospect, is a thing of memory. Deeper than that, because prior to it, is a dynamic which is more innocent and instantaneous than is sheer ego. In the original function of action, Man when he acts is not in the present or the past, is not prudentially conscious, but is in sheer imaginative thought of a future in which he does not yet exist, is in search of bringing that future into existence through action. 'The reason why a child first distinctly wills to pursue its own good is not because it is his, but because it is good.' 'Man when he acts is always absolutely independent of, and uninfluenced by the feelings of the being for whom he acts, whether this be himself or another.'

30 Cavell, *Must We Mean What We Say?*, p.326.

Select Bibliography

Jean-Christophe Agnew, *Worlds Apart*, Cambridge, 1986.

John Barton, *Playing Shakespeare*, London, 1986.

John Bayley, *The Uses of Division*, London, 1976.

Isaiah Berlin, *Vico and Herder*, London, 1976.

Ralph Berry, *On Directing Shakespeare*, London, 1989.

Bernardino M. Bonansea, *Tommaso Campanella: Renaissance Pioneer of Modern Thought*, Washington, DC, 1969.

Peter Brook, *The Empty Space*, Harmondsworth, Middlesex, 1972.

Giordano Bruno, *On the Infinite Universe and Worlds*, 1584, in D.W. Singer, *Giordano Bruno*, New York, 1950.

Giordano Bruno, *The Ash Wednesday Supper* (*La Cena de la Cenari*), 1584, translated by S.L. Jaki, The Hague, 1975.

Giordano Bruno, *The Expulsion of the Triumphant Beast*, 1584, translated by A.D. Imerti, Lincoln, NB, 1992.

Edmund Burke, *Reflections on the Revolution in France*, 1790, Harmondsworth, Middlesex, 1978.

Ernst Cassirer, *The Individual and the Cosmos in Renaissance Philosophy*, translated by M. Domandi, Oxford, 1963.

E. Cassirer, P.O. Kristeller and J.H. Randall Jr (eds), *The Renaissance Philosophy of Man*, Chicago, 1948.

Terence Cave, *The Cornucopian Text*, Oxford, 1979.

Stanley Cavell, *Must We Mean What We Say?* Cambridge, 1976.

Brian P. Copenhaver, 'Astrology and Magic' in *The Cambridge History of Renaissance Philosophy*, ed. C.B. Schmitt and Q. Skinner, Cambridge, 1988.

Thomas Creech, translator, Titus Lucretius Carus, *His Six Books of Epicurean Philosophy*, 3rd edn, London, 1683.

Jonathan Dollimore and Alan Sinfield, *Political Shakespeare*, 2nd edition, Manchester, 1994.

Pierre Duhem,, *Medieval Cosmology*, edited by Roger Ariew, Chicago, 1987.

Philip Edwards, 'Person and Office in Shakespeare's plays', *Proceedings of the British Academy*, vol.56 (1972), pp. 93–109.

Arturo B. Fallico and Herman Shapiro (eds), *Renaissance Philosophy*, vol.I, *The Italian Philosophers*, New York, 1967.

Marsilio Ficino, *Commentary on Plato's Symposium*, translated by Sears Jayne, Dallas, Tex., 1985.

E.H. Gombrich, *Art and Illusion*, London, 1983.

Edward Grant, *Much Ado About Nothing; Theories of Space and Vacuum from the Middle Ages to the Scientific Revolution*, Cambridge, 1981.

Stephen Greenblatt, *Renaissance Self-Fashioning*, Chicago, 1980.

Stephen Greenblatt, *Shakespearian Negotiations*, Oxford, 1988.

William Hazlitt, *Characters of Shakspeare's Plays*, 1817, London, 1970.

William Hazlitt, *Lectures on the English Poets*, 1818, London, 1967.

Agnes Heller, *Renaissance Man*, London, 1978.

Richard Hooker, *Of the Laws of Ecclesiastical Polity*, 1593, edited by A.S. McGrade, Cambridge, 1989.

Emrys Jones, *Scenic Form in Shakespeare*, Oxford, 1971.

Sister Miriam Joseph, *Rhetoric in Shakespeare's Time*, New York, 1962.

Michel de Montaigne, *Essais*, 1603, translated by John Florio, Everyman's Library, 3 vols, London, 1980.

Maurice Morgann, *Shakespearian Criticism*, edited by D.A. Fineman, Oxford, 1972.

John Middleton Murry, *Shakespeare*, London, 1948.

Nicholas of Cusa, *On Learned Ignorance*, 1440, translated by Jasper Hopkins, Minneapolis, MN, 1981.

Carlos G. Norena, *Juan Luis Vives*, The Hague, 1970.

Douglas Oliver, *Poetry and Narrative in Performance*, London, 1989.

Michael Polanyi, *Personal Knowledge*, London, 1973.

George Puttenham, *The Arte of English Poesie*, 1589, edited by G.D. Willcock and A. Walker, Cambridge, 1936.

John L. Russell, 'Action and Reaction before Newton', *British Journal for the History of Science*, vol.IX (1976), pp.25–38.

Carol Rutter (ed.), *Clamorous Voices*, London, 1988.

Wilbur Sanders and Howard Jacobson, *Shakespeare's Magnanimity*, London, 1978.

Rupert Sheldrake, *The Presence of the Past*, London, 1988.

G. Gregory Smith (ed.), *Elizabethan Critical Essays*, 2 vols, Oxford, 1967.

Robert Sorabji, *Matter, Space and Motion: Theories in Antiquity and their Sequel*, London, 1988.

Marion Trousdale, *Shakespeare and the Rhetoricians*, London, 1982.

Brian Vickers, *In Defence of Rhetoric*, Oxford, 1988.

David Williams (ed.), *Peter Brook: A Theatrical Casebook*, London, 1992.

Index